Praise for *Torn*

"*Torn* is an insightful, well-supported by meaningful research, and compelling appeal to all of us to be understanding, supportive, and compassionate as we navigate the challenges met by families and individuals wrestling with their beliefs and affiliation with The Church of Jesus Christ of Latter-day Saints. Jeff Strong is a caring and faithful Latter-day Saint and committed disciple of Christ who seeks not only to inform but to heal and unite. To those for whom these issues are relevant, *Torn* will be a detailed road map for positive engagement and dialogue."

—S. Michael Wilcox, renowned Latter-day Saint author, speaker, and institute teacher

"Jeff Strong is a truth-seeker, treasured friend, and fellow believer. With deep faith and conviction, Jeff asks, 'Who is the Church for?' That question is difficult. It makes us wrestle deeply. It requires honesty, especially if people we love choose other paths. But the answers will heal us—individually and collectively. In love, Jeff reminds us we need each other. We need eyes to see and ears to hear so we can truly minister and ensure all God's children, no matter their journey, feel they belong in the nourishing body of Christ and know in whom they can find healing and wholeness."

—Ally Isom, business & community leader; former director of Institutional Messaging, Church of Jesus Christ of Latter-day Saints; former deputy chief of staff to Utah governor

"For fifteen years I've had countless conversations with people in faith crisis, and this is a book I wish I'd had from the start. Drawing on groundbreaking research into the tensions that are leading our loved ones out of the Church, it provides essential maps and mental models—identifying pain points, diagnosing problems, and suggesting solutions, all while speaking the truth in love. For anyone wrestling with questions, struggling with aspects of our culture, or wanting to learn the healer's art, this book is required reading. I'll be rereading it—and recommending it—often."

—Jared Halverson, BYU professor and host of the *Unshaken* podcast

"In the restored Church, we are encouraged to seek learning by study and by faith. This book exemplifies that dual approach, offering solid data to illuminate and inform the complexities of contemporary Latter-day Saint religious life. Yet, as the Apostle Paul reminds us, all our efforts will amount to nothing if not motivated from first to last by love. It is in that respect that *Torn* truly shines. Jeff Strong really loves people in all their glorious messiness, and that love is shimmeringly apparent on practically every page. This is a book that centers both head and heart. *Torn* will help us all—no matter where you stand on matters of faith—better understand and love one another."

—Patrick Q. Mason, author of *Planted:*
Belief and Belonging in an Age of Doubt

"In a time when conversations about faith can feel especially tense or tender, *Torn* opens the door to more compassion, clarity, and understanding. Drawing from compelling research and lived experience, Jeff translates complex data into practical wisdom for everyday life. With unflinching honesty and deep love for our community, he invites us to examine our fears, rigidity, and blind spots while pointing us toward something brighter, a way rooted in Jesus's gospel of love. Nourishing for believers across the spectrum, *Torn* guides us toward deeper connection, greater resilience, and real transformation in our hearts, our relationships, and our communities."

—Aubrey Chaves, cohost, *Faith Matters* podcast

"A faith crisis is a terrible thing to waste. Too often today it leads to the fracture of families and friendships. Jeff Strong's pathfinding research shows not only that this need not be the case, but that these very struggles offer opportunities for deeper trust and more authentic connection. They are both invitations to grow for both the disciple and the doubtful. This is not just an important book. It is a road map to fuller Christianity."

—Joseph Grenny, cofounder of The Other Side Academy
and The Other Side Village; *New York Times* bestselling author

"As someone who has wrestled with questions and doubts throughout my life, I was deeply touched by the tone and wisdom Jeff Strong brings not only to those who struggle but also to their families and friends. I left the Church for eight years as a young husband and father, and I remain profoundly grateful for a loving wife, children, parents, and extended family who never condemned me but instead made room for my doubts and for a complicated, often painful, spiritual journey.

In *Torn,* Strong reframes disaffiliation not as a failure of faith but as an earnest effort to deepen spiritual roots and live the gospel of Jesus Christ more fully. His perspective offers both compassion and clarity at a time when so many feel polarized or misunderstood.

I came back to the Church because I love the gospel and I want our Church to thrive. This book points us, as a community of Saints, toward a more mature faith—one grounded less in conformity and fear and more in love, understanding, and the teachings of Jesus Christ. *Torn* has the power to heal relationships, soften hearts, and help us grow together into a more Christlike community."

—Roger Kay Allen, PhD, psychologist and
cofounder of The Human Development Institute

"*Torn* is the indispensable guide to healing our community. Working with LGBTQ Latter-Day Saints and their families, I've discovered the struggle for understanding and belonging, rather than a crisis of faith, is the deep wound causing individuals to leave. Jeff Strong's disruptive research on disaffiliation, paired with his compassionate approach to ministry, is a healing balm for those navigating faith challenges and a comprehensive guide to becoming effective and loving healers in the Body of Christ."

—Allison Dayton, founder of Lift+Love

"We often measure the health of the Church by listening primarily to those who remain while overlooking those who have left or are quietly struggling. Jeff courageously addresses this blind spot—not as a critic outside the faith but as a devoted disciple who loves the Church and its doctrine. *Torn* does not undermine belief; it invites us to examine how culture shapes belonging, trust, and spiritual experience. By giving voice to those who wrestle in silence, this book calls us to a needed self-reflection. Its message is timely and vital—strengthening our ability to build connection, preserve faith, and minister more like Christ."

—Rob Ferrell, BYU Education Week instructor;
former mission and stake president

"With beautiful imagery, Jeff Strong shatters our cones of light and encourages us to step into a new world of transformation—one step at a time. For anyone who desires to have 'eyes to see,' this is MUST read."

—Steven A. Hitz, author *Igniting the Holy Flame*

"Ever since Jeff Strong engaged with a comprehensive spectrum of 20,000 current and former Latter-day Saints in the largest and most detailed survey ever conducted about our experiences, I have been on tenterhooks waiting for the publication of what it revealed. This book does not disappoint! It decisively lays to rest the frustrating myths that once-loyal members who leave are lazy learners who do not try hard enough, want to sin, and get deceived by foolishness. Instead, it accurately presents the principled and painful processes involved, and the real reasons for our concerns. Everybody who wants the Church's culture and community to be healthier, kinder to those who leave, or thrive in the 21st century will find the information they need here."

—Peter Bleakley, host of the *Mormon Civil War* podcast

"Jeff Strong's book thoughtfully explores the culture and shared experiences we all encounter as members of The Church of Jesus Christ of Latter-day Saints. Because of our long and trusted friendship, I know the sincerity and integrity behind his words. Over the past decade, I have wrestled to better understand why Jesus Christ needs His church, and Jeff articulates many of the same feelings and questions I've carried. This is an honest, faith-affirming work that offers clarity, hope, and a healthier perspective on discipleship within the Church."

—Ryan Seare, stake presidency counselor and former bishop

"Words are powerful and Jeff's words have the power to bring much healing to many who are hurting—a sense of identity and belonging, validation of their unique yet communal experience and perhaps even a flicker of hope for ongoing connection to Christ through his instrument on this earth. What an amazing book!"

—Catharine Payze, Latter-day Saint psychologist

He Anointed the Eyes of the Blindman,
© Walter Rane. Used by permission of the artist.

Torn

**Why People We Love
Are Leaving the Church and
What We Can Learn from Them**

Jeff Strong

Coolstream Publishing
Midway, Utah

Cover design by Cole Melanson
Graphics design by Jeff Strong
Print design by Marny K. Parkin
Ebook design by Marny K. Parkin

ISBN 979-8-9951426-0-7

First edition

The Proceeds of This Book Will Be Donated to Charity

The author is donating 100 percent of the net proceeds from the sale of this book to the Jeff and Sara Strong Foundation, a charity established to provide scholarships for education and training that expand employment opportunities. These scholarships may support vocational training, community or junior college programs, or university study and are awarded in accordance with the foundation's mission to develop character, respond to those in need, and enhance people's capacity to provide for themselves and help others.

If you would like to learn more about the foundation's purpose and scholarship programs or to apply for a scholarship, you may do so by visiting the book's website (tornbyjeffstrong.com) or via the QR code provided.

CONTENTS

FOREWORD

by Steve Young

Jeff's book is vital to our spiritual journey. His title invites us to consider *not* how we can fix those we love who are leaving the Church but what we can learn from them. I don't know anyone who hasn't experienced loved ones leaving the Church, whether immediate or extended family or close friends. It's a universal experience.

Is our purpose to sift the good people from the bad or to join Jesus as a healing force in all directions? The sifting paradigm takes us to a country-club mentality where there's gatekeeping and othering, letting in the elect and keeping out the rest. Christ isn't looking for a country club. He's looking for a hospital, knowing that one day we're the doctor and the next we're the patient and that we're all ministering to each other. Jesus invites us to join Him in His healing work. But we get in the way when we act as sifters, damning ourselves and our growth. God wants to connect with all His children.

Are we open to learning from those who leave, as Jeff's title suggests? Or do we double down on our transactional thinking, which is the root cause of disconnect?

When someone we love leaves the Church, we can feel threatened. When I can uncover and address my underlying, fear-based thinking, however, I can work on building a healthier relationship that's based on respect for the other person's unique journey.

Instead of trying to fix those who leave, might we learn something instead? We can learn about them, about ourselves, and about God. Let's think about these one at a time. But first, I've got to confess that I'm not speaking as an expert. I'm just a fellow traveler trying, making mistakes, and trying again.

Learn about the other person. Instead of seeing those who leave as lazy or trying to sin, as Jeff points out, the data shows the opposite. Those who leave often try harder to find and follow personal inspiration. Instead of rushing to judgment to make ourselves feel better, we can become curious. The North Star is our *relationship*, not our expectation that others will conform to a set of prescriptive rules. Who knows, when we become curious, we might even feel a touch of "holy envy." That phrase was coined by the late Krister Stendahl, Lutheran bishop of Stockholm, in response to opposition against the building of a Latter-day Saint temple there. Stendahl felt "holy envy" when he thought about the love for ancestors and God that lies at the heart of temple worship. If a Lutheran bishop can be humble enough to listen and even advocate for a faith not his own, maybe we can muster enough humility to be curious about others' spiritual journeys.

Learn about ourselves. It's hard to listen when we feel threatened. My anxiety is the price I pay for trying to keep bad things from happening, my sleepless sacrifice on the altar of outcomes I can't control. That fear-based thinking gets in the way of our relationships, but we can learn to identify and face our fears and move to a healthier paradigm. "There is no fear in love; but perfect love casteth out fear" (1 John 4:18; see also Moroni 8:16). If we forget ourselves and really listen to others, we might see where we can be more accepting, more loving, less quick to judge or condemn—and more like Christ. Instead of the judgmental "You chose to leave, so therefore you have been sifted," we can have the humility and vulnerability to look closely at what we are doing that pushes people away. Not to blame ourselves— that's transactional thinking too. Just so we can learn and grow and do better.

Learn about God. God knows the gospel of Jesus Christ is true but allows His children to choose for themselves. Always. If God is that patient with our growth, what are we doing putting up guardrails for others' growth? Why do we try to compel others to see things our way? Are we living by checklists and merit-badge theology while missing the whole point of the gospel?

It all comes back to Moroni 7:47: "The pure love of Christ . . . endureth forever." As we seek for transfigured eyesight, we will see every human as the glorious, eternal being they are. We can't do that when we judge. We can't aid the Savior in His healing work unless we see things the way He does.

Jeff's book is a call to the higher, holier work of leaving behind the language and behaviors of transaction that seem rational in fear-based thinking but have nothing to do with the rationality and higher logic of heaven.

Leave behind the sifting. Leave the world of transaction and rise to a place of connection. As I often say, we are not loving others onto our path. We are just loving them. No agenda, no expectations, no transactions.

In football, in business, in our churches, and in our families—love can heal whatever is torn.

Steve Young is an NFL Hall of Fame quarterback, cochair of the Forever Young Foundation with his wife, Barb, and author of The Law of Love *and* The Law of Love in Action.

INTRODUCTION

When Worlds Go in Different Directions

One unremarkable morning, I opened my email as I typically do and was startled to see a message from my son Elder Cale Strong. He had entered the Missionary Training Center only days earlier—and it wasn't P-day. I couldn't believe what I was reading. He was coming home.

My mind raced to find an explanation that made sense. Confusion, fear, and grief washed over me. I lingered at my desk, slowly going numb—somehow knowing, even then, that Cale's relationship with the Church was ending. What I didn't know was that my family would soon be torn—first Cale and later Zach and Samantha, three of our five children.

This opened my eyes to something unfolding across our Church community. In time, I came to understand that what began in our family with Cale was part of something much larger—a rare and historic shift touching nearly every Latter-day Saint home.

This book explores why so many sincere, believing Latter-day Saints feel torn between their personal sense of faith, integrity, and what is good and their desire to belong to, love, and be faithful to the Church—and how Church culture can compound or relieve these difficult tensions.

I believe the gospel of Jesus Christ is universal. The Church and its culture are shaped by time and place, and the experiences and perspectives Latter-day Saints have are not the same everywhere, which is important to remember to avoid overgeneralizing as we explore this together.

These tensions, for those who experience them, show up for so many of us in very personal ways: the sadness when someone we love steps away, the confusion of not knowing what happened or why, the conflict we feel in our own Church experience, the strain these differences place on our relationships and families, and the helplessness of not knowing what to do.

What I did not yet know that morning—but I would come to understand over time—is that what was happening was something more significant than an individual faith crisis. It was a trust crisis between a people and their church. When trust and belonging erode, even the most sincere belief struggles to sustain people spiritually, leaving many feeling unseen, disconnected, and hungry. Many are hungry now, and not because they don't believe in or love the Church but because they are searching for belonging, purpose, and spiritual nourishment—things they feel increasingly hard to find in the Church because of the tensions created by the culture.

If this feels close to home—or stirs discomfort, sadness, or recognition—you are not alone, and you are not failing. You are paying attention. This book does not ask you to resolve huge and complex problems or to choose sides. It invites learning, honesty, patience, and a trust that clarity can come with time and that there is power in the small and simple things.

Culture is an instructive word. It comes from the Latin word *colere,* which means to till, tend, or cultivate the soil to grow things. Healthy soil anchors, protects, and provides nourishment. Soil becomes compacted and depleted over time—the natural outcome of doing its job. Church culture serves a similar purpose and works in a similar way. And like soil, it can be examined, prepared, and cultivated to enhance what is good and life-giving in it.

This book is not a critique of the gospel of Jesus Christ, nor a rejection of the Church's mission. It is an examination of how Church culture—shaped by habits, assumptions, traditions, and unspoken expectations—can sometimes drift from the spirit and example of Jesus Christ. Throughout these pages, I am careful to distinguish between the gospel, which I believe is eternal and life-giving, and culture, which is human, adaptive, and therefore capable of both great good and real harm.

In a church, culture and institution are deeply intertwined. Doctrines, leadership, policies, teachings, and member assumptions shape one another. So, in focusing on culture, I am not exempting these other things. I am focusing on the lived experience of the gospel— where doctrine is interpreted, policy is felt, and belonging and belief are either strengthened or strained.

At the heart of our cultural struggle, the problems in our "soil," is a difficult but inevitable tension: how to honor our cherished, time-tested traditions while giving our faith the room it needs to bloom and grow in a changing world. This conflict sits quietly and stubbornly in four questions our Church community wrestles with:

- ➤ Who is the Church really for?
- ➤ How does the Church best prepare us for the challenges of real life?
- ➤ How do we honor God's gift of agency in a culture that expects us to comply?
- ➤ How can we be one when we are so different?

These tensions and the disaffiliation they can cause remain unspoken in our Church community because talking about them is uncomfortable.[1] And while silence may feel safer, it diminishes us. It isolates people in their pain and keeps understanding and healing out of reach. Fyodor Dostoevsky wisely said,

"Much unhappiness has come into the world because of . . . things left unsaid."[2]

The way forward for us begins by refusing to leave things unsaid.

Falling Upward[3]

Cale's story is just one among so many that could be told. Together, these stories reveal an age-old human conflict: the pain of being torn between living in two worlds moving in different directions. Cale's story is also my story.

For years, I allowed myself to be led too much by Church culture and drifted from Jesus Christ's gospel into a cultural version of that gospel—a version that failed when Cale left and the foundation I built on cultural sand and my own hubris was washed away in the flash flood of real life. When we fall, God can teach and lift us in our failures and disappointments. That truth saved me. For decades, my trusted and beloved Latter-day Saint "map" had guided my life. But when my missionary son removed his name tag, took off his garments, left the Church, and, for a time, distanced himself from our family, that map failed me.

Just days earlier, Cale had given a powerful farewell talk as I proudly presided as his bishop, imagining him returning to that same pulpit two years later. That future was on my map. What followed was not.

Months later, searching for clarity, I leafed through his scriptures and found an undonated tithing slip with a ten-dollar bill—a quiet, piercing lesson of a sudden ending and the answers I did not have as to why. My wife, Sara, and I were unprepared for what unfolded. But what Cale endured was far worse. Some who once loved him became harsh and judgmental, their rejection nearly destroying him.

At the time, none of us understood what he carried: the weight of expectations from faith and family colliding with the convictions rising inside him. He wrote in that email: "I honestly want to do the right thing. I'm trying to seek the truth. I just don't think this is where my life should be right now. This is the point where my beliefs are the only ones that matter. I can't lean on the beliefs of others anymore."

Why did Cale choose to step away? For deeply personal reasons that are his to hold and share. The story here is not the private calculus of any one person's journey but the simple and unsettling fact that many people leave—thoughtfully, sincerely, and for reasons that make sense to them. This book is not about evaluating why individuals leave but understanding the culture and conditions that shape so many of those decisions.

What This Book Is Really About

Knowing how many people are leaving and why matters. And what matters even more is understanding what we can do, personally and collectively, to create a Church community where faith can flourish and endure for more of us.

At its core, this book shares that the crisis of trust so many Latter-day Saints are experiencing today is rooted in a Church culture that has become so compacted and depleted that even deep, committed belief struggles to survive. More specifically, it reflects the tension surrounding whether one's questions, experiences, and conscience can coexist with belonging in the Church. The good news is that culture, like soil, can be cultivated to nourish. That is my hope.

In simple terms, this book makes three assertions:

1. Many of our members are leaving, or quietly disengaging, not because they no longer care about faith or the Church but because their lived experience in the Church has, for them, become intellectually, relationally, and spiritually empty.

2. History, doctrine, and leadership are hugely consequential factors. Culture powerfully shapes how these things are taught, lived, and

experienced, often in ways we do not intend, want, or even recognize. Culture can either deepen trust and discipleship—or erode them.

3. Ordinary, faithful members like you and me have more influence than we realize in cultivating a healthier, more Christlike culture. Creating room for more people to gather and faith to grow is how we honor our heritage, affirm our beliefs, and demonstrate our commitment to the Church.

This book flows from a heart beating with gratitude, respect, love, and *concern* for Latter-day Saints and our Church. It seeks to help us better understand one another and stay connected during a time of real strain. And, perhaps, to restore relationships lost.

It is not about attacking anything. It is about tending our shared cultural soil so that faith in Jesus Christ and trust within the Church can flourish for more of us. It is merely a new expression of an old idea—what it means to be a disciple of Jesus Christ in His Church today.

It is written *to* faithful, active Latter-day Saints who love the Church and are trying to make sense of what they are seeing and feeling. This includes worried parents, leaders and teachers seeking to help others, and members feeling tension in their Church experiences. It is also written *for* those who have stepped away but still hope the Church community and its culture can become healthier and more life-giving, for those who stay and those who leave.

If you find yourself in any of these places, by the end of this book, my hope is that you will know you are not alone. I believe you will understand more clearly why so many are leaving, what many experience along the way, and how you can respond with faith, honesty, and love—without abandoning your convictions or adopting theirs.

The messages and stories in this book are supported by world-class research, including one of the largest and most in-depth studies ever conducted on Latter-day Saint disaffiliation and culture (see Strong and Dotson, *Why People Are Leaving,* 2025, in appendix A). But more importantly, they are grounded in the scriptures, our doctrines, and our lived experience—the voices, emotions, insights, and hopes of the thousands walking this path.

The Shape of the Journey

This book is organized around the work of tending the soil. There are four parts:

> **Part 1—Examine the Soil:** How many are leaving, who they are, and why they are leaving

> **Part 2—Prepare the Soil:** How culture creates conditions that impact the way faith takes root

> **Part 3—Cultivate the Soil:** How to balance the tensions that often push people away

> **Part 4—Bring Forth Good Fruit:** How Jesus Christ can help us transform our culture

The metaphor of soil is the central arc of this book. I will often draw on other metaphors, but, ultimately, all tie back to culture as soil. Like all powerful metaphors, it gives us greater understanding, helping us cut through complexity and sensitivity.

Hope in Christ

Whoever you are and however you feel about all this, one thing we all share is hope. Hope is born in the tension between what is and what could be. It draws us forward in ways silence and avoidance never can by refusing to accept the present as the end. Anne Frank said it so well:

"Where there's hope, there's life."[4]

This book ultimately argues for the great potential of our Church community to embrace, guide, and lift its members. Our Church and its culture have real and sustaining strengths. And for nearly two hundred years, the Church has been a place of deep faith, belonging, and growth for millions.

The gospel of Jesus Christ is a lesson in cultivation. Christ restores what is wounded, strengthens what is weak, and makes possible the growth of God's children—even in difficult soil. Cultivation is an act of love. It is how living things remain alive. And it is our work as members of the Church.

The tension you or those you love experience can feel heavy and disorienting. It certainly felt that way for us. But over time, we began to see that God was mindful of us, even in our darkness. That darkness taught us to recognize light. And with more light, I began to see my son more clearly—not through the lens of Church culture but as he truly was.

Faith became a choice. And choosing to see and trust Cale, rather than judge him, opened my eyes. I remembered who he was—my son—and that I knew him. Remembering this gave me greater understanding and hope. In many ways, he became my teacher.

Not long ago, I read a story in *Home By Another Way,* by Barbara Brown Taylor about a group of believers who gathered to strengthen one another's faith. Their discussion commenced with an invitation to think about a time when someone had been Christlike to them. And they began to share their stories. Of this experience, one woman said, "There was one about a friend who stayed put through a long illness while everyone else deserted and another about a neighbor who took the place of a father who self-destructed. One after another, there were stories of comfort, compassion, and rescue."

She said that those who attended felt the Savior's spirit, the warmth of each other's company, and the sense that all was right with the world. She then added, "Until this one woman stood up and said, 'Well, the first thing I thought about when I tried to think who had been Christ[like] to me was, who in my life has told me the truth so clearly that I wanted to kill him for it?' She burst our bubble, but she was on to something vitally important that most of us would be glad to forget."[5]

Christ is there to comfort us and lift our burdens. And He is sometimes there, through His example, teachings, and prodding, to confront us with the truth. If I didn't believe Latter-day Saints wanted and could handle the truth, I wouldn't have written this book.

Some readers may feel this book places too much emphasis on Latter-day Saint culture. Disaffiliation is deeply personal and complex, significantly shaped by secular society, our history, and individual choices. Those realities matter, but they are largely outside our community's control. Culture is not. From both my experience and our research, it is clear that Latter-day Saint culture is both a strength and, at times, a weakness—and we aren't discussing it enough. If we want more people to stay, grow, and thrive in the Church, making our culture more Christlike may be the single biggest lever we have.

I realize that what I am sharing here involves complex, sensitive matters. Consider reading this book with a sense of humility, learning, hope, and love. Consider how you might help create a healthier, more Christ-centered church community where more of us can stay and be loved and lifted and where our relationships with those who choose to leave are respectful and loving.

I do not presume to tell anyone what to think or do. I write as one beggar telling another where I found bread,[6] and I do so in a spirit of love, faith in God, and with great hope in us as a people and a Church. And I try to do that through His perspective, which sometimes forces us to confront difficult truths. If we are willing to see clearly and keep Christ and His teachings at the forefront, especially when it's difficult to do so, I believe we can make progress on this problem that has so far been beyond our reach.

A Short Reading Roadmap

If you prefer to discover a book as you go, feel free to skip this page and begin with chapter 1. If you'd like an overview of the journey, the following is your roadmap. This book is intentionally sequenced, with each part building on the preceding one.

Part 1—Seeing Clearly What Is Happening

Chapters 1 and 2 clarify what is happening with disaffiliation in the Church community today. Drawing on data, research, and lived experience, we identify the disaffiliation patterns people sense but struggle to articulate. Some readers may see this material as weighty, but spending time here is worthwhile because it lays the foundation for what follows.

Part 2—Understanding the Landscape

Chapters 3 through 6 explore the broader landscape upon which disaffiliation is taking place. In these chapters, we explore the cultural, social, and institutional forces shaping how belief is formed, sustained, or strained within our society and Church. The goal is to gain a broader perspective before we explore the core tensions.

Part 3—Engaging the Core Tensions

Chapters 7 through 10 constitute the heart and soul of the book. They examine four tension-causing questions about the Church's culture and its impact on people, relationships, and beliefs, inviting healing, renewal, and Christ-centered balance.

Part 4—Living What We Are Learning

The final chapters focus on integration and how increased understanding can shape everyday discipleship and strengthen trust, connection, and peace.

However you choose to read it, my hope is that this book brings deeper understanding and connection with the gospel of Jesus Christ and those you love.

Part 1

Examine the Soil

How Many Are Leaving and Why

CHAPTER 1

WHAT IS HAPPENING

**"In God we trust.
Everyone else must bring data."**

In this climate of disaffiliation, before we can respond to one another with understanding, compassion, and trust, we must slow down long enough to clearly see what is happening. There are conflicting narratives in our Church community about the scale and seriousness of disaffiliation,[1] and the resulting confusion inhibits the shared understanding that allows wisdom, humility, and love to guide us. The data in the next two chapters provides a foundation—one that helps us see the scope and shape of this problem so that what follows rests on clarity rather than speculation or anecdote.

Science, Data, and Faith

Before diving into how many are leaving and why, let's briefly consider the role data can play in matters of faith. Centuries ago, the prophet Alma taught that the heavens declare the existence of God. "All things denote there is a God; yea, even the earth, and all things that are upon the face of it, yea, and its motion, yea, and also all the planets which move in their regular form, do witness that there is a Supreme Creator" (Alma 30:44).

Later, scientist Johannes Kepler noted the same thing in the elegant laws of planetary motion. Modern scientists still marvel at the fine-tuned constants—the delicate and exact balance of gravity, energy, and the fundamental forces of nature—that allow life to exist in the universe and on Earth.[2] President Russell M. Nelson summarized the beautiful harmony of science and faith: "There is no conflict between science and religion. Conflict only arises from an incomplete knowledge of either science or religion—or both."[3]

A spirit of honest inquiry should guide us as we face one of the most pressing challenges in the Church today. Many of us have seen it with our families, friends, and congregations. The questions come naturally: How many are leaving? Why are they leaving? What does it all mean?

Why Trust This Research?

Our study is perhaps the most in-depth ever done on disaffiliation within the Church. Our surveys included over twenty thousand respondents, mostly in the United States, and dozens of one-on-one interviews. It was conducted and reviewed by a cross-disciplinary team of world-class research professionals deeply familiar with Latter-day Saints, religious belief, psychology, organizational culture, and the study of lived religious faith, including in our Church. We followed best practices and subjected our findings to external review by a variety of experts—all of whom deemed the research appropriate and the findings reliable.[4] A summary of the methodology is available in appendix A.

Like all research, ours has limits. In presenting our findings, I strive to be transparent about those limits. But the patterns our study reveals are consistent and compelling. When compared with national studies (to which I also refer) from Harvard University and the Pew Research

Center, two of the world's most trusted research organizations, our conclusions are consistent and unmistakable: *Faithful* members are leaving, and the pace is quickening.

Why People Love the Church

Though this chapter heavily emphasizes how many are leaving and why, it would be incomplete and imbalanced without including a few positives. In our survey, we asked what people most valued about the Church. What thousands of Latter-day Saints told us closely mirrors my own positive experience. Their testimony of the gospel, their relationship with Jesus Christ, the sense of belonging and support in the Church community, and the plan of salvation were most often mentioned. The chart below provides an informative and inspiring glimpse into the hearts and minds of thousands of today's Latter-day Saints and what they love about the Church.[5]

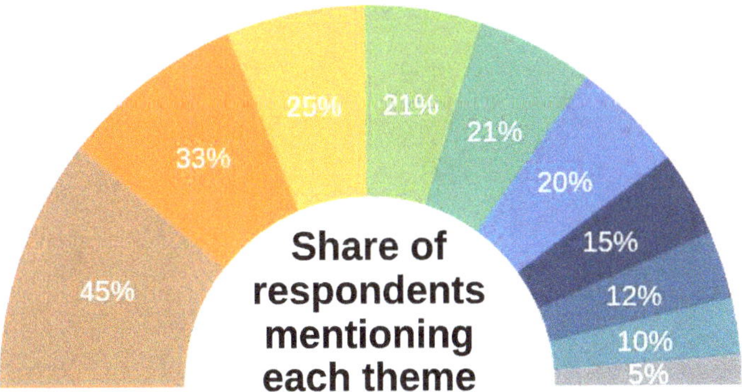

Source: Strong and Dotson, *Why People Are Leaving*, 2025.

Testimony	The truthfulness of the gospel and a relationship with Jesus Christ
Community	Belonging, support, and friendships in the Church community
Plan of Salvation	The guiding doctrine that provides direction, purpose, and an eternal perspective in life
Atonement	The enabling and redemptive Atonement of Jesus Christ as a source of peace and hope
Prophets	Continuous revelation and guidancefor Church members
Covenants	Covenants that bind us to God and provide a path to eternal life
Temple	A place for sacred ordinances and spiritual connection and growth with God
Scriptures	Foundational sacred documents that guide beliefs and practices
Priesthood	Authority and ordinances essential for spiritual growth and connection to God
Sacrament	Renewing covenants and fostering a close relationship with Jesus Christ

These factors tie many of us to the Church. You may find it reassuring and helpful to keep them in mind as we turn our attention to the challenges. As you read what follows, resist the urge to explain it away or solve it too quickly. For now, the goal is simply to see clearly what is happening so we can respond with wisdom, humility, and love.

How Many Are Leaving?

Equally clear is that too many of us are not experiencing the Church in the same way. Based on our research and the findings of Harvard and Pew, we estimate that about 40 percent of once-active, faithful members in the United States have stopped participating over the past twenty-five years.[6] These are *not* members who have always been inactive. These are members who were highly active and stopped participating—members who've experienced disaffiliation.

Source: Strong and Dotson, *Why People Are Leaving,* 2025.

To be thorough in our survey, we approached this question in three ways. First, we directly asked respondents if they had stopped participating. Second, we asked for an estimate of how many in their immediate and birth families had stopped participating. Third, we asked how many of their Latter-day Saint high school friends had. All three approaches produced similar results and suggested a number greater than 40 percent.

Projections for How Many *Active* and *Faithful* Members Have Left the Church

2025 Strong/Dotson Study

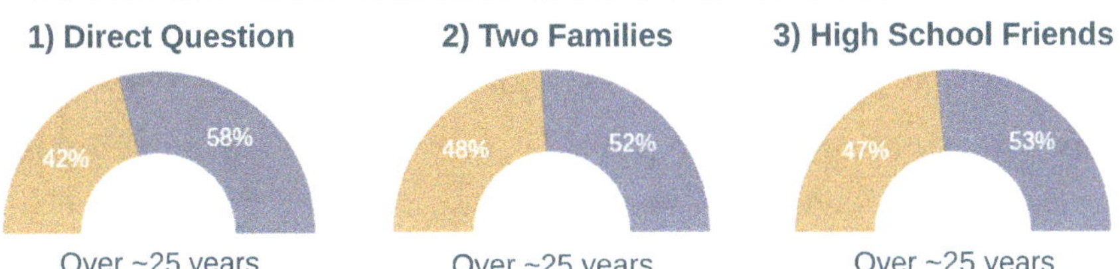

Source: Strong and Dotson, *Why People Are Leaving*, 2025.

National Research Organizations

To validate this finding, we compared our estimate to the findings of independent, national reports by Harvard's Cooperative Election Study[7] and Pew's American Religious Landscape Studies.[8] Both revealed similar disaffiliation rates—55 percent for Harvard over a much shorter time frame and 46 percent for Pew. While no study can perfectly quantify this shift, the convergence of independent data sources suggests a 40 percent estimate is a reasonable one.

To further test the validity of our findings, we shared our results with past and present Church researchers who had first-hand knowledge of Church research and statistics, and asked if our general projections and insights were reliable. All of them confirmed they were. Taken together, these independent findings converge on the same conclusion: A substantial share of once-active members have disengaged, and the scale of this shift is significant. If this feels sobering, that is understandable. Clarity is not criticism. It is the beginning of wisdom, and it helps us respond to real people and issues with more understanding, insight, and kindness.

Our study was not designed to estimate disaffiliation or understand Church member experience outside of the United States, as important as that is. Some valuable and instructive information is available in appendix D and on our website.[9] Though the data is much more limited and what is happening can vary greatly by country, the pattern of disaffiliation or, in many countries, inactivity, appears to be just as pronounced as in the United States, if not worse. Though, thankfully, some countries appear to be thriving.

Why Are They Leaving? The Four Waves

For those who love and trust the Church, exposure to those who don't can be unsettling. It's important to keep in mind that the sacred and treasured experiences we have in the Church are not diminished or undermined by the perspectives of those who experience the

Church differently. The idea in hearing from them is not necessarily to agree but to understand. So, if your perspective and beliefs are different than what follows, and for many of you they will be, that is, of course, okay.

It is also important to note that the way any of us explain our decisions or motives to others is sometimes subject to our own biases and perceptions and our deep need for inner congruency and validation. This complicates how we might interpret people's explanations for their choices. And for most of us, motives are more complex than we might understand, acknowledge, or communicate. Keep this in mind as you review the insights that follow.

Every story of disaffiliation is personal, unique, and complicated. Yet when you study the responses of thousands of voices, patterns emerge—patterns we can learn from.

In our study, we sought to establish clarity on both the *main* reason people step away and *all* the contributing factors. We also sought to go beneath the numbers to understand the experiences people have when they go through a faith transition and what we can learn from them that might help us make a difference. I touch on each of these in the pages that follow.

Importantly, I have done my best to present these insights from the perspective of those who shared them, using *their* words as much as possible. This does not mean I agree or disagree with their views; I am simply relaying what they shared.

Our research suggests that there are four primary reasons most people step away. I refer to these reasons as "waves" because the factors that lead people to leave are dynamic, cumulative, and often experienced in interaction rather than isolation. Like waves, their impact depends not only on size but on timing, overlap, and the individual's position when they arrive. Each represents a cluster of related factors that influenced their decisions.

4 Primary Reasons People Cite for Stepping Away

Source: Strong and Dotson, *Why People Are Leaving*, 2025.

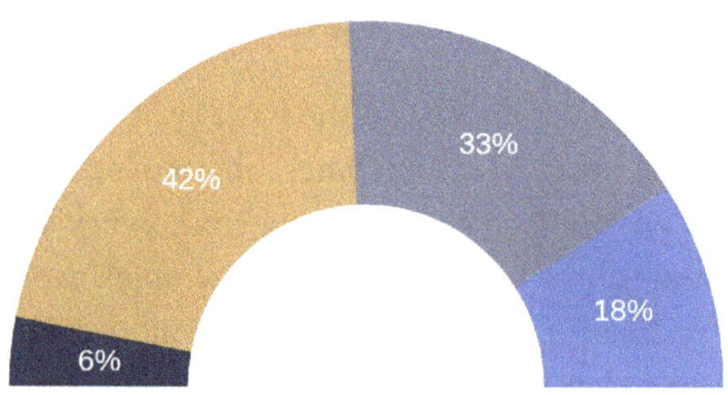

Wave I **Lifestyle**	**Wave II** **Church History**
"I couldn't keep living this way."	*"The Church isn't what it claims to be.*
Wave III **Social Issues**	**Wave IV** **Church Experience**
"Even if the Church were true, I couldn't support this."	*"The Church isn't led by Christ, and it's not life-giving."*

Wave I—Lifestyle Dissonance

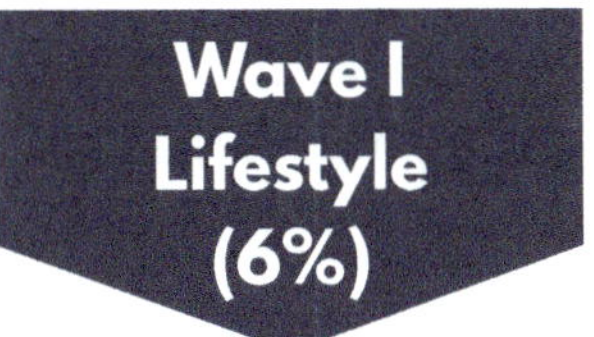

"I couldn't keep living this way." [10]

Most Frequently Cited Issues

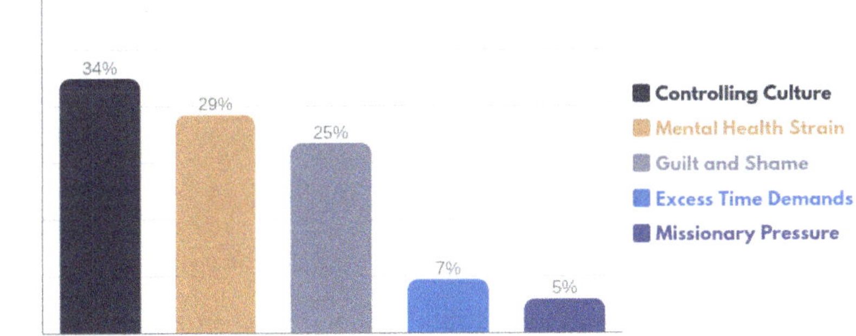

Strong and Dotson, *Why People Are Leaving*, 2025.

Wave I is the main reason approximately 6 percent of people step away from the Church. It is also a contributing factor for another 20–30 percent. The following information provides a helpful, general profile for those most significantly influenced by Wave I factors.

What People Describe

Wave I people describe a growing sense that the demands and rhythms of Church life have become unsustainable, emotionally draining, or misaligned with their capacity and season of life. This wave is quiet and cumulative; it begins not with doubt but with depletion. These members experience burnout, spiritual fatigue, guilt around rest or personal challenges or weaknesses, and a sense that membership has become constant output with too little replenishment. For many who step away, a significant part of this is the culture they feel smothered and controlled by and are not allowed to question.

What People Say

> "I felt controlled and manipulated. There was no room for my thoughts or decisions."[11]

> "I was burning out."

> "I felt overwhelmed and overstretched by time commitments."

> "I got tired of giving so much."

> "I didn't want the expectations or standards."

Typical Triggers

> High-demand callings layered upon family or work strain

> Mental health challenges amplified by perfectionism or guilt

> A culture of constant engagement where rest feels like failure

Relationship to Other Waves

Wave I (Lifestyle) is rarely the cause of departure. It is often the earliest pressure point and, unfortunately, reduces resilience if members later experience the other waves.

Critical Insights

Wave I disaffiliation does not ask "Is it true?" but "Can I survive this?"

Wave I is both spiritual and practical. People are not rejecting sacrifice; they are questioning whether the type of sacrifice they are giving builds connection with God or just depletes them. When lived membership no longer feels life-giving, people become vulnerable to deeper Church concerns they once had the capacity to manage.

Wave II—Church History and Truth Claims

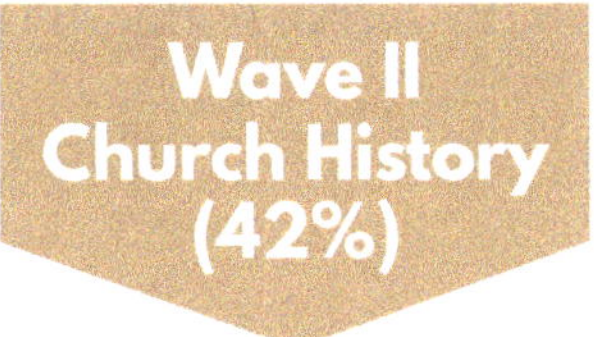

"The Church isn't what it claims to be."

Most Frequently Cited Issues

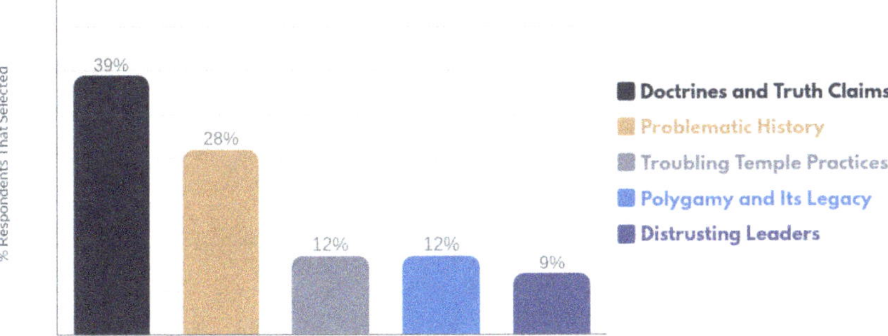

Strong and Dotson, *Why People Are Leaving*, 2025.

Wave II (Church History), the largest wave, is the main reason people are stepping away from the Church (approximately 42 percent). It is also a contributing factor for another 40 to 50 percent.

What People Describe

These people encounter historical, doctrinal, or institutional information that conflicts with what they were taught or assumed about the Church's origins and truth claims. For many, the deepest rupture is not learning of troubling things; it is concluding they no longer know who or what to trust. They are often less disturbed by the actual historical problems (although for many those are troubling enough) and more disturbed by how they believe Church leaders have handled them.

What People Say

> "There were too many concerning things I was never told."

> "The Restoration facts didn't match what I was taught."

> "I believe some of the doctrines and practices were and are wrong."

> "I felt misled."

> "I didn't know what to trust anymore."

Typical Triggers

> Polygamy, racism, Book of Mormon and Book of Abraham translation

> Prophetic fallibility

> Aspects of the temple endowment

> Learning of minimized or withheld historical information

> Official Church explanations perceived as incomplete, defensive, or misleading

Relationship to Other Waves

Wave II (Church History) disaffiliation rarely begins in isolation. It often confirms intellectually what other waves have stirred and becomes the framework people use to articulate why they can no longer stay. Using Wave II as the primary explanation for leaving simplifies the conversation.

Critical Insights

Wave II issues destabilize belief, but it is the loss of trust that ultimately brings withdrawal.

This wave is about inaccurate information and institutional distrust. Many people can live with complexity and imperfection. What troubles them is the perception that they were asked to build their lives on a simplified or inaccurate narrative and later learned that complexity or errors may have been known but not fully shared. The deeper question becomes whether the institution can be trusted to give them the complete truth, even about the problematic things.

Wave III—Church Social Positions and Moral Conflict

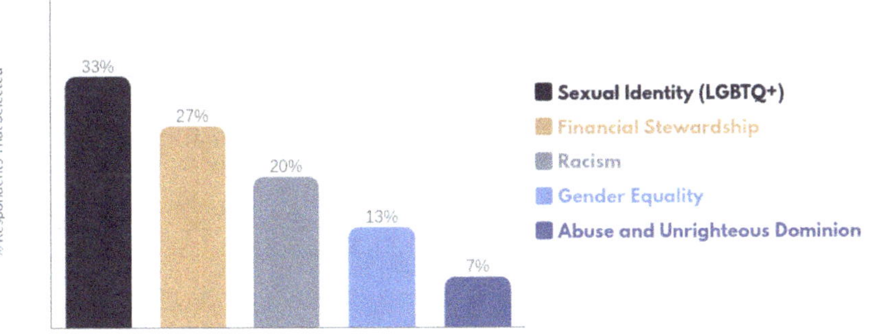

Strong and Dotson, *Why People Are Leaving*, 2025.

Wave III (Social Issues) is the second largest wave and a primary reason (approximately 33 percent) people step away from the Church. It is also a contributing factor for another 50 to 60 percent.

What People Describe

Wave III people experience a collision between Church doctrines, positions, policies, or culture and their conscience, particularly when they perceive harm to vulnerable individuals. This wave is experienced as a moral cost. It is not abandoning faith, but honoring conscience.

What People Say

> "I couldn't reconcile certain things with the teachings and example of Jesus Christ."

> "How the Church handles its money feels morally wrong to me."

> "I felt complicit when I remained silent."

> "I had to choose between my conscience and my church."

Typical Triggers

> LGBTQ+ treatment and theology, particularly if it involves the individual or loved ones

> Financial transparency, priorities, and the for-profit business ventures of the Church

> Paying tithing to the Church as a requirement for baptism and temple ordinances

> Gender inequality and exclusion

> The handling of abuse or harm and a perceived bias for protecting the institution

Relationship to Other Waves

Wave III (Social Issues) disaffiliation often serves as a catalyst, making it permissible for these members to ask questions previously avoided due to a sense of loyalty to the Church or a fear of what they might discover. It frequently leads into Wave II (Church History) inquiry and activates Wave IV (Church Experience) disillusionment when moral concerns are rebuffed by defensive Church leaders or other members.

Critical Insight

Wave III reframes the foundation of belief from truth claims to moral credibility.

Wave III is where belief becomes ethically costly. These members do not primarily seek change; they seek moral integrity. When sustaining the institution feels like a violation of their conscience, Church loyalty becomes heavy for them. This wave is powerful because many feel they cannot outsource moral responsibility without compromising their conscience and values.

Wave IV—Church Experience and Spiritual Depletion

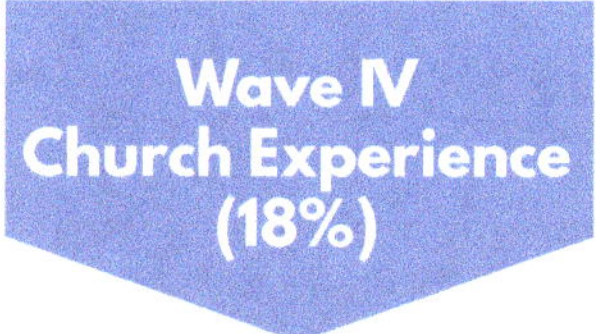

"The Church isn't led by Christ, and it's not life-giving."

Most Frequently Cited Issues

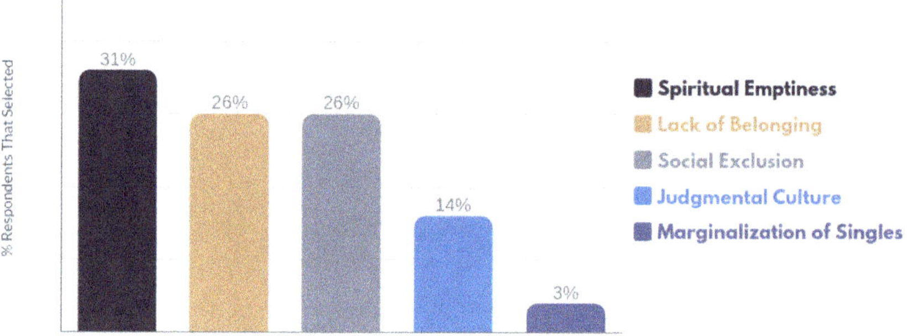

Strong and Dotson, *Why People Are Leaving*, 2025.

Wave IV (Church Experience) is the reason approximately 18 percent of people step away from the Church. It is also a contributing factor for another 30 to 40 percent.

What People Describe

These disaffiliated members describe Church participation that is no longer spiritually nourishing, Christ-centered, or life-giving, even when belief in God and Jesus Christ remains. This loss of spiritual nourishment is often both experiential and relational. For many, this includes disillusioning experiences with leaders. This is less about being offended by random or one-off incidents and more about seeing a pattern of leadership being less informed by discipleship and pastoral care than by institutional loyalty and order.

What People Say

> "I wasn't encountering Christ anymore."

> "I felt spiritually starved."

> "The Savior felt eclipsed by the institution and by Church leaders."

> "I needed the living bread and water of the Savior and could no longer find them here."

Typical Triggers

> Worship that feels procedural rather than spiritually alive

> Too much focus on prophets, obedience, and temples over other gospel priorities

> Leadership that prioritizes compliance over care

> Inability to speak honestly without repercussions

Relationship to Other Waves

Wave IV (Church Experience) disaffiliation often precedes Wave II (Church History) emotionally and follows Wave II intellectually. Our research suggests it is *one of the strongest influences of departure*—a last straw.

Critical Insights

Wave IV asks, "Can I grow here without losing myself—and without losing my faith?

People are evaluating outcomes, or fruits, not claims or policies. Many can live with ambiguity about Church history or social issues, but few can endure a faith community that feels spiritually empty. This wave often becomes decisive because *it takes the question beyond belief to spiritual nourishment and purpose.*

An Integrative Perspective of All Four Waves

The four waves are not separate explanations for why people leave. They are different points of collision between sincere people and a cultural environment that struggles to allow and effectively deal with complexity, conscience, and concerns.

Most people do not leave because of one wave. They leave when multiple waves converge and endurance finally gives way. Culture rarely creates the initial question, but it powerfully influences what happens once the questions come. Of course, we all remain fully responsible for our choices. Over time, the journey is less about losing belief and more about losing trust that the institution and community can engage truth, vulnerability, and moral concern with Christlike kindness and wisdom.

An Important Pause on Key-Issue Depth

This book does not attempt to examine each important and complex issue shaping the contemporary Latter-day Saint experience. Questions surrounding Church history, race and racism, gender and women's roles, and sexual identity within the Church deserve thoughtful, sustained attention that extends beyond the scope of this book. Fortunately, many highly capable authors have already examined these subjects with depth, rigor, and integrity. Readers who wish to explore these issues more fully are encouraged to consult the works cited in the endnotes and others, each of which offers thoughtful and substantive engagement with these vital topics.[12]

The Accelerating Pace of Disaffiliation

Perhaps the most alarming finding in our research is not just the total number leaving but the speed at which they are leaving. Using the decade 2000–2009 as a baseline, the rate of disaffiliation in our survey multiplied dramatically in over the next three successive five-year periods. The exact rates of this acceleration (3×, 6×, and 11×) should be interpreted cautiously. It is possible that a survey bias may exist here. People who have been out of the Church longer (i.e., they left before 2010) may have been less likely to take our survey. If true, the acceleration rate could be somewhat overstated. The important point is not the exact magnitude of the acceleration but that it appears to be happening—a conclusion supported by numerous other credible studies.[13]

Disaffiliation Appears to Be Accelerating

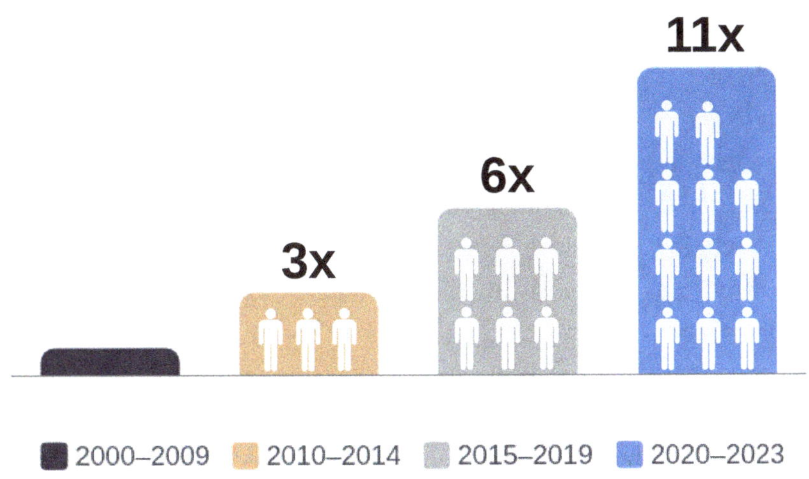

Source: Strong and Dotson, *Why People Are Leaving*, 2025.

When applied across thousands of wards and branches, the impact of disaffiliation is significant. A bishop in Utah told us, "I used to worry about a few individuals drifting each year. Now it feels like entire pews are emptying." The rate of departure suggests something more than isolated concerns. It reflects an unusual and broad shift in how members experience the Church in a changing world.

Demographics and a Changing Church Composition

The Harvard CES report also helps clarify not only how many people are leaving the Church but *who* is leaving and how disaffiliation patterns are changing. Analysis of the HCES study, synthesized by Alex Bass, shows that disaffiliation is accelerating at both ends of the age spectrum.[14] Members aged thirty-five and under are leaving at substantially higher rates than previous generations did at the same life stage, while members sixty-six and older are also disaffiliating at faster-than-average rates. This suggests that disaffiliation is no longer confined to young adulthood and may reflect a broader, life-course dissatisfaction.

In recent years, an emerging narrative suggests that younger adults, particularly Generation Z (roughly 1997–2012) are returning to religion in large numbers. While this claim reflects real pockets of renewed religious activity, reliable research does not support it. Gen Z remains the least religiously affiliated generation on record, with roughly one-third identifying as religiously unaffiliated, and young adults continue to disengage from organized religion at higher rates than older groups.[15]

What has changed is not the overall level of affiliation but its *composition*: Fewer people participate casually or by inheritance, while a smaller group engages more intentionally and visibly.[16] At the same time, many who disaffiliate continue to express belief in God or spiritual openness, suggesting that what is eroding is not their faith but their confidence in religious institutions as the primary custodians of belief.[17]

Disaffiliation in the Church today is not evenly distributed across age or gender. While men were historically more likely to drift away, that pattern has now reversed among younger members. Generation Z women are leaving at higher rates than men—a striking break from the past. Recent surveys show that young women are more likely to stop identifying as Latter-day Saints and fully disengage rather than quietly go inactive.[18]

Their reasons differ as well. Men who leave tend to cite intellectual or historical concerns, while women more often point to cultural and structural tensions, especially around gender roles, authority, and social issues.

At the same time, a paradox remains: The women who stay are typically more religiously committed than the men who do.[19] The result is a Church increasingly shaped by deeply devoted women on the inside alongside a growing exodus of women at the margins—a dynamic that may represent the most serious retention challenge of the coming decade.

In addition, Bass's analysis shows that members with higher levels of formal education are disaffiliating at higher rates than those with less education.

One of the more sobering statistics from the HCES study is the replacement ratio: For every convert joining our church in the United States, how many step away? It appears from their research that our replacement ratio may be insufficient to offset the losses. However, with exceptionally strong convert baptisms in 2024 and the highest convert baptism year ever in 2025, it may be that the long-term decline in convert baptism since the mid-1990s is reversing.[20] I certainly hope so. Taken together, these trends suggest that contemporary disaffiliation is systemic rather than episodic, indicating a sustained shift in how increasing numbers of members currently experience the Church.

Beneath the four waves of disaffiliation lies a quieter and more complex dynamic. Using data from the Pew Research Center's Religious Landscape Studies, Alex Bass conducted an analysis to identify distinct belief-and-experience segments among Latter-day Saints.[21]

One segment, described as Devout Traditionalists, is characterized by strong literal belief, high institutional trust, close alignment with

Church authority, and deep comfort within prevailing Church culture—members who are a very important part of the Church.

Bass's analysis estimates that Devout Traditionalists may have once made up approximately 50 percent of U.S. Latter-day Saints in the late 2000s and early 2010s. Today, that same segment appears to represent closer to 23 percent of Church membership—suggesting a significant decline of roughly half over two decades. It is less likely that Devout Traditionalists are leaving the Church, though some may be. It is more likely that people who were once Devout Traditionalists may be changing in their mindset and approach to religion. At the same time, Pew data shows that this group reports significantly higher levels of life satisfaction, emotional well-being, family stability, and positive religious experience than other Latter-day Saint segments. If you are in this segment, this probably reflects what you feel.

In many ways, this is cause for celebration. It is a gift when a faith community works deeply and consistently well for those within it. What remains less certain but increasingly important is what this divergence means for the broader Church community.

> **If a culture continues to be shaped primarily around the needs, assumptions, and experiences of a shrinking minority for whom it works exceptionally well, how does that culture remain life-giving for a growing majority whose beliefs, questions, or moral experiences are no longer attended to?**

I don't believe there are any easy answers to this question, but it helps illuminate why the same Church culture can feel sustaining to some and draining to others.

The Human Cost

Behind every statistic is a real person, and behind every person is a family and a community. The cost of disaffiliation is not only measured in numbers but in broken trust, strained relationships, and spiritual loss.

A father in his forties explained: *"I spent years trying to hold on. I didn't want to leave. But eventually, I realized the Church I had loved for so long wasn't nourishing me anymore. I felt spiritually empty."*

A mother described her experience: *"I stopped going not because I lost faith in God but because every Sunday I felt invisible. Nobody asked what I was going through. Nobody seemed to care."*

A returned missionary reflected: *"The history shook me, but it was the culture that drove me out. I could have stayed if I felt safe wrestling with my questions and concerns. I felt alone and even ashamed."*

These stories help illustrate two crucial truths: (1) Disaffiliation is not casual. It is rarely a quick decision. It is a journey of struggle, grief, and, finally, resignation. (2) We each experience the Church and the gospel differently.

Understanding the Four Waves

Taken together, the four waves reveal not separate causes but a shared pattern: When sincere questions, moral tension, or vulnerability arise, Church culture powerfully shapes whether those experiences lead to growth, prolonged endurance, or disengagement. This is why the chapters that follow focus less on resolving individual issues and more on understanding the cultural conditions that influence how faith is lived, tested, and sustained.

What Do Latter-day Saints End Up Believing?

Eighty-six percent of those who took our survey characterized themselves as currently or previously "very active" in the Church. So, where are they now in their belief? Fifty-six percent continue to participate in the Church but have very different ways of believing, as shown in the graphic on the next page.

These are all active members who are in the same pews and classrooms, worshipping and serving together despite differing beliefs but sometimes experiencing significant tension, which we will return to

Which statement best describes your current beliefs?

Among respondents who self-identified
as previously being completely or mostly active

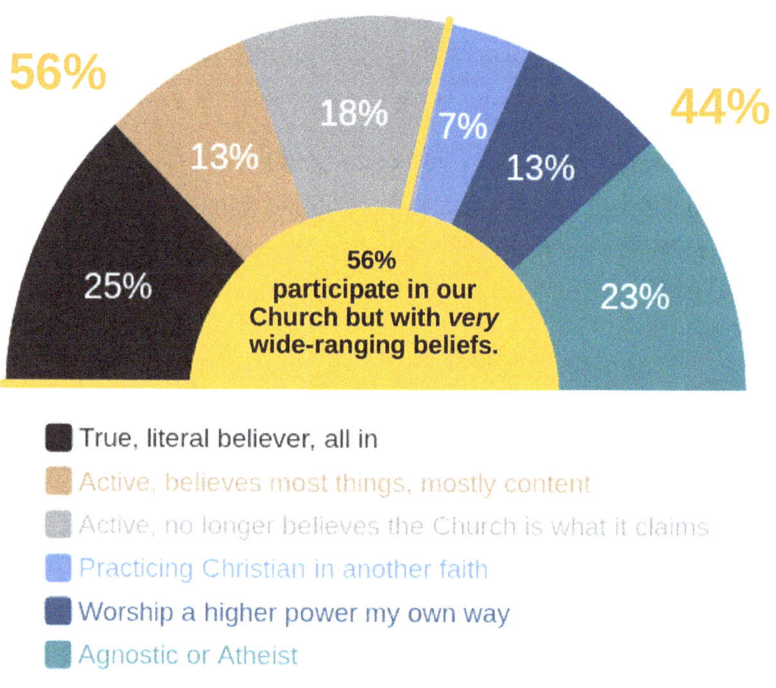

Source: Strong and Dotson, *Why People Are Leaving*, 2025.

later. Forty-four percent stop participating. Some remain practicing Christians (7 percent), some believe but don't participate in organized religion (13 percent), and some are agnostic or atheist (23 percent).

The vast majority who stop participating say they are at peace with their decision, though, as we will see in chapter 2, their transition is most often full of mixed emotions, including a sense of loss, anger, and grief but also an increased sense of freedom, new possibilities, and relief.

They commonly find meaning and purpose through family, close relationships, community, work, service, nature, hobbies, and personal values. Many maintain values like ours and continue to hold spiritual beliefs and engage in religious practices.[22] Many do not. And over half who step away say the Church can do nothing to cause them to return. They are at peace with their decision and have moved on.

Our Crossroads

For many, experience in the Church community is deeply torn between faith and conscience, honesty and belonging—between two worlds pulling them in different directions. Before we can talk about solutions, we must first understand what people are experiencing. If we ignore this reality, our loves ones will continue to leave our Church community.

We are at a crossroads. The direction we choose will quietly shape whether future questions are met with trust and growth—or silence and departure. There exists a path that is harder and slower yet far more hopeful: intentionally cultivating a culture where people feel safe to wrestle, question and learn, and bring their whole selves—a culture that treats diversity of experience and belief not as a threat but as part of the living body of Christ.

The crisis is real, the losses painful. But the path forward is within reach. The gospel of Jesus Christ is a gospel of renewal. Christ restores what is broken and heals what is wounded.

Disaffiliation may feel like decline, but it can also be a refining fire, exposing what is not working and inviting us to build something more faithful to Christ's vision.

> **"Come unto me, all ye that labour and are heavy laden,**
> **and I will give you rest."**
> **(Matthew 11:28)**

That promise of rest is still available—for those who stay, for those who leave, and for the Church itself.

Understanding *what* is happening and *how many* are affected is an important first step. Chapter 2 now turns inward. It explores what this journey feels like from the inside and why culture often determines whether sincere questions lead to deeper faith or departure.

Key Chapter Takeaway

Disaffiliation is widespread, accelerating, and deeply consequential not because belief itself is weak but because cultural conditions often fail to engage people through disruption, inquiry, and change. Culture powerfully shapes whether faith disruption leads to growth or withdrawal, underscoring why cultural renewal is so important.

Reflection Questions

1. What disaffiliation have I noticed in my family or faith community over time?

2. How have I typically interpreted the magnitude and causes of disaffiliation?

3. Whose experiences with disengagement or leaving have I struggled to understand and why?

Application Suggestion

Resist the urge to immediately explain, defend, or resolve any tension you might feel as you read this next chapter. Instead, choose someone you know who is experiencing what is described. Spend time simply trying to understand this experience without correcting it or reframing it.

Pay attention to where discomfort arises within you. Notice the instinct to simplify, categorize, or move too quickly toward certainty. Stay present with complexity a little longer—not to abandon faith but to make space so that deeper understanding and compassion can take root.

CHAPTER 2

WHEN BELIEF IS TORN
How Culture Breaks What Questions Cannot

**"We are a question-asking people
because we know that inquiry leads to truth."
—President Dieter F. Uchtdorf**

As I began to understand the magnitude and causes of disaffiliation, I felt discouraged. But given what I saw unfolding in my own family, the mission Sara and I led, and in the Latter-day Saint community around me, I also felt deeply motivated to understand. I couldn't set it aside and move on. I wanted to make a difference. I knew I had to spend time walking in other people's shoes. The research and experiences I share throughout this book are part of that walk.

As I did that, in time, I came to realize it was not what I imagined—and that gave me hope. I offer that encouragement to you as we dive a little deeper into what people are experiencing. Of course, the truth matters, and sometimes we must pay a price to obtain it.

**"The truth will set you free,
but first it will make you miserable."[1]**

The hard truth is that people are suffering. It is valuable for anyone affected, directly or indirectly, to understand what that suffering feels like from the inside so we can respond with compassion.

Individuals and families are strained. Fewer are finding solace in the Church. Facing this truth with honesty can feel miserable, but beyond that misery lies the possibility of renewal in the gospel and in our Church community.

Candor and Pain

Responding wisely to disaffiliation also requires us to see clearly how our culture may turn reasonable questions or concerns into crises. We must be humble and honest. Honesty is an essential thread in the fabric of trust. Candor is often the most uncomfortable form of honesty. Yet candor and the pain it may bring are not our enemies; they can be our teachers.

Sara once gave a stake conference talk about the important role pain plays in our lives. She drew from Dr. Paul Brand and Philip Yancey's *The Gift of Pain,* which shows that pain is a God-given warning system. Without it, as Brand observed in his leprosy patients, unnoticed injuries lead to devastating harm.

Brand and Yancey put it simply: "Silencing pain without considering its message," they warn, "is like disconnecting a ringing fire alarm to avoid receiving bad news."[2] Sara reminded us that we often fear pain (failure, criticism, and disappointment) in life and in the Church and respond by denying or numbing it rather than learning from it. Yet, in Jesus Christ's teachings, we can take painful experiences and turn them into opportunities for learning, change, and healing.

Many of us feel some degree of pain in our Church experience. In all this, regardless of the reasons, know you are not alone. Our relationship to the Church is rarely driven by a single motive. Some who step away do so with deep sincerity and a desire to live with integrity; others take a step back with a mixture of conviction, pain, exhaustion, unresolved questions, and relational strain—as most of us do when life gets complicated.

The same complexity exists among those who stay. Many remain grounded in genuine faith and devotion to Christ, while others stay partly because of fear, habit, social pressure, or the cost of leaving. Most live somewhere in between. This book is not an attempt to sort people into moral categories or excuse personal responsibility. It is an effort to understand how culture shapes experience—and how that shaping can either help strengthen or diminish belief.

Whether you are among those who've left or those who've stayed, we all share a similar sense of loss and many of the same questions. Pain may feel isolating, but it is, in reality, shared and can instruct us if we let it. And if you experience pain while reading this book or from what is happening in life or with your loved ones, consider this:

> Pain helps us locate and diagnose what needs attention.

> Pain is a teacher. It can help us adapt and become resilient.

> Pain, when faced honestly, can become a pathway to healing, gratitude, and peace.

Rather than disconnect our ringing fire alarms, we can ask: What is this pain trying to teach us about the condition of our cultural soil? If we are willing to accept candor and pain as our teachers, we can face the reasons driving today's disaffiliation.

Beyond the Numbers

The numbers tell us something significant is happening, and they correct the idea that disaffiliation is rare, fringe, or driven primarily by moral failure or apathy. But the numbers alone cannot tell us what this journey feels like.

This chapter draws on the thousands of first-person accounts we received in our surveys and further explored in one-on-one interviews.[3] Together, they reveal that faith transition is not a single decision but a prolonged, deeply serious experience—one shaped less by questioning than by the cumulative effects of culture on conscience, trust, and, ultimately, belonging.

What emerges is not a story of people trying less but of people trying longer than they thought possible, often until something finally gives way. And it is a difficult and uncomfortable process where those who experience it and continue to participate in the Church experience conflict, a loss of belonging, and cultural discomfort. This invites us to consider what it is about our culture that causes people to feel all of this.

What People Going through Faith Transition Experience

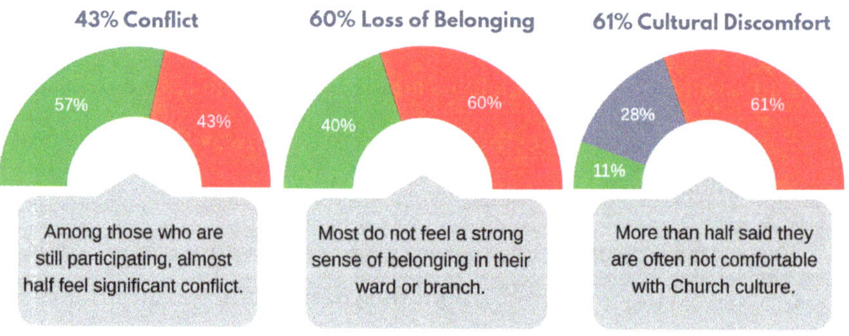

Source: Strong and Dotson, *Why People are Leaving*, 2025.

The Journey That Starts Early, Takes Years, and Involves Many People

While concerns about the Church or Church experience often emerge early, disaffiliation unfolds slowly. Thirty-five percent of Latter-day Saints report experiencing a significant concern in childhood or adolescence, with 62 percent doing so by the end of their twenties.

However, relatively few act on those concerns while children or teenagers. Instead, many carry them forward into adulthood, often spending a decade or more wrestling with them before stepping away. As a result, disaffiliation is concentrated later, with most departures occurring in their twenties (29 percent), thirties (29 percent), and forties (20 percent)—well after initial concerns first arise.

What they encounter when they seek understanding often changes the trajectory of the journey. Encouragingly, many receive support. But many encounter criticism when they open up—and that criticism has consequences. For some, it comes as a warning to "be careful." For others, it's more direct: a rebuke, a dismissal, or a reframing of sincere questions as weakness or even sin. In either case, the effect is similar. Their openness narrows. Trust thins. Those who feel criticized or reprimanded for seeking understanding often become careful and guarded.

The negative responses they often encounter are rarely driven by malice. More often, they are driven by concern or defensiveness—the instinctive reaction that naturally arises when a question feels threatening, destabilizing, or too close to home.

When questions challenge beliefs that feel central to our identity or sense of stability, we tend to become defensive. I did. When this defensiveness goes unchecked, it becomes destructive. My mistakes have taught me that it's often rooted not in conviction but in feeling unprepared or insecure in my answers.

Those in search of understanding reach out to spouses and friends, parents, and Church leaders to different degrees and with very different outcomes. Interestingly, parents and leaders, who may have the most to offer, are sought out far less and are perceived to be dramatically less helpful than spouses and friends. When faith is closely bound up with identity, certainty, and belonging, honest questions can feel like an attack rather than an invitation.

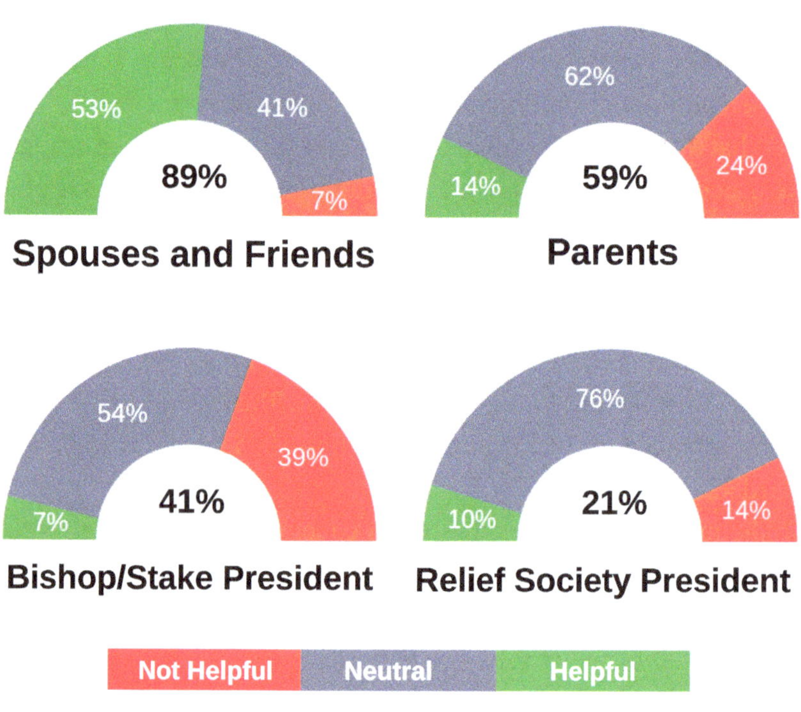

Source: Strong and Dotson, *Why People Are Leaving*, 2025.

In those moments, the impulse is often to shut the conversation down. Questions are reframed as a lack of faith. Inquiry is recast as disloyalty.[4] Moral concern is interpreted as pride, worldliness, or spiritual weakness. Usually, these responses are not intentionally critical; they are protective. But they are deeply consequential. People quickly learn which questions are welcome and which are not. And they learn who they can trust with their deepest thoughts and feelings—and who they cannot.

I believe we can do better. We can greatly benefit from the wise counsel and reassurance of the Christian theologian Paul Tillich, who observed, "Doubt is not the opposite of faith; it is one element of faith."[5] What threatens faith is not questioning but a religious culture that cannot make room for it.

> **"The hardest part wasn't losing belief.**
> **It was realizing who I couldn't be honest with."[6]**

If this feels heavy, it's because these experiences involve real people and real pain. For a moment, simply understanding this and feeling some empathy is enough.

Trying Harder, Not Less

Another common assumption collapses under closer examination: that people leave because they simply stop trying or become lazy. The data shows the opposite. People pray more. Study more. Serve more. Seek the guidance of the Holy Ghost more. At first, when answers do not come, many assume the problem lies with them—that they lack faith, humility, worthiness, or spiritual capacity. This self-blame is often reinforced by a culture that teaches, implicitly if not explicitly, that good people do not have these kinds of concerns or needs—a persistent, inaccurate cultural belief.

For a time, that assumption holds, often for years. People double down. They try harder. They wait longer. They quietly endure. But endurance has a cost. Over months and years, self-blame compounds. Silence deepens. The effort required to remain present while withholding one's real questions becomes exhausting. Over time, the mindset begins to shift. As people continue to wrestle honestly, many come to a painful realization: The problem is not their lack of effort or sincerity. The vast majority spend countless hours over many years wrestling with their questions and concerns.

Faith Transition Is a Serious, Sustained Process

How Much Time and How Long Did You Spend Wrestling With Your Concerns?

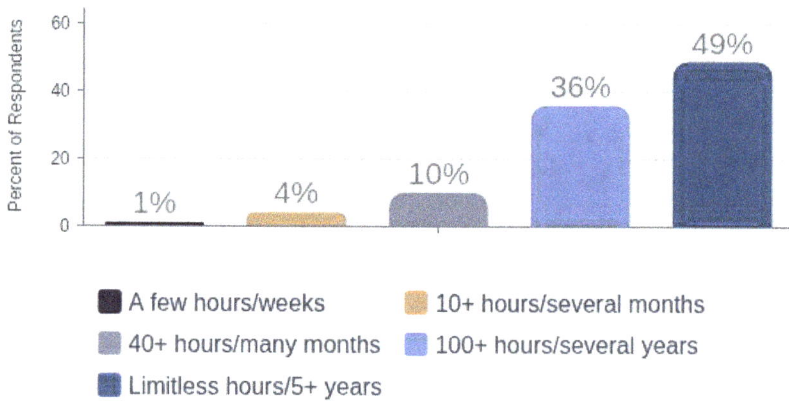

Source: Strong and Dotson, *Why People Are Leaving*, 2025.

The deeper conflict lies in the culture they trusted—a culture that struggles to engage questions with openness, humility, and compassion. That realization is often accompanied by grief and sometimes anger—not the anger of rebellion but the anger that follows the betrayal of trust. They slowly realize it is not *they* who are broken but the culture that won't tolerate their questions.

If effort preserved belief, most of these individuals would still be fully active. Leaving, for the majority, is not the beginning of disengagement. It is the end of endurance.

The Moral Disruption

Contrary to popular belief, most faith transitions do not begin with questions about Church history. They begin with some disruption regarding moral integrity. Sometimes this comes through direct experience: watching a vulnerable person excluded or shamed, seeing abuse mishandled, observing unrighteous dominion practiced by a leader and seeing it go uncorrected, or witnessing institutional protection at the expense of people.

Other times it comes through an accumulation of tension, particularly around the limited voice and roles of women, the complex issues of sexual identity, our problematic history with racism, financial stewardship, and cultural dishonesty. What matters even more than the issue itself is the internal shift it produces.

"At some point, it stopped being about questions and became about conscience."[7]

This internal shift rarely initially produces disbelief. What it produces is *permission*—the permission to ask questions previously off-limits—deferred or suppressed because asking felt disloyal, unsafe, or spiritually risky. For many, that search includes serious study, credible research, and the honest use of the moral compass God has placed within them. Faith and inquiry are not enemies. The light of Christ does not bypass reason. It deepens its. As Alma taught, "Now, as I said concerning faith—that it was not a perfect knowledge—even so it is with my words" (Alma 32:26). Scripturally, faith has never required certainty or remaining ignorant. But that is often what our culture requires.

Once permission is granted, many let go of this false cultural belief and begin to more openly and actively seek answers to their questions. This search *almost always* begins with the hope of finding a reason to believe, to stay, and to preserve everything they have loved and believed about the Church.

Seeking Answers but Finding Problems

Most members experiencing a faith transition actively seek information and perspectives. Their experience across a variety of sources varies dramatically. Nonofficial Latter-day Saint[8] and non-Latter-day

Saint religious[9] resources are the most frequently utilized and the most often found to be helpful. They also frequently consult official Church[10] resources, but a significant number of people find them unhelpful. Social media and ex-Latter-day Saint resources are less frequently utilized but are found to be more helpful than not by a significant number of people. Overall, most describe official Church resources as the least helpful, typically because they are seen as incomplete, selective, defensive, or disconnected from lived reality. This is a tremendous opportunity for us to do better.

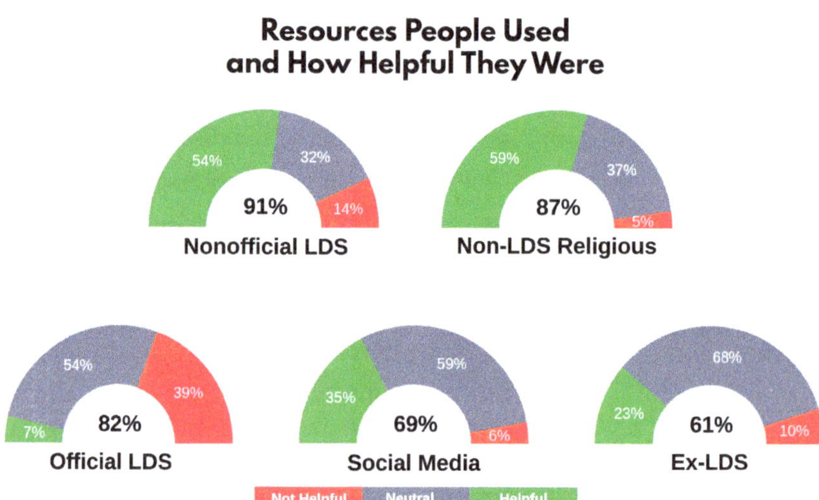

Source: Strong and Dotson, *Why People Are Leaving*, 2025.

One of the most difficult and least-discussed dynamics we observed in the data was that for many sincere seekers, increased involvement in the Church does not resolve their concerns—it sometimes intensifies them. This pattern appears consistently across survey responses and interviews. This is not because they lose spiritual sensitivity or encounter hidden facts. It's because proximity sometimes exposes patterns of defensiveness, institutional self-protection, and moral inconsistency that erode trust through first-hand, lived experience rather than arm's-length, abstract speculation.

For some, this proximity comes through leadership. Serving as leaders closely with other more senior Church leaders can be deeply inspiring or deeply disillusioning—not because of imperfection, which people expect, but because they see a pattern first-hand: Their perception that some issues of moral-integrity are sometimes dismissed or managed rather than confronted and repaired. For many, this creates a painful dissonance between what they experience and the Christ-centered ideals they have been taught by Church leaders to believe in and strive toward. It is certainly possible that they may not have had visibility to all of the complexities involved.

At this stage, the crisis is no longer informational. The question shifts from *Is this true?* to *Can I rely on this institution to tell me the truth—and to do what is right when it is costly*?

Across thousands of stories, a remarkably consistent pattern emerges—not as a rigid formula but as a lived sequence many recognize only in hindsight:

› **Moral-integrity disruption**—a moment when conscience is stirred by something significant, such as harm, information, dishonesty, or institutional self-protection

› **Permission to ask**—questions once deferred or suppressed are now approached openly, not to dismantle belief but to preserve integrity and with the hope of finding answers

› **Intensive seeking**—sustained prayer, study, reflection, seeking the Holy Ghost, and engagement with others, including Church sources and leaders, often over years

› **Relational or cultural breaking point**—repeated defensiveness, silencing, or dismissal erodes trust, and belonging becomes conditional

Typical Stages of Disaffiliation

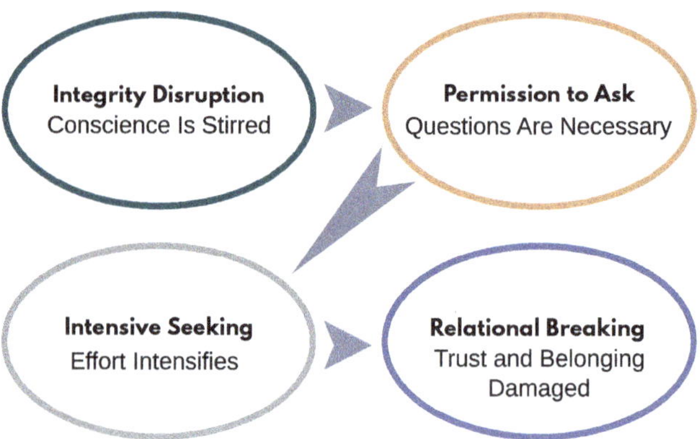

Source: Strong and Dotson, *Why People Are Leaving*, 2025.

**For most, departure does not follow doubt.
It follows disillusionment.**

Silence as the Cost of Belonging

Many people participate long after belief fractures. Our research suggests that approximately one-third of members attending sacrament meetings each week no longer believe the Church is what it claims to be. They attend meetings. They hold callings. They listen carefully, editing themselves internally, not because they are deceptive but because they understand the personal and relational cost of being open or disruptive.

Our research provides an unusually sobering window into this reality. Among those who experience a faith transition, only about 12 percent describe themselves as comfortable in the Church. Roughly 65 percent report that they still participate but do so in a state of internal conflict. More people remain in discomfort than feel genuinely at home.

A question I've heard many faithful members raise is: If they are so uncomfortable, why don't they just leave?

> Because families matter. Because relationships matter. Because leaving would mean abandoning a church and a people they have loved and given themselves to with their whole hearts for decades or a lifetime. Because silence feels safer than honesty or withdrawal.

This reveals a crucial tension: Many believe that someone with doubts or concerns can remain valued in the Church, which is encouraging. But a greater number do not believe that someone who holds nontraditional beliefs—even if they live Church standards and express themselves respectfully—would be accepted if they spoke openly. Belonging requires silence.

Silence can preserve relationships. Silence can protect families. Silence can keep doors open. But silence exacts a price. Over time, people describe feeling thinner—present but unseen, engaged but increasingly unreal. The strain of maintaining belonging while suppressing conscience becomes unbearable. This is where many people feel most deeply torn—between integrity and inclusion, between conscience and community, between honesty and home.

The Hidden Mental and Emotional Cost

Beneath these patterns lies a quieter cost. Faith transition is often accompanied by loneliness, anxiety, grief, and emotional exhaustion. Many seek counseling not because they have failed spiritually but because they are trying to survive the strain of prolonged internal conflict, the fear of relational rupture, and the pain of being rejected by a community they have loved and that has nurtured them. The fracture in friendships, marriages, parent/child relationships can be real and painful.

This is not evidence of pathology. It is evidence of seriousness and consequences. People are not disengaging from meaning. They are grappling with it, often in isolation. In many cases, the psychological burden is not created by the question itself but by the prolonged requirement to carry it silently. At the very time they need their church community most, they are often met with rejection and are pushed to the margins. *This is a significant factor in why many step away.*

Some voices in our research express deep anger—anger born of betrayal, grief, and harm. These voices are real, and they matter. The dominant emotions are sorrow, exhaustion, and loss. Some do leave in anger and protest. More leave in grief and disillusionment.

God and the Church: A Critical Divergence

One of the most revealing findings from our research is that, for many, faith transition strengthens their relationship with God even as it weakens their relationship with the Church. After a faith transition, a slight majority report a deeper, more personal connection with God. At the same time, about nine in ten report a weaker relationship with the Church.

How did your faith transition impact your relationship with God and the Church?

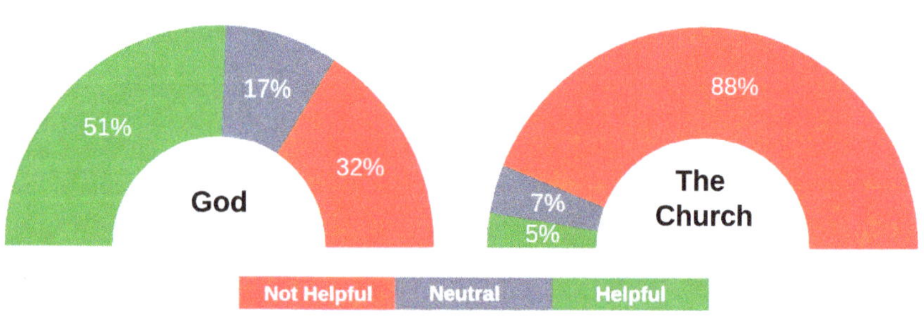

Source: Strong and Dotson, *Why People Are Leaving*, 2025.

This divergence is critical. While this is not true for all who step away, it suggests that faith transition is not primarily a loss of spirituality or belief. It is often a loss of institutional trust. One respondent said simply:

**"I didn't leave because I stopped believing.
I left because I couldn't keep pretending."**

Preparing the Soil

For some of you, this chapter may feel unsettling because it is difficult to comprehend the complicated faith described when, for so many of us, our faith has been uncomplicated, meaningful, and sustaining. Latter-day Saint author Neylan McBaine helped me understand the importance and value of what we can do individually to ensure the difficulties described in this chapter are not endured in vain: "Honoring the suffering of one by telling her story is a way of honoring and relieving the suffering of all who have had similar experiences."[11] Taking these experiences seriously does not diminish our faith or invalidate the real and sustaining experiences many of us have had. It asks us whether a community that has blessed us so abundantly can also be strong enough to listen and extend goodwill to those having a very different experience.

This chapter is not about resolving questions or prescribing solutions. It is about understanding what faith disruption actually feels like when it unfolds inside real people. Without that understanding, efforts to explain, defend, or fix almost always miss the mark. With it, we are better prepared to examine why cultural conditions can either help people endure disruption with faith—or quietly push them toward withdrawal. That work begins in chapter 3.

Key Chapter Takeaway

For many, honesty can become a casualty of belonging. Questions, doubts, or moral tensions are often met with discomfort or dismissal, eroding trust until endurance gives way to exhaustion.

A healthier community is one strong enough to listen sincerely and compassionately.

Reflection Questions

1. When have I felt pressure to stay silent to belong? When have I seen this in others?

2. How do I usually respond when someone I love shares faith questions or concerns?

3. What might it look like to listen without correcting, fixing, or defending?

Application Suggestion

Rather than focusing on the scale of change happening around belief, bring your attention back to what is within your reach. Choose one relationship, one conversation, or one moment where belief feels unsettled or strained for someone you know.

See them with compassion rather than alarm. Ask yourself: *How might I respond differently if I assumed this wrestling reflects sincerity, courage, and a desire for integrity—not weakness or failure?* Let that assumption guide how you listen, speak, and remain present.

PART 2

PREPARE THE SOIL

Create Soil
Where Seeds Can Take Root:
Helping People Stay

CHAPTER 3

SEEING

We will now step back from *what is happening* to the *landscape it is happening on*: the forces—beneath and beyond disaffiliation—reshaping how belief is formed, experienced, and sustained or not sustained in today's world and in our Church. It will help us better understand the things creating conditions that can prevent or trigger disaffiliation.

Healthy soil can produce deep roots and sustain growth. For our cultural soil, this means several things: Being able to see disaffiliation clearly. Recognizing what culture is and how it nourishes or depletes religious experience. Understanding the significant societal factors changing the relationship between spiritual needs, religious beliefs, and churches, and ensuring our beliefs are truly centered in Christ's teachings.

We can engage with these issues more confidently and successfully when we are informed. We can contribute to a cultural soil that sustains more of us. We will touch on each of these things in part 2, starting with seeing.

Being human is to sometimes confuse what we see with the fullness of truth. Perspectives that help us see can also blind us to what lies beyond them. As Daniel J. Boorstin observed,

**"The great obstacle . . . [is] not ignorance
but the illusion of knowledge."[1]**

A Bike Ride in the Dark

One evening, after a long day of dealing with some significant challenges in the mission, I went on a bike ride to decompress. I set off on my bike at sundown, lost track of time, and went farther than planned. As darkness settled in, I turned toward home. I rode briskly, without a light, seeing just well enough by the faint starlight. As I rode, I wondered, *Why do we sometimes miss what later feels obvious, even when we are sincere, thoughtful, and well-intentioned?*

I found myself approaching a couple walking toward me on the bike path. Curiously, they both had headlamps on, creating triangular cones of light that began at their foreheads and illuminated only the space directly in front of them, contrasting with the darkness. I had no light of my own but could see them clearly. What surprised me was this: They didn't seem to see me at all. I slowed down, drawing quietly closer.

Not until my front wheel pierced the edge of their cones of light did they notice I was there. Yet I had seen them from a hundred yards away. Their light was much brighter than mine but far more limited in scope. It was not the darkness that prevented them from seeing me. We shared the same darkness. It was their light.

The Need to See

The limits of our cones of light can impact us in simple ways. I met a man who stepped away from the Church. I later learned I knew his mother. In one of our conversations, he shared a beautiful letter he had written to her—a thoughtful, intelligent, loving, deeply respectful attempt to help her understand his journey. When I later spoke with her, I could feel how deeply she hurt—not from anger toward him but from the painful distance that now lay between them. Both were trying; both had reached toward the other with sincerity and love, yet the ease and warmth they once shared had faded and their relationship seemed cautious, measured, and always touched with some sorrow.

She could not understand how someone she loved so dearly could walk away from something so sacred to her, just as he struggled to understand the depth of her devotion to something he saw as so flawed.

They were experiencing the same pain from opposite sides of a chasm, each seeing yet not seeing enough, longing to be close again but unsure how to bridge the space between them. They were not wrong or mistaken, but simply human with yet incomplete understanding. The healing and reconciliation they longed for was just beyond their reach, not because God withheld it from them but because they could not see beyond what they *could* see.

When we are less able to see, it often isn't because we don't have light but because we do. The illusion that we already see clearly is often what prevents us from seeing more. This was the cause of my initial misunderstanding of what Cale experienced and what he needed from me to learn and grow. I had to be open to the possibility that I did not have all the answers.

An Opportunity for Us to See More Clearly

Like everyone, Latter-day Saints sometimes miss things for this very reason. For example, in our research, three out of four active Latter-day

Saints substantially underestimated how many young adults are leaving the Church.[2] Strikingly, those who considered themselves very devout were twice as likely to answer incorrectly.

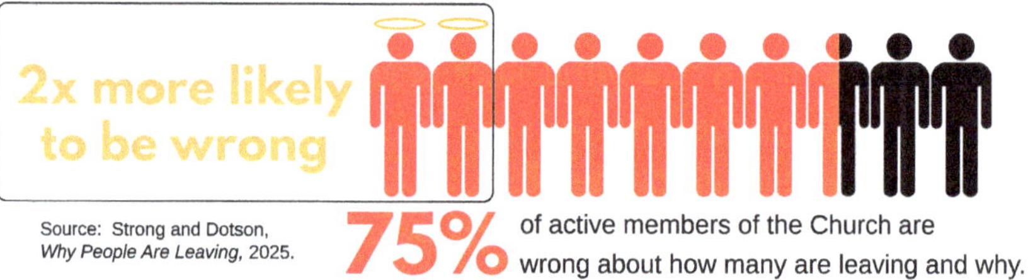

This suggests how prone human beings are to see through the lens of hopes and expectations rather than the realities in front of us.

This wasn't the only misunderstanding our research revealed. We asked members to identify the most common reasons people leave the Church. A large majority were unable to identify those reasons. In fact, they most often selected the less common reasons.

Less Common

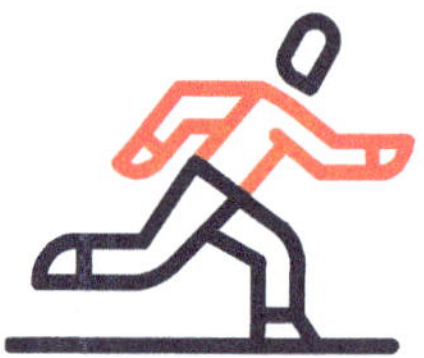

1. They lost their testimony because they sinned, stopped praying and reading scriptures, and lost the Spirit.
2. They don't want the responsibilities and constraints of membership.
3. They were led away by the things of the world.

More Common

1. They feel like they don't belong.
2. They don't believe in the Restoration or have concerns about some Church teachings.
3. They are not experiencing the fruits of the gospel in their Church experience.

Source: Strong and Dotson, *Why People Are Leaving*, 2025.

And, again, the more active and devout the member, the more likely they were to be wrong.

It is puzzling why good and intelligent people don't see this more clearly. Perhaps we prefer not to look—often letting our yearnings and desires overshadow truth. That's human nature, and Latter-day Saints are human too. We could feel discouraged by this, but we don't need to. Acknowledging our weaknesses, and even laughing at them, can help us see more clearly. Winston Churchill once quipped about a colleague, "Occasionally he stumbled over truth, but hastily picked himself up and hurried on as if nothing had happened."[3] I know that feeling well. But the truth isn't going anywhere; it will be there tomorrow, patiently waiting for us.

It is exciting to know that seeing more accurately empowers us to make a meaningful difference. I am hopeful because the Church is taking positive steps toward a greater focus on Christ, making adjustments to its programs, and increasingly encouraging its members to seek personal revelation and exercise their God-given agency. These are good things, and I believe they are helping.

Seeing but Not Seeing

Sometimes the very light that guides us can blind us, narrowing our vision just when we need to see more. Of course, none of this means that light and darkness are interchangeable or that truth itself is uncertain. God is the source of all light, and His understanding is complete. What is limited is not truth but our human ability to fully comprehend it. Each of us sees something real but not everything that is real. The invitation, then, is not to abandon conviction but to hold it with humility—to trust the light we have received while remaining open to the possibility that God is illuminating more than we can yet see.

All of this reveals a simple truth: We cannot respond wisely to what we do not yet see clearly. The good news is, we can all learn to see more than we currently see. Humility and faith can expand our vision.

Humility allows us to trust the light we have while remaining open to seeing beyond that light. Faith gives us the desire and confidence to pursue what lies beyond our current cone of light.

King Benjamin cast some light on the limits of our sight and the greatness of God's sight. His words are an inspiration to me: "Believe that *man doth not comprehend* all the things which the Lord can comprehend" (Mosiah 4:9, emphasis added). Of course, we understand less than God. His light encompasses not only our light but also what we see, with our limitations, as darkness. Because we experience it as darkness, we may misunderstand or fear it, rejecting the possibility that truth and goodness exist beyond our current light. If we think this way, we may avert our eyes and stop seeking. Worse, we may turn away and run from it because we fear what might be out there in the dark. It may not be darkness at all, but learning. If we don't look, we can't see. And if we can't see, we can't fully understand, even though it might be clear if we just look. This matters because if we misperceive how many are stepping away from our Church and why, we may not respond in the ways they need us to, and we can do more harm than good.

What we choose to give our attention to also matters. The prophet Jacob highlighted our tendency to sometimes not see crucial things because of what we *want* to look at, including the problem of looking beyond the mark or beyond Christ Himself. He taught, "The Spirit speaketh the truth and lieth not. Wherefore, it speaketh of things as they really are. . . . But behold, the Jews . . . sought for things that they could not understand. Wherefore, because of their blindness, *which blindness came by looking beyond the mark*, they must needs fall" (Jacob 4:13–14, emphasis added).

Paul similarly warned the Corinthians to be aware of when their "minds should be *corrupted from the simplicity that is in Christ*" (2 Corinthians 11:3, emphasis added). Both prophets saw then what we sometimes experience now—how our natural appetite for complexity or mystery can become a blind spot, keeping us from recognizing the transforming power of what is plain and simple and how it can cause us to *over*look Christ.

Many of us are sincerely interested in things like the signs of the times, end-of-time prophecies, unresolved doctrinal questions, seeking sensational spiritual experiences or knowledge, and the reassurance that comes from having clear and confident answers to deep and abstract theological questions. These interests can be meaningful, but they are less essential than the simple message Jesus taught—love others, forgive offenses, serve quietly, care for the poor and needy, and repent daily. Once we recognize this pattern of looking beyond the mark in ourselves, the Savior's attributes become essential. They are how He teaches us to see more fully.

The Attributes of Christ

As a mission leader, one of the things Sara beautifully taught the missionaries was the power of Christlike attributes. She would choose one attribute to discuss with the missionaries at each zone conference. She felt inspired to do this because many of them saw His attributes as abstract ideas, not powerful, useful realities with real benefits. Most of the missionaries were, as I once was, laser-focused on the cultural version of the gospel at the expense of the transforming simplicity of Christ's gospel, too easily satisfied with completing the "checklist" of good things we do to be good missionaries or Latter-day Saints.

The attributes of Christ are simple yet powerful. They are the very qualities that steady, guide, and carry us through the challenges of life, including the need to see more completely. Because of their simplicity, we naturally tend to overlook them, yearning instead for what seems more elaborate, exciting, or mysterious.

It was one of the highlights of my mission to watch Sara teach these principles, to see the missionaries come alive as they discovered the real meaning and practical application of these insights, and then to watch new goodness, wisdom, and strength flow into their lives through a steady stream of real-world experiences. These attributes help us in daily life—and broaden how we learn. They help us see the Savior more clearly so we can follow Him. And, as illustrated by my bike ride, the Christlike attributes of humility and faith play a most essential role in helping us to see more.

Learning by Faith

Each Christlike attribute has the power to transform us. I focus here on humility and faith because they are the attributes that expand what we see. Without them, we either become overconfident in what we know or paralyzed by what we don't—either way, seeing too little.

My understanding of faith expanded significantly through a 2006 talk by Elder David A. Bednar called "Seek Learning by Faith," based in part on Doctrine and Covenants 88:118: "Seek learning by study, and also by faith." I had long known how to learn by study. But I realized, surprisingly, that I had no idea what it meant to learn by faith. Thankfully, a wise, loving friend helped me understand it not by giving me answers but inspiring me to ask good questions, trusting me, and trusting God enough to let me find my own way. The spirit of this is captured so well by Patrick Overton, who said,

> **"When you walk to the edge of all the light you have and take that first step into the darkness of the unknown, you must believe that one of two things will happen—There will be something solid for you to stand on, or you will be taught how to fly."[4]**

It has been my experience that God can teach us anything, but what He teaches us often waits beyond our current light until we have the humility and faith to take that first step.

Our learning is a *never*-ending expansion of our understanding. The Savior shared this foundational truth with Joseph Smith: "That which is of God is light; and he that receiveth light, and continueth in God, receiveth more light; and that light groweth brighter and brighter until the perfect day" (Doctrine & Covenants 50:24). A little at a time, line upon line, if we are willing, God expands our sight. We can have the humility to ask, seek, and knock. We can have the faith to step into the darkness of our unknown. And today, reaching those who are leaving clearly requires us to obtain light and knowledge beyond our current understanding and perceptions, just as I had to do with Cale.

Jesus's Warnings About Spiritual Blindness

This principle of learning by stepping beyond what we can see lies at the heart of Christ's repeated warnings about spiritual blindness. He told His disciples that "they seeing, see not" (Matthew 13:13–15). He chastised them after they'd witnessed miracles, asking, "Having eyes, see ye not?" (Mark 8:18). He even called out the Pharisees and teachers of the law, warning against blind guides leading the blind (see Matthew 15:14; 23:23). His concern was clear: He knew that even the devout need help recognizing spiritual blindness—not in others but in *themselves.*

Experience is an important part of learning. It's the essence of learning by faith. The best treasures of knowledge in life, the game-changing ones, are often those we obtain as we learn by faith. This requires us to take a step into what feels like darkness because it is unknown to us. When we do this, the Holy Ghost can give us further intelligence from God. With faith, we follow His principles in a way that carries us beyond our current understanding. We can do this through scripture study, reflection, and prayer and also nonreligious education and study of worthwhile material and our powers of reasoning and critical thinking. When we act in this way, with faith, before we know or see, new learning comes as we act—a manifestation of our faith as we leave our light and enter our "darkness." We do not yet see or know; we trust—and our sight grows as we move forward. This requires both humility and faith.

It is our inevitable human pride that sometimes prevents us from even knowing we need to take that step, our fear that too often prevents us from taking it. If we fail to do this, we stop learning. We stop growing in truth and light. We remain inside the limits of what we already know, holding on to past lessons and traditions while missing important opportunities to learn and grow—the very things that could expand our sight.

Being led too much by the past or our traditions—because doing so somehow makes *us* feel safe or more self-assured—when responding to those who leave the Church or those who are having conflict in their Church experience is another way to not see. We may incorrectly assume ulterior motives, minimize sincere concerns, equate honest inquiry with weakness, or begin to treat people we love as if they are suddenly unsafe or suspect. All these things can be harmful to them and to us and limit our sight.

The harm isn't in having light and loving the things we can see with that light. There is great value in it. It provides stability, direction, confidence, and peace. It helps us see everything *in our cone* more accurately and vividly. I am deeply grateful for my Latter-day Saint perspective and knowledge. The harm comes when we assume our understanding is complete and dismiss other's light as darkness because it does not match ours. This can cause us to disconnect and miscommunicate with people whose understanding includes things ours does not. We may amplify their tension, a tension that often leads them away from the Church.

And, of course, we experience our own tension when we can't see completely. We may feel either naively self-assured or slip into confusion, frustration, fear, and even anger. Those who step away often sense these negative things from us. It causes them to feel misunderstood and inaccurately judged, even though that is rarely our intention. Trust and relationships can be compromised. If there are things we aren't seeing, we all lose. But we *can* see our loved ones as they *really* are if we are willing to, and that can make a huge, positive difference.

The most capable, intelligent, and wise people I know often share a common characteristic: They have a well-developed sense of how much they *don't* know. Sir Isaac Newton, who contributed extensively to the search for truth in many scientific fields, beautifully expressed this when he said, "I seem to have been only like a boy playing on the seashore . . . whilst the great ocean of truth lay all undiscovered before me."[5]

A nineteen-year-old once taught me this principle with a scripture and a drawing that illustrated the same truth. In sharing, he expanded my seashore, opening me to an ocean of further learning. The more we recognize our limits, the more God can open us to new truths.

Seeing Those Who Leave

Our limits apply to what we *think* we know about those leaving. Here are some of the important things I have learned. Many are still reaching for the same light we seek—though outside of *our* cone. This is often because the very things they loved, things that became part of them as members of the Church (in their homes, in seminary classes, from friendships and leaders, on missions, and at Church), are now missing for them in the Church.

Many of the things they seek and love—truth as it really is, the power and peace of living a Christlike life, inclusiveness, learning and coming to belief through their own choices and experiences, growth without man-made or worldly limitations, finding real meaning in life, being true to the light of Christ within them, and following their desire to be and do good—are rooted in Christ's gospel. Many of them love these principles—enough to make the painful choice to step away when they can no longer find them in the Church.

Seeing this with humility and charity changes how we see them: We see far better motives than we might have assumed, and we recognize that our efforts to love them and share the gospel were not wasted. We may realize that the truth and light, the belief and goodness that came with those teachings, took root in them, after all. What did not take root were certain aspects of our history, tradition, practices, and culture.

One source of frustration for those who leave or are in conflict is the belief that we misunderstand their experience in the Church and their choice to step away—that we view their choice as irresponsible or rebellious when it may instead come from a desire for truth, goodness, and integrity.

If you don't see or feel these things as they do, that they would leave or feel conflict may seem unbelievable, yet it is real for them, just as our own experiences are real for us. I know this may be difficult to accept, and that's okay, but considering and respecting their perspective can help us see them with more humility and love. Making room for different perspectives does not diminish our own.

When we consider with love and curiosity those who leave and those who are in conflict but stay, recognizing the light they carry and seek, it preserves relationships, expands our sight, and changes and softens *us* for the better. Unfortunately, they often see our ignorance and feel our judgment. But just as easily, they can feel and see our learning and love.

In the end, we are all in this together. We are all walking in the dark with only a small cone of light before us. Christ invites us to walk humbly, to step forward in faith, and let Him expand our sight. That expansion begins with the humility to see more clearly what is happening among us—how many are leaving and why. When we see this accurately, we can stop underestimating and misunderstanding the problem. We can avoid offering the wrong remedies. And we can learn to love and listen instead of misjudging. In that humility, we can create a community where people feel understood, valued, and like they belong. Christ does not just expand our light; He shatters the illusion that we are seeing clearly, expanding our vision to see a little more as He sees.

Seeing clearly is not a threat to faith; it is one of its most sacred prerequisites. Every meaningful act of discipleship begins with the willingness to notice what is actually happening rather than what we wish were happening. When we confuse what we are familiar with for truth or what we feel certain about with righteousness, we risk mistaking our limited perspective for God's full vision.

The invitation of this chapter is simple but demanding: Slow down, listen more carefully, and resist the urge to quickly explain away any discomfort. In our families and congregations, seeing others begins with being curious about them rather than wanting to correct them and with humility rather than certainty that we already know all there is to know. When people feel truly seen—without being immediately categorized, fixed, or judged—trust grows and understanding becomes possible. Only then can healing begin.

Seeing does not require agreement. It requires honesty. Honesty paired with faith opens the door to deeper connection, wiser judgment, and a more Christlike way of being together. With a better feel for how many are leaving our Church and why and the need to see the challenge honestly and accurately, we turn our attention to our Church culture: what it is, why it is the way it is, and how it can influence our experience in the Church community.

Key Chapter Takeaway

Cultural assumptions and beliefs are often mistaken for eternal truths, narrowing our vision and producing defensiveness rather than Christlike awareness. Humility expands our sight by helping us distinguish the gospel from culture and showing us where we can learn more.

Reflection Questions

1. What cultural beliefs might I be mistaking for eternal truths, limiting my ability to see more clearly?

2. Whose lived experiences in the Church have I been slow to truly see?

3. How might greater humility and faith change the way I interpret others' faith journeys?

Application Suggestion

Choose one situation where you feel confident you already understand someone else's experience or motivations. Notice what assumptions you may be carrying into that interaction—about belief, faithfulness, intent, or outcome.

In one conversation this week, practice setting those assumptions aside. Ask a sincere, open question and listen without correcting, interpreting, or steering the response. Seeing more completely often begins not by adding new explanations but by noticing where our own perspective has quietly limited what we can see.

CHAPTER 4

NOURISHING

**"Tradition is not the worship of ashes,
but the preservation of fire."**
—Jean Jaurès

Though often invisible, culture is a powerful influence. While a healthy Church culture can nourish faith and keep the fire burning, an unhealthy culture can smother that same fire, even when our intent is to protect what we believe. For many, our culture has been a source of strength, identity, and belonging. For others, it has felt heavy, confining, and misaligned with their deepest spiritual needs. Both experiences are real. Both deserve respect.

This chapter explores what culture is, how it works, and why it plays such a significant role in whether people stay—or feel they cannot. Tradition is one important part of culture. And when tradition becomes fused with culture in ways we don't notice, it can either preserve the fire or quietly smother it.

As we have seen, people step away for complex, personal, and deeply sincere reasons. But culture shapes how those reasons are experienced, especially when someone is trying to stay. A healthy culture can hold people in Christ even amid tension and uncertainty. An unhealthy culture can amplify strain until leaving feels like the only way to breathe. If we want more people to stay rooted—both in Christ and in one another—culture is something we must understand and cultivate intentionally.

Tradition and Change— A Shared Human Struggle

My dad loved *Fiddler on the Roof*. I grew up listening to him repeatedly sing the beautiful songs from the soundtrack. To me, he was Tevye. Set in the Jewish community of Anatevka, the story follows Tevye, a father and a milkman, as he tries to hold on to his family and his cultural and religious traditions amidst the pressures of external social and political forces and the change that life unexpectedly brings to their village and family.

I recently went to the play at the Hale Centre Theatre in Sandy, Utah. After fifty-two years, I still knew every song! I was drawn into the story and music in an unexpected way. As an older man, I now felt a surprising kinship to Tevye—sharing his frustration, heartbreak, and deep love as a husband and father fighting for his family and what he believed in, with few answers and everything stacked against him.

The story brings to life the themes of love, sorrow, resilience, adaptation, and the tension between tradition and change. Ultimately, it portrays the universal human experience of navigating change while striving to preserve one's identity, values, and beliefs. While tradition is just one element of culture, it is, perhaps, the most important. Tevye's opening monologue captures it well:

> Here in Anatevka we have traditions for everything . . . how to eat, how to sleep, how to wear clothes. For instance, we always keep our heads covered and always wear a little prayer shawl. This shows our constant devotion to God. You may ask, how did this tradition start? I'll tell you—I don't know! But it's a tradition. . . .

Because of our traditions, everyone knows who he is and what God expects him to do.[1]

One scene captures that struggle with heartbreaking clarity. Chava, Tevye's beloved daughter, marries Fyedka, a Christian. In doing so, she crosses a boundary her father cannot move past. Chava leaves, torn between her love for Fyedka and the only world she has ever known. Tevye remains behind, equally torn between his daughter and the traditions that give his life meaning.

In the play, Chava is given no voice. She simply leaves. Her silence mirrors the experience of many who step away from the Church. They are still sincere, still acting from a place of conviction, but no longer able to remain within the world that formed them. Tevye's pain and Chava's pain are, in many ways, the same pain: the pain of losing something precious when two worlds move apart faster than hearts can adapt.

A Fiddler on the Roof Church?

I grew up in a kind of *Fiddler on the Roof* home. We understood who we were and what was expected of us. And like Tevye, we often struggled with the change part. In many ways, members of the Church are living a *Fiddler on the Roof* moment—a season where we are wrestling with how to hold fast to what matters most while responding to a rapidly changing world and membership.

Faithful members are experiencing tension between what they believe, value, and feel called to do in their discipleship and what they perceive they are *expected* to believe, value, and do within Church culture. A couple of common examples are being loyal to the Church and its leaders versus following one's conscience after a lot of listening, study, and prayer. Or worshipping in a Church that places a high value on certainty and conviction as opposed to more humble, evolving, and nuanced beliefs. These tension can be deeply uncomfortable, especially when the culture seems to move in one direction while personal spiritual growth pulls in another.

That night at the Hale Theatre, I felt hope in one important truth: We are not the first people to carry this burden. Communities of faith have always faced the challenge of preserving what is sacred while adapting to new realities. Perhaps that means God's hand is in this moment, inviting us to learn, adjust, and more intentionally cultivate our culture.

What Culture Does—Soil That Nourishes

Let's return to the root of the word itself. *Culture* comes from the Latin *cultura*, derived from *colere*, meaning "to cultivate the soil."[2] Over time, the meaning evolved from care of land and crops to cultivation of the mind, character, and communal life.[3] Today, *culture* most often refers to the shared patterns of meaning, belief, and behavior that shape how a community lives.[4]

Soil as a metaphor for culture is a particularly helpful way to think about Church life. Like soil, culture provides stability and nourishment. When it is healthy, roots deepen and the plant becomes resilient. When it becomes compacted or depleted, even good plants struggle—not because they are weak but because they cannot breathe or access nutrients. Cultivation is not about tearing everything up; it is about tending—loosening what has hardened, enriching what has been depleted, and protecting what is life-giving.

How Culture Works

Let's look at Edgar Schein's framework to see how culture functions.[5] He described culture as operating on three interconnected levels: artifacts, values, and underlying beliefs. Artifacts are the visible expressions of culture—what we say and do, the practices and patterns that sit on or above the surface of the soil. In Church life, artifacts might include how we speak about faith, the rituals we observe, the buildings we worship in, or the ways we signal belonging and commitment. Artifacts matter, but on their own, they rarely explain why a culture feels nourishing to some and constraining to others.

Values sit beneath artifacts. They represent what a community prioritizes—often deeply shared and rarely questioned. In Latter-day Saint culture, values such as devotion, family, service, sacrifice, reverence, and loyalty have shaped generations of faithful living. These values guide behavior and give coherence to communal life.

At the deepest level we find underlying beliefs—the reasons we hold certain values and practices. These beliefs may be conscious or unconscious, but they shape how we understand God, truth, authority, growth, and belonging. In Latter-day Saint culture, beliefs such as the reality of continuing revelation, the centrality of Jesus Christ, the eternal nature of families, and the covenant path of discipleship profoundly shape our values and behaviors.

When beliefs shift, values and artifacts usually follow. When beliefs become distorted, exaggerated, or incomplete, the culture becomes compacted or depleted. Cultivation must begin at this level. Focusing only on surface behaviors without tending underlying beliefs is like pruning a plant while ignoring the condition of the soil.

When Culture Becomes Unhealthy

Culture, even in the Church, can become unhealthy in predictable ways. Sometimes untrue or incomplete beliefs take root. Sometimes good values become exaggerated or misplaced until they lose their original purpose. Sometimes traditions that once served us well no longer do.

Cultivation means retaining truth while modifying our traditions to serve their intended purpose—and pruning what harms growth. One example is the evolution of Church discipline. In earlier periods, discipline was often public and applied to relatively minor transgressions. Over time, greater pastoral care, privacy, and emphasis on healing replaced shame. The doctrine of repentance did not change, but the cultural expression of it did—moving toward nourishment rather than fear.

President Russell M. Nelson repeatedly called the Church to deeper repentance and greater spiritual self-reliance, teaching us that spiritual vitality requires personal revelation and a willingness to let God continue to move us forward.[6] In a cultural sense, those teachings can function like cultivation—loosening what has hardened and restoring what has been depleted.

Why Culture Is Often Overlooked

One reason we often overlook culture despite its influence is that it is intangible and difficult to measure. Urgent demands crowd it out, and unless leaders are unusually attentive, culture is often assumed healthy by default. Attention shifts toward managing behavior instead of cultivating belief.

I repeatedly saw this in my experience as a mission leader. Many youth and young adults were clear about the checklist behaviors expected of them but far less clear about the truths, principles, and spiritual purposes underlying those expectations. Over time, this can produce outward compliance without inward nourishment or growth—soil that appears healthy on the surface but lacks depth and resilience.

Beyond these general challenges, Latter-day Saints face two additional ones. First, our culture tends to defend itself vigorously, especially among those for whom it works well. Second, we sometimes blur the line between culture—which can and should evolve—and eternal doctrine, which only God defines. And while these are challenges, they are also opportunities for growth.

To sustainably influence culture, we must begin with beliefs. Correcting untrue beliefs and adapting traditions that no longer serve their purpose is the most effective way to cultivate healthy growth. Truth—things as they really are, were, and are to come—endures. Everything else changes. President Gordon B. Hinckley captured this beautifully when he taught, "A growing church, spreading across the earth in these complex times, needs constant revelation from the throne of heaven to guide it and move it forward."[7] What worked in the past may not work in the future—and this is particularly true of culture.

Beautiful yet Complicated

Latter-day Saint culture has many real strengths worth preserving and cultivating. It has provided millions with identity, continuity, and belonging. Shared language, rituals, and practices connect generations and anchor faith during times of uncertainty. Cultural rhythms such as baby blessings, baptisms, missionary service, temple worship, communal worship, and funerals create meaning, stability, and solidarity across time.

Culture preserves what is sacred, promotes social cohesion, and transmits values from one generation to the next. It provides continuity during times of disruption and anchors life with rituals that connect us to God and one another. For nearly two centuries, these elements of culture have blessed Latter-day Saints around the world. They are worth honoring and preserving.

At the same time, like all cultures, ours is complicated. Culture can resist needed change, elevate conformity above growth, or become inflexible in ways that marginalize those who are different. It can cling too tightly to past tendencies even when over time circumstances or even doctrine have changed. Consider the significant changes initiated by the Church around race, the role of women, standards for youth, missionary practices, teaching curriculum and practices, ministering, and historical transparency—yet our culture adapted slowly, holding on to inherited patterns longer than those changing realities required. When these resisting tendencies go unexamined, trust can erode—and people feel less nourished and less at home.

Seeing both the beauty and complexity is essential. Culture is not a villain. It is a human creation shaped by faith, history, fear, and love. Acknowledging its weaknesses is not an act of disloyalty; it is the first act of cultivation.

Why Our Culture Is the Way It Is

Latter-day Saint culture emerged from specific historical contexts. Early converts brought with them religious traditions from Protestant Christianity and frontier life, for both good and ill. Persecution, isolation, and the struggle for survival shaped behaviors meant to protect their faith, families, and community. Over time, these responses became embedded cultural patterns. Much of what we experience today—both the blessings we cherish and the burdens we struggle with—can be traced to those formative moments and the beliefs, values, and behaviors they produced.

One observer of Latter-day Saint culture, Kyle Nelson, describes this reality with compassion and clarity: "We can look at specific things that are both good and annoying or hurtful in our culture now and trace them to a specific context where they made sense. This understanding extends much grace to the culture and the community that collectively grew it—it is an embodied, lived reality that came together mostly without malice or ill intent. The community of Saints 'grew up' through the very real things that made us what we are today."[8]

Culture always involves growth—and pain. Understanding this helps us accept that tension and conflict are inevitable while also recognizing our responsibility to cultivate something better. As Kyle notes, this perspective gives us the wisdom to recognize that there will be seasons of discomfort, stagnation, reformation, and renewal. Cultivation is not failure; it is normal, necessary, and good.[9]

Fear has also played a significant role in shaping our culture. Fear of sin. Fear of mistakes. Fear of criticism. Fear of losing our children, our way of life, our freedoms, and even our faith. Often motivated by love, these fears produce behaviors meant to protect what matters most. But fear tends to elevate protection above nourishment. For example, we have a tendency sheltering our youth from potentially harmful things rather than preparing them to face and overcome those things. Over time, fear can compact the soil—turning us inward, amplifying expectations of conformity, and placing obedience above love. In some cases, fear has led to overcorrection, secrecy, and misjudgment—not only of those who leave but of those who remain faithful.

The Spirit works through faith, not fear. In my experience, we recognize and follow the Holy Ghost far more readily when we act in faith. While fear was rational for early Saints facing persecution, many of our fears today may be outdated overreactions—or signs of diminished trust in God. For example, our long-term cultural practice of avoiding difficult historical questions to protect faith has actually created more doubt and loss of trust in an age where information is instantly accessible and when the Church is also being more transparent.

Formative markers produced positive results but also some unintended side-effects.

The Beauty and Complexity of LDS Culture

Formative Markers

- Intense persecution
- Difficult westward migration
- Ultimately, growth and success
- Prophetic leadership

Intended Results

- Protectiveness, solidarity, loyalty
- Self-reliance, commitment
- Faith, self-assurance, prosperity
- Reverence, inspiration, blessings

Unintended Side-Effects

- Fear, conformity, secrecy
- Insularity, ignorance
- Hubris, resistance to change
- Fealty, lack of critical thinking

As Kyle observes, overreaction to fear can sometimes bring about the very outcomes we fear most. There is love buried in these responses—we love our families, our members, and the Church. But when fear governs culture, nourishment gives way to control.[10]

Those inherited patterns matter because they shape how we respond to change now. When a culture is formed in hardship, it naturally learns to prize stability and protection. Those instincts can preserve what is sacred but also make adaptation feel dangerous, even when adaptation is exactly what nourishment requires.

What once made sense can lose relevance as the Church and world change. We are no longer the small, isolated, pioneer-corridor church of the past. Change pounds on our door—and that is a call for cultivation. What once protected us may now need turning or enrichment so the soil can nourish today's plants.

The Tension of Two Worlds Going in Different Directions

This tension—and our desire to escape the uncertainty of change— often pushes us toward tradition. We are a conservative Church; we change carefully. That steadiness can be a gift. But it can also go too far. The Savior taught this in His parable of the wine bottles: New wine must go into new bottles so both are preserved (see Matthew 9:17). On another occasion, He forcefully challenged religious traditions that overshadowed God's word and elevated human commandments as doctrine, warning of confusing tradition with truth.[11]

The Lord also warned Joseph Smith that we can lose truth and light through adherence to tradition. "The glory of God is intelligence, or, in other words, light and truth. Light and truth forsake that evil one. . . . And that wicked one cometh and *taketh away light and truth*, through disobedience, from the children of men, and *because of the tradition of their fathers*" (Doctrine and Covenants 93:36–39, emphasis added). Most of us understand how we can lose light and truth when disobeying God's laws. Tradition itself is not the problem; the danger arises when traditions are treated as truth rather than as vessels meant to carry truth forward. How do we lose light and truth due to our traditions?

From my experience in life and in Church leadership, some traditions tend to diminish light and truth in predictable ways—not because they are malicious but because they are human. Over time, traditions can introduce distortion, subtly overshadowing or misrepresenting doctrine. They can harden into rigidity, resisting renewal and further revelation. They can foster cultural bias, shaping interpretation in ways that narrow vision. They can encourage complacency, assuming inherited forms are complete or flawless. And when these tendencies go unexamined, they often lead to division, as fear of difference replaces trust and charity. When this happens, what once unified can begin to fracture, and what once nourished can begin to deplete.

One simple example is this: Over time, valuable Church programs or practices can shift from being tools that serve spiritual growth to being treated as ends in themselves, where participation and completion matter more than whether hearts are actually being changed and people are being lifted.

Doctrine & Covenants 93 also includes a surprising and instructive scolding. The Lord corrected Frederick G. Williams, Sidney Rigdon, Newell K. Whitney, and Joseph Smith for neglecting to bring up their children in "light and truth," which led to serious problems in their families (see verses 40–50). Section 93 came in 1833, three years after the Church was organized. During those years, these leaders worked hard to build the Church. Perhaps this invites us to consider if building the Church and teaching truth and light are always the same thing.

While traditions can be valuable, the question is: As change accelerates, are we striking the right balance? How healthy is our soil? The plants themselves are telling us about the soil. Listening to them is essential if we hope to improve it before more wither or leave.

Our research surfaced an important signal. Nearly half of active members report some level of discomfort with Church culture, while only a small minority describe themselves as very comfortable. This imbalance does not imply disloyalty or lack of faith; rather, it suggests that for many, the soil feels increasingly compacted or depleted, especially when personal spiritual growth pulls in directions the culture does not easily accommodate.

Source: Strong and Dotson, *Why People Are Leaving,* 2025.

Here are a few examples of things that cause some to feel uncomfortable:

➤ They question or disagree with some of the teachings common in the culture—for example, the culture often emphasizes that God has a plan for our individual lives, while many believe God expects us to create our own plan using divine principles and the Holy Ghost.

▸ They often hold different views of what it means to be Christ-centered—the culture places high importance on obedience, ordinances, covenants, and the temple, while many, especially those on the margins, are more moved by humility, faith, love, and serving others.

▸ They sometimes have different religious values and behaviors than the prevailing culture. The culture emphasizes we are the only true church and that proselytizing missionary work and seeking converts is critical, while many believe it is more important to be humble, to respect other faiths as equals, and to focus on ministering and serving, not just converting.

▸ They feel we are missing the important influence of women in the Church. Many faithful Latter-day Saints cannot reconcile this tension. In the scriptures, women stand at the center of God's work, entrusted with decisive responsibility at moments when the future of divine purposes hang in the balance.[12]

Yet, in the modern Church, the public voice and influence of women are often limited. For many, this contrast creates confusion—not about doctrine or priesthood responsibilities but about culture—about whether the Church community today fully reflects the pattern revealed in scripture and the vital role God consistently relied on women to play.

At critical moments, our Heavenly Parents have relied on the agency, courage, spiritual discernment, and leadership of women to move the work of salvation and eternal progress forward. Many women and men in the Church today see unrealized opportunities to do the same—and feel the Church community is diminished when those gifts are not fully received.

When a culture leaves substantially more people feeling uneasy than at home, it signals that something deserves attention and cultivation—not as an indictment but as an early warning that the soil may be compacting or depleting for a significant portion of the roots. That raises a hard question: How do we get the culture right when different people need different things? We will expound on that in chapter 10. For now, the message is simple: Prevention matters. The time to cultivate healthier soil is before the roots wither—and before new or bigger storms arrive.

Culture always feeds something. The only real question is whether it is nourishing faith—or slowly starving it. When culture is healthy, it creates space for growth, belonging, and transformation. When it becomes compacted or depleted, even sincere devotion can feel heavy, constrained, or exhausting. Former General Relief Society President Julie Beck said it well:

"To nurture means to cultivate, care for, and make grow."[13]

The work is not to discard culture but tend it. We must individually and collectively shape the soil through our words, expectations, and priorities. Small choices—how we welcome others, respond to questions or disagreements, and balance structure with grace—either loosen the soil or harden it further.

Healthy soil matters most before the storms arrive. But storms also prepare the ground for new growth. Our calling is not to preserve yesterday's soil but to cultivate today's—loosening what has hardened, enriching what has been depleted, and protecting what still gives life. This is the preventative work before us: to tend the soil now so that more of us can grow, stay, and remain rooted in Christ—and in one another—when the winds come.

Key Chapter Takeaway

Well-intended traditions can quietly harden into compacted or depleted soil, leaving some spiritually underfed even while fully participating. Faith flourishes when Church culture is actively tended and evaluated by whether it genuinely nourishes growth.

Reflection Questions

1. In what ways does my experience with Church culture feel nourishing—or depleting?

2. Which cultural habits or traditions strengthen faith, and which quietly deplete it?

3. How might others experience the same Church culture differently than I do?

Application Suggestion

Choose one "artifact" of Church culture you regularly experience—how people speak in meetings, how callings are discussed, how questions are handled, or how belonging is signaled. Evaluate it by one question: *Does this nourish faith in Jesus Christ—especially for someone whose experience differs from mine?*

Then reflect on what value or belief may be sustaining it and whether it is true and Christlike or just culture. If you sense it limits nourishment, consider one small, relational way you could influence that pattern—through tone, language, inclusion, or example. Cultural change often begins not with correction but with modeling a better way.

UNDERSTANDING

**"The wise man in the storm prays to God,
not for safety from danger,
but for deliverance from fear."
—Ralph Waldo Emerson**

Storm feels like the right word when nearly 40 percent of a community disappears—and when the pace of that departure is accelerating. Faced with something so unsettling, it's natural to respond with confusion and fear. Human instinct often tells us to step back, deny what we see, disengage, or wait for the storm to pass. But storms don't stop because we avoid them. Avoidance prolongs exposure and deepens damage.

There is another response—one that does not require certainty, defensiveness, or retreat. We can choose to face the storm, seeking to understand what is happening, why it is happening, and how we might respond with wisdom, faith, and compassion. Understanding is a strength. And it is one of the most faithful responses available to us.

A Storm Mindset

During our mission, we published a monthly newsletter featuring brief reflections from the missionaries—small insights gathered during their service. One month, Sister Carlene Tausinga shared a piece she titled "Be the Buffalo."

She wrote about storms—how they are unavoidable in both missions and life and how our response to them shapes not only outcomes but character. She explained that buffalo and cattle respond very differently when storms approach. Cattle tend to turn away and scatter in search of shelter. In doing so, they often remain in the storm longer—exposed, isolated, and distressed.

Buffalo, by contrast, do something counterintuitive. They turn into the storm. They gather, lower their heads, and move forward as one. By facing the storm directly, they reduce exposure and pass through it more quickly. Their strength is not just physical—it is collective. Carlene ended with a simple invitation: When storms come, be the buffalo.

Her counsel applies far beyond missionary service. As a Church community, we face storms that tempt us to scatter—into silence, defensiveness, withdrawal, or judgment. But we can choose to move forward together, turning toward reality with courage, humility, and faith.

Storms We Have Faced Before

Our history offers perspective. This is not the first time the Church has encountered storms that felt existential, unsettling, or overwhelming. Repeatedly, progress has required courage—not just to endure hardship but to change direction when necessary.

Several moments stand out:

> **Expulsion from Missouri (1830s):** Violence and persecution forced the Saints from their homes, forging resilience and solidarity through shared suffering.

>   **Martyrdom in Nauvoo (1844):** The deaths of Joseph and Hyrum Smith shook the Church to its core, forcing a painful reckoning and a leap into an unknown future.

>   **Pioneer Migration (1847–1870):** Tens of thousands crossed the plains under extraordinary hardship, forming a spiritual and cultural identity that still shapes the Church today.

>   **Turning Points in Practice (1890 and 1978):** The end of polygamy and the extension of priesthood and temple blessings marked profound change—difficult, controversial, and, ultimately, life-giving.

>   **Becoming a Global Church (1960s–present):** Rapid worldwide growth required adaptation across cultures, languages, and contexts, reshaping what it means to be a Latter-day Saint.

None of these moments were easy. Each demanded faith, humility, and a willingness to let go of the present to go forward and secure the Church's future. In every case, growth came not from denial but from engagement with reality.

Today's storm is different in form but not in essence. It, too, presses us to understand our moment honestly and decide how we will move forward. It consists of four things.

First: Disruptive Technology

The first of these forces has changed almost everything about how we live, connect, and believe. In the past few decades, five familiar technological developments have reshaped daily life and, with it, the way people experience faith and church:

>   **World Wide Web (1989):** The web shrunk the world by transforming access to information, communication, and commerce.

>   **E-Commerce (1990s):** Amazon and others redefined convenience, transparency, and consumer choice, raising expectations in many areas of life.

> **Social Media (mid-2000s):** Platforms like Facebook, Instagram, and TikTok transformed how people connected, shared, evaluated, organized, and came to an identity.

> **Smartphones (2007):** Smartphones put the world in the palms of our hands, changing how we managed time, relationships, commerce, communication, and priorities.

> **Artificial Intelligence (2020s):** AI is now reshaping how we learn, solve problems, and even think about the future and is likely to have an impact greater than the internet itself.

As much as these advances have shaped everyday life, they have had a dramatic though less visible impact on belief, religion, and our church communities. Their influence can be seen in three powerful ways:

> **Voices and Diversity:** Amplified personal voices allow for much greater expression but also challenge traditional authority. Exposure to diverse peoples and beliefs fosters understanding while also creating new tensions within and between communities.

> **Information and Connection:** The rapid spread of information increases learning and tests established convictions, leading some to reconsider long-held traditions, beliefs, and practices. At the same time, new ways of connecting are redefining how relationships and communities are formed.

> **Accountability and Global Reach:** Greater institutional visibility holds leaders to higher ethical standards and raises expectations for transparency. And as cultural and geographic barriers diminish, new connections emerge—alongside fresh conflicts—as diverse groups interact more closely.

Second: Growing Spiritual and Emotional Challenges

The technology storm is only one part of the storm we face today. Equally powerful—and often more personal—are the spiritual and emotional burdens that shape how we experience faith, community, and meaning.

Despite unprecedented prosperity, access, and freedom, many are experiencing deep emotional and spiritual hunger. We may be living in one of the most psychologically and relationally difficult periods of the past seven decades. Political polarization, mental health struggles, rising suicide rates, the distorting effects of social media, and global conflict have combined to create an undercurrent of loneliness, fear, and despair. More than ever, we are searching for meaning, purpose, and belonging—the very things faith, the gospel, and the Church are meant to offer.

David Brooks describes this moment as a *relational crisis*. He observes that when we hunger deeply for meaning, connection, and purpose, we often reach instead for what he calls "shallow food"—achievement, status, consumption, entertainment, or moral superiority. These substitutes can provide momentary distraction or validation, but they cannot nourish the soul. Rather than satisfying deep hunger, they often intensify it.

"Deep **hunger** cannot be satisfied with **shallow** food."

David Brooks

Belonging
Trust
Truth
Meaning
Life

More Loneliness and Despair

Connectivity
Choice
Possessions
Entertainment
Knowledge
Convenience
Time

Brooks also notes how social media amplifies this dynamic. Platforms designed to connect people often do the opposite. As he puts it, "My life is better than yours—that's Instagram. Your opinions are stupider than mine—that's Twitter."[1] Social media rewards comparison, outrage, and performance rather than empathy, humility, and genuine connection. What might have been tools for building relationships instead deepen isolation and division.

The data confirms the depth of this crisis.[2] Brooks cites, and national research organizations confirm:

> ❯ Thirty-five percent of Americans over the age of forty-five report being chronically lonely.

> ❯ Only 8 percent of Americans say they have meaningful conversations with their neighbors.

> ❯ Trust in neighbors among millennials has dropped to just 18 percent.

> ❯ Suicide rates have increased by approximately 30 percent since 1999, and by roughly 70 percent among teenagers in recent years.

> ❯ More than 45,000 Americans die by suicide each year, while approximately 72,000 die annually from opioid addiction.

> ❯ Life expectancy in the United States has begun to decline rather than rise, a rare and troubling reversal.

These are not abstract trends. They represent millions of lives marked by isolation, anxiety, despair, and unmet spiritual hunger.

My experience has been that Latter-day Saints are subject to these same pressures. We are not insulated from loneliness, depression, or exhaustion simply by virtue of faithful belief or activity. Many are deeply committed yet quietly struggle. The hunger Brooks describes exists within the Church just as it does outside it.

This is where culture matters. If we are living in a compacted and nutrient-depleted Church culture, the shallow nutrients such soil produces cannot sustain those who are already hungry. Structure without nourishment, expectation without belonging, and activity without meaning may temporarily organize a community, but they do not feed the soul.

As much as many of us love our experience in the Church and are deeply nourished by it, others are experiencing something very different. For them, organized religion in general—and our Church specifically—feels unable to meet the depth of their hunger. This may be what President Dieter F. Uchtdorf was warning against when he said:

> This beautiful gospel is so simple a child can grasp it, yet so profound and complex that it will take a lifetime—an eternity—of study and discovery to fully understand it. But sometimes we take the beautiful lily of God's truth and gild it with layer upon layer of man-made good ideas, programs, and expectations. Each one, by itself, might be helpful and appropriate for a certain time and circumstance, but when they are laid on top of each other, they can create a mountain of sediment that becomes so thick and heavy that we risk losing sight of that precious flower we once loved so dearly.[3]

God's truth nourishes. The gospel of Jesus Christ is sufficient. But when culture becomes layered, compacted, and overly managed, it can unintentionally obstruct the very nourishment people need. Jesus Himself framed the problem—and the solution—clearly:

"I am the bread of life: he that cometh to me shall never hunger, and he that believeth on me shall never thirst."
(John 6:35)

When people are starving for meaning, connection, and hope, culture that fails to nourish—or worse, distracts from Christ—becomes not just ineffective but harmful. We must understand this if we hope to respond wisely and compassionately to the storm we now face.

Third: Declining Institutional Trust

Alongside personal and spiritual burdens exists a broader cultural shift regarding institutions themselves. One of the defining realities of our time is how many people—especially younger adults—have lost confidence in the institutions that once guided, protected, and represented them. This is not unique to religion. It spans governments, corporations, media, education, and community organizations. Churches are caught in this broader storm.

Understanding this context matters. Simply being aware of these forces can dramatically increase empathy and help us understand why people respond to churches differently than they once did. For many, trust has been eroded not by doctrine but by experience. Six factors consistently emerge as drivers of this erosion:

1. **Dogmatic Fundamentalism:** When institutions demand certainty, compliance, and unquestioning loyalty, credibility often collapses when lived experience exposes complexity or contradiction.

2. **Insular Communities:** Groups that become inward, transactional, or tribal can feel disconnected from real life, weakening trust in both leaders and institutions.

3. **Misjudging "Outsiders":** The gap between rhetoric about outsiders and people's lived experiences with them is now highly visible, especially online.

4. **Broken Trust:** Abuse of power, financial misconduct, or lack of transparency—even once—can permanently damage confidence.

5. **Harming the Marginalized:** When belonging feels conditional, even unintentionally, institutions communicate exclusion to both those harmed and those who love them.

6. **Spiritually Dead Institutions:** When compliance and appearance overshadow meaning and transformation, institutions feel lifeless

rather than life-giving, echoing Paul's warning that "the letter killeth, but the spirit giveth life" (2 Corinthians 3:6).

These dynamics influence how many, especially young adults, experience institutions, including some organized religion, today. Acknowledging this does not diminish the positive experiences many of us have had. It creates space for humility and understanding.

What the Data Shows

Multiple independent research organizations document the same trend. Gallup reports that church membership in the United States has declined from approximately 73 percent in 1930 to 47 percent in 2020, with participation among younger adults significantly lower.[4] Pew reports that the share of Americans with no religious affiliation grew from 16 percent in 2007 to 28 percent in 2023, driven less by loss of belief in God than by disengagement from organized religion.[5] The National Opinion Research Center's General Social Survey shows those who never attend church rising from 5 percent in 1972 to 32 percent in 2023. Even more striking, the percentage of Americans who report having "hardly any confidence" in organized religion nearly doubled—from 24 percent in 2016 to 44 percent in 2023.[6]

While these trends are sometimes dismissed as evidence of declining faith or righteousness, the data suggests something more complex: a widespread breakdown in trust, credibility, and institutional confidence.

Why Institutional Failure Matters

This erosion of trust has been reinforced by high-profile institutional failures over the past several decades. These examples help explain why tolerance for secrecy, inconsistency, or abuse has dramatically declined.

> **Catholic Church Sexual Abuse Scandal (2000–present):** Widespread abuse and systemic cover-ups devastated victims and shattered global trust in church leaders.[7]

> **Wells Fargo Unauthorized Account Scandal (2016):** Employees opened millions of fraudulent accounts to meet sales quotas, harming customers and violating laws.[8]

> **Boy Scouts of America (BSA) Sexual Abuse Scandal (2018–2020):** BSA was complicit in thousands of abuse cases, including many in Latter-day Saint troops, harming thousands of boys, leading to lawsuits, bankruptcy, and lasting reputational damage.[9]

These broader failures shape how people interpret concerns closer to home:

> **Ensign Peak Advisors / SEC Settlement:** The illegal use of shell companies to obscure the size of Church investment holdings raised concerns about transparency, even as leaders acknowledged mistakes and corrected practices.[10]

> **Church Sexual Abuse Cases:** Legal cases in Arizona, California, and elsewhere have raised difficult questions about reporting, clergy-penitent privilege, and our Church's responsibility to protect victims.[11]

> **Church Commercial and Real Estate Development (City Creek):** Large-scale retail development funded through Church-affiliated business entities prompted questions about institutional priorities despite legal and financial justifications.[12]

People interpret these events differently. Some view them as understandable imperfections in a human institution; others experience them as evidence of misplaced priorities. Either way, awareness is widespread, and trust is shaped by how institutions respond to failure.

Fourth: Changing Religious Values and Pathways to Belief

Declining institutional trust and the other forces shaping our moment are also reordering religious values and changing how people come to belief. Religious belief has never been static.

In every generation, people come to faith—and sometimes leave it—in ways shaped by the culture, questions, and pressures of their time. To meet people where they are with the hope of the gospel and the value of Church participation, we must understand how these shifts are reshaping belief today.

Traditionally, four primary pathways have shaped religious conversion and commitment: Information, Experience, Credentials, and Community. All four still matter, but their relative influence has changed. Historically, the Church has emphasized Information and Credentials. The Restoration narrative, doctrinal explanations, priesthood authority, and prophetic leadership provided clarity and confidence. For many, these pathways were decisive.

Today, their influence is declining not because information or authority no longer matter but because people now evaluate them differently. In an age of radical transparency and access, information is constantly tested for honesty, completeness, and the *fruit it produces*. Credentials alone no longer persuade; authority is trusted when it is experienced as service, humility, and moral consistency. Many now believe that being *right* only matters if one is also *good*.

At the same time, Experience and Community have become far more influential. People increasingly ask: *Does this faith help me become whole? Does it produce peace, meaning, and love? Do I feel seen and valued here? How does it treat people on the margin, people who don't fit in?* These questions are not hostile to belief; they are deeply human.

Pathways to Belief Are Changing

INFORMATION

Our Restoration narrative, doctrines, and theology form the cornerstone of testimony.

As LDS history, theology, and doctrine become more readily available and questioned by critics, some members grow skeptical, seeking what they view as honesty and transparency over defending or rationalizing, weakening the traditional influence of information.

EXPERIENCE

Personal spiritual experiences, worship, prayer, and the Holy Ghost strengthen belief.

As information grows complex and less trusted, experience matters more. People rely on what they personally live and can verify—the fruits of connection, gospel living, church activity, and personal growth.

CREDENTIALS

Priesthood keys, prophetic authority, and revelation inspire trust and belief.

Institutional leaders are increasingly viewed with some distrust. People value humility, authenticity, and servant leadership—goodness and contribution over authority, power, and being right.

COMMUNITY

Belonging strengthens belief through shared purpose, worship, rituals, sacrifice.

Community remains vital but must be inclusive, healing, and authentic. Conditional belonging drives people away; genuine love draws them in.

This shift presents both a challenge and an opportunity. Our historical pathways to belief will be less decisive for many people going forward. If we hope to remain a living church where belief is passed along to others, we will need to adapt—without surrendering truth—by allowing experience and community to bear fuller witness to the gospel's power.

Large and Powerful

Shifting values are not the only challenge we face. The Church's size, global reach, and institutional strength also shape how members and nonmembers experience it. As with other large institutions, rising visibility brings heightened expectations for trust, transparency, and accountability.

Many who leave the Church—and many who stay while feeling conflicted—perceive a gap between what the Church teaches and what they sometimes observe institutionally. They recognize devotion and sacrifice yet do not always see corresponding engagement with the suffering, inequality, and division that mark modern life. For example, calls for peacemaking in contrast to persistent political division in the Church, significant investment in temples in contrast to the plight of the homeless, some who prioritize serving the dead over serving the living, and caring for members in the fold more than for people outside of the fold.

Institutions naturally work to preserve themselves. The Church, led and staffed by real people, is no exception. Institutional self-preservation can occasionally overshadow responsiveness to human need. Critics sometimes describe this as caring more about being right than being good or focusing on the next life more than improving this one.

Public perception reflects this tension. A 2023 Pew study found that Latter-day Saints are viewed less favorably than any other major religious group in the United States.[13]

While misunderstanding and bias play a role, this disparity invites humility and reflection. Other religious communities with distinctive beliefs face skepticism yet maintain higher favorability, suggesting that behavior, tone, and transparency matter greatly.

Fewer Americans View Latter-day Saints Favorably Than Any Other Religion or Group

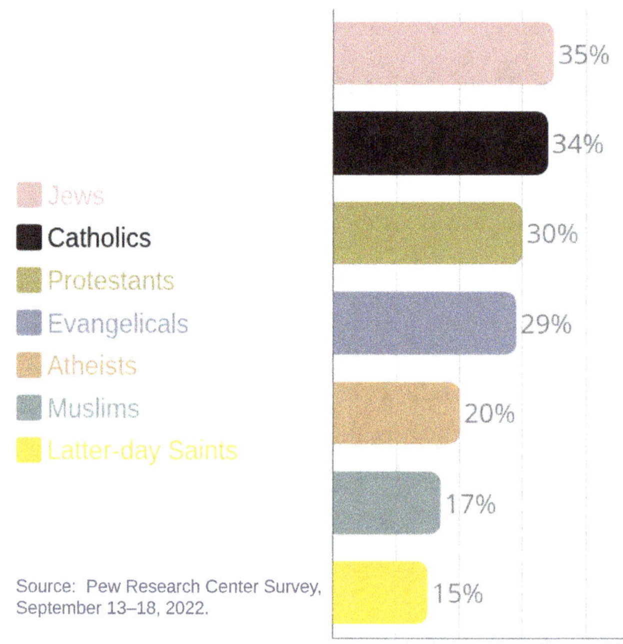

Those who know Latter-day Saints personally often describe them as kind, generous, and service oriented. The gap between personal experience and public perception underscores both how misunderstood the faith remains and how much opportunity exists to build trust through Christlike engagement.

Opportunities to Respond More Effectively

Understanding the storm does not lead to despair. It creates the conditions for wiser, more faithful responses. Culture is always being shaped, and individual choices—especially those made by leaders—can either crowd out the gospel or allow it to flourish.

In India, conversions rarely follow a linear pattern of instruction and testimony. One man I met was embraced first by friendship. What was done *right* was prioritizing experience and community; what could have gone *wrong*—imposing rigid cultural expectations—was avoided. Experience and community opened the door for doctrine to take root.

In South Africa, a stake presidency counselor I spoke with described the discouragement members felt when visiting leaders insisted on pushing Wasatch Front cultural norms. What went *wrong* was confusing culture with righteousness. What went *right* was local leaders recognizing the disconnect and caring enough to help local members work through these negatives.

In Soweto, a young mother shared how small she felt when comparing her modest circumstances to the polished affluence of General Relief Society and Young Women leaders in Salt Lake City, leaving her feeling like she didn't belong. The harm was unintentional but real. We can be more aware of how visible differences in culture and affluence can wound even when no offense is intended.

Closer to home, a Relief Society president in the United States was handed a preselected list of counselors. What went *wrong* was the message that her inspiration was secondary. What went *right* was her awareness of the dissonance—and the opportunity it created for leaders to reconsider how authority and revelation are shared. Revelation flows both ways.

In each case, culture shaped outcomes and affected how real people experienced the Church. When culture eclipsed the gospel, people felt diminished. When leaders allowed the gospel to breathe—prioritizing dignity, agency, and love—people felt strengthened.

Conclusion

Understanding is strength. Each storm we face becomes less threatening when we face it and get through it together. Like the buffalo that turn into the storm together, we find courage not by retreating but by moving forward with open eyes and hearts, anchored in Christ, bound by love, and committed to lifting one another.

Key Chapter Takeaway

Faith disruption is increasingly shaped by forces outside the Church, yet it is often misread as personal weakness. A faithful response begins with understanding how belief formation is changing, and responding with empathy and awareness rather than judgment.

Reflection Questions

1. What forces outside the Church have most shaped my own faith journey?

2. How might technology, social change, or trust in institutions be shaping others' beliefs today?

3. When faith is disrupted, do I tend to judge motives—or seek understanding?

Application Suggestion

Choose one disruptive force discussed in this chapter that you feel least fluent in. Spend a short, intentional amount of time learning about it to understand how it shapes belief today. Ask someone whose experience differs from yours: *"How do you feel this force is influencing people's beliefs in a way that might be different now from in the past?"* Listen without correcting or defending. Your goal isn't agreement; it's understanding. The more clearly you understand the landscape, the more wisely you can respond when someone you love is navigating it.

CHAPTER 6

BELIEVING

"The greatest source of failure in life comes from this: It is easier to be almost right than to be right; to wish, than to gain. In place of gold, there is always something almost as good, and which glitters equally. . . . Illusion can be had on easy terms, though the end of deception is failure and misery."

—David Starr Jordan

A Gospel of Transformation

We believe the Savior is the way to peace, happiness, and eternal life. Whatever glittering counterfeits might entice us, He is the rock on which to build. The test is whether our conviction is just words or whether it shapes our beliefs, values, and behaviors. The danger is

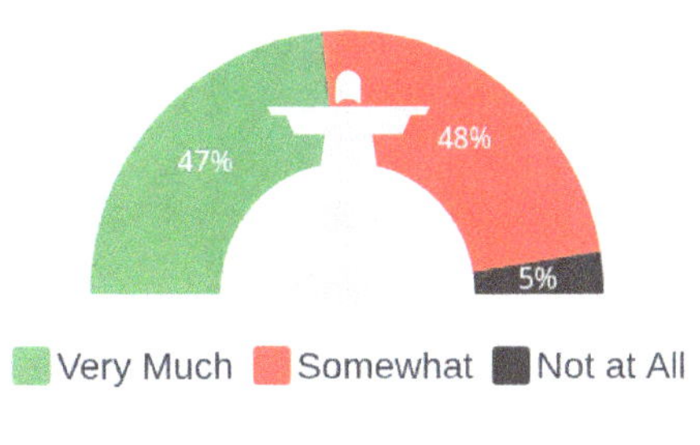

Source: Strong and Dotson, *Why People Are Leaving*, 2025.

not in abandoning the gospel but in drifting toward something that seems almost as good and shines just as brightly yet leaves us unsteady and at risk of falling.

Jordan's warning hits close to home. Our church bears the Lord's name. We genuinely want to follow Him. And yet our research shows that a majority of active members see the Church as *only somewhat / somewhat not* Christ-centered.[1] Have we embraced something "almost as good" that causes us to overlook Him?

This gap between our intentions and reality invites attention. It calls us back to the journey of finding Christ as the rock upon which to build our faith.

The difference between gold and glitter became much clearer to me when Cale left. Through that experience, I learned what mattered most and what I could rely on: My faith had to rest in God, not in certitude—the unbending conviction that if I believed and lived the one right way with enough faith, devotion, and exactness, God would shield me and my family from painful experiences, spiritual trials, and the refining fire of uncertainty. I also learned that obedience without love cannot give life; and becoming fully who God wants us to be requires the courage to be different, even from the norms of our Church culture. Those were parts of my old map, which failed thirteen years ago—and for many who leave, it is a similar map they are walking away from now.

A Story of Transformation

Perhaps the most compelling evidence for the truth and goodness of the gospel of Jesus Christ is its ability to transform us. We can be among those who "awake unto God" (Alma 5:7), experience a "mighty change of heart" (Mosiah 5:2), and become "a new creature in" Christ (2 Corinthians 5:17). This transformation is self-evident. For so many of us, this is why we can say with conviction that we believe or know. Like many of you, I have been blessed to experience this in my own life and to see it happen in the lives of so many people I know well and care about.

One of those people is Josh, a university student who joined the Church in our mission. His story illustrates the transformative power of following Jesus Christ. "If I had been told I'd be a college graduate, married, and pursuing a career in Alaska while striving to follow Jesus, I would have laughed. I was lost—into drugs, partying, and wasting money. I was in debt, on academic probation, and my health was deteriorating. I hit rock bottom. Missionaries found me, but I brushed them off. Their persistence and love paid off. We became friends. They invited me to lessons, church, and sports night. My walls crumbled. As I read the Book of Mormon and prayed, I felt hope returning. I became happier. Even my mom noticed I was smiling again.

"After reflection and soul searching, I chose Him and accepted the missionaries' invitation to be baptized. I see God's hand in this. I now understand I am a loved child of God. I have become a devoted husband, transformed by the Atonement. The gospel changed everything, and I'm forever grateful."

His Path. His Gospel. His Way.

**"The path of salvation has always led
one way or another through Gethsemane."[2]
—President Jeffrey R. Holland**

The path we climb to become like our Heavenly Parents is steep. Life comes with uncertainty, opposition, difficult decisions, and consequences. It is normal to long for certainty and comfort, but seeking an easier way leaves us vulnerable to cultural shortcuts that cannot provide Christ's truth and light. President Spencer W. Kimball taught, "Being human, we would expel from our lives physical pain and mental anguish and assure ourselves of continual ease and comfort, but if we were to close the doors upon sorrow and distress, we might be excluding our greatest friends and benefactors."³ The children of Israel struggled with this yearning to be free of challenges, but God reminded them, "Behold, I have refined thee, but not with silver; I have chosen thee in the furnace of affliction" (Isaiah 48:10).

Christ is light that shines through the darkness. At the Last Supper, despite the agony awaiting Him and in anticipation of the coming uncertainty and opposition His Apostles would face, Jesus used His last peaceful moments to succor *them*. Thomas was the one who said, "Lord, we know not whither thou goest; and how can we know the way?" Jesus answered,

"I am the way, the truth, and the life."
(John 14:5–6)

He is the way, but it's not an easy way. Following Him requires intent and focus. President Russell M. Nelson taught: "There is nothing easy or automatic about becoming such powerful disciples. Our focus must be *riveted* on the Savior and His gospel. It is *mentally rigorous* to strive to look unto Him in *every* thought."⁴

This truth applies not only to us as individuals but also to the Church community itself. When Jesus visited the Nephites, He taught them plainly: "If it so be that the church is built upon *my gospel,* then will the Father show forth his own works in it" (3 Nephi 27:10, emphasis added). He must have known how easy it would be for His followers to lose focus. There are so many things that glitter, competing for our attention with the promise of fulfillment.

The scriptures repeatedly show this pattern of drift. Alma 4 describes a people who, despite being humbled by affliction, became affluent and quickly slipped into pride, inequality, and neglect of the poor. Helaman 3 records how even during peace and prosperity, "pride entered into the hearts of people who professed to belong to the church of God," leading to persecution within the community. Yet the more humble, persecuted people grew stronger in faith and joy by yielding their hearts to God.

These stories encourage us to reflect on the degree to which we are focused on the Savior versus the culture or even the Church. The danger comes when we prioritize the institution or culture over discipleship itself. From Zarahemla to our wards and stakes, the lesson is clear: Both individuals and communities must resist the pull of the glitter and stay focused on Christ. Do we sometimes mistake outward compliance for the inner change that is the real work of the gospel? Do we sometimes confuse conformity and sameness with being one in Christ? When 40 percent of our active members leave and less than half of us believe the Church is Christ-centered, it should cause us to reflect on whether the Father is showing forth His works in our community to the degree that He could be.

The Problem with Culture

Cultural beliefs are often the starting point of spiritual drift. The "easy" version feels more enticing than the hard truth. Is there a "diet pill" version of the gospel instead of the exercise-and-nutrition version? Culture can become so pervasive that we may not even notice how deeply it shapes us. David Foster Wallace captured this with his parable: "There are these two young fish swimming along, and they happen to meet an older fish swimming the other way, who nods at them and says, 'Morning, boys, how's the water?' And the two young fish swim on for a bit, and then eventually one of them looks over at the other and goes, 'What . . . is water?'"[5]

Culture is *always* powerfully influential but not always for good. It can normalize what is unhealthy or even wrong. We often see its power most clearly at the extremes, when it pushes people beyond what is normal or good. The Holocaust is a terrible but instructive example of the power of culture. Nazi culture extolled conformity, detached people from personal moral responsibility, and rationalized atrocity. In her book *Eichmann in Jerusalem: The Banality of Evil,* Hannah Arendt argues that the Holocaust wasn't driven by inherent evil but by thoughtless adherence to norms. *Banal* means ordinary.

This "banality of evil" shows how culture can make the unthinkable seem normal. Leaders like Rudolf Höss and Franz Novak admitted that they detached emotionally from their atrocities by thinking of their victims as inventory, revealing the blinding power of culture.[6]

In contrast, Danish culture, rooted in democratic values and human rights, inspired ordinary citizens to smuggle most of the nation's Jews to safety in Sweden. These two responses show the danger *and* potential of culture. It can blind us to evil or inspire extraordinary goodness. We can learn from these examples, stepping back to ask how we can ensure that our culture is helping us become what Christ expects—small but vital reflections of His extraordinary light. I believe it most often does, but that is not all it does.

When We Confuse Culture and Tradition with Truth

Part of the challenge is that we sometimes confuse culture and tradition with truth and goodness—or even with doctrine itself. The results can be simplistic, untrue, and inconsistent with Christ's character and teachings. I have heard well-meaning members and leaders perpetuate harmful cultural beliefs: that faith aligns only with one political party, that worthiness is measured by outward appearance, that missionaries should only return early in a pine box, or that having doubts means a person is doing something wrong. Such expressions wound people, create barriers to belonging, and lead people away from the true gospel. Culture can shape us subtly, often without malice but in ways that limit our spiritual strength and eclipse Christ.

When we step back, we can see these attitudes for what they are—symptoms of a deeper issue: the tendency to let culture speak louder than Christ. If our culture is to serve Him, it should reflects His compassion, truth, and welcome to every child of God.

Pride and Spiritual Blindness

Elder David A. Bednar taught, "We always must be on guard against a pride-induced and exaggerated sense of self-importance, a misguided evaluation of our own self-sufficiency, and seeking self instead of serving others. As we pridefully focus upon ourselves, we also are afflicted with spiritual blindness and miss much, most, or perhaps all that is occurring within and around us. We cannot look to and focus upon Jesus Christ as the "mark" if we only see ourselves."[7] It is vital to see and remember that the people mentioned in Alma and Helaman who strayed were members of the Church, the covenant people. All were taught and led by God's living prophets. All had, in some form, access to the scriptures or scriptural teachings. *None of those vital things were enough to prevent them from drifting off course.* Perhaps that's why the sacrament prayer very simply reminds us weekly to *always* remember the Savior. His spirit, teachings, actions, and invitations are the critical compass for us, and our eyes and hearts must stay vigilantly fixed on Him. He is the reliable star that can lead us through the dark.

A Path of Truth and Light

Truth is "things as they really are" (Doctrine and Covenants 93:24). Light is the effect God's truth creates in and around us. It comes to us and into us as we live His truth. The Church's own description captures it well: "The Light of Christ is divine energy, power, or influence that proceeds from God through Christ and gives life and light to all things."[8] The Lord revealed to Joseph Smith that this light "proceedeth forth from the presence of God to fill the immensity of space . . . the light which is in all things, which giveth life to all things, which is the law by which all things are governed" (Doctrine & Covenants 88:12–13). We are drawn to this light because it is *life-giving.* The Apostle Paul said it so well: "Ye are all the children of light, and the children of day" (1 Thessalonians 5:5).

While looking for a way to make this idea more accessible for our missionaries, I discovered the "heliotropic effect"—the way plants always grow toward sunlight. Place a plant in a dark room with a single window, and it will turn toward the light because it needs light to survive. Sunlight sustains life not just for the plant but all living things around it as the plant transforms light into food for itself and oxygen for the things around it.

What does the heliotropic effect look like for people? It looks like *environments that encourage and nourish growth,* where *everyone feels drawn toward their highest potential,* much like a sunflower reaching for the sun. People, like plants, need what is truly life-giving.

It seems to me that in a world that too often feels designed to defeat us, people do not often leave places or communities that provide encouragement, nourishment, and growth for them—and yet, many of our friends and family are leaving the Church.

The journey of becoming like our Heavenly Parents involves acquiring more truth and light—light that comes from Jesus Christ. The Lord warned that truth and light can be lost "through disobedience . . . and *because of the traditions of their fathers*" (Doctrine & Covenants 93:39). Things that increase our light are righteous. Things that decrease our light are sinful. And the levers for both are not limited to standards and commandments. They include any belief, attitude, or behavior that impacts our light—in other words, culture. Part of our work is to create a culture of light.

We can think of our loving Heavenly Parents as having created a kind of "fiber-optic" conduit that conveys truth and light from Them to us through the Savior, bringing increase—growth, wisdom, contribution—and ultimately joy.

God's Truth and Light → Jesus Christ → Us → Increase and Joy

Our culture sometimes forgets that the Church is not a substitute for His light.

Increasing or Decreasing in Light?

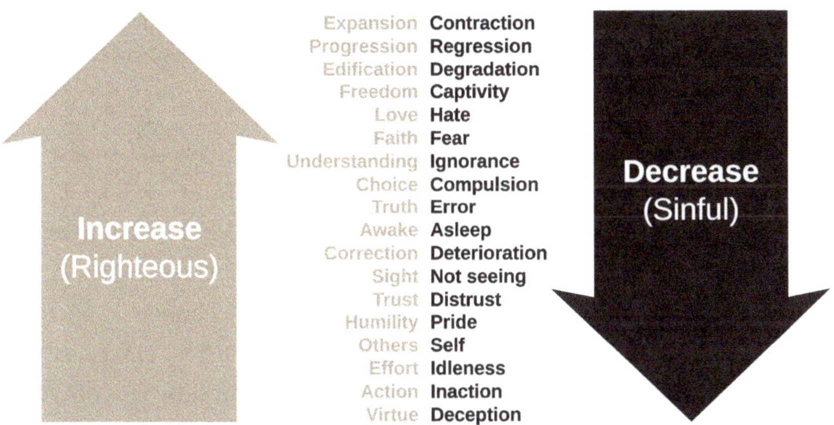

Getting in the Way

The lost 116 pages of the Book of Mormon translation shed some light on this. When Martin Harris lost the pages, Joseph Smith was deeply troubled, but the Lord reassured him that God's work was not dependent on any individual, *even Joseph as the prophet*: "Remember, remember that it is not the work of God that is frustrated, but the work of men" (Doctrine and Covenants 3:3). Light comes from God through Jesus Christ to us. Our role as members, individually and collectively, is important but limited—and it begins with not getting in the way of that light. The work of eternal life is God's work, and *He* will do it.

In our great love for the Church, we must remember not to insert ourselves or the Church in place of Christ between God and our fellow members, an easy mistake to make in our zeal. It is too common in our culture. One person I interviewed who left the Church described it this way: "The Church is using Christ to attract people to the Church rather than using the Church to lead them to Christ." Another said,

"I need the Savior's living water and bread of life, and all I am getting is a steady diet of 'Church stuff.'"

If these statements seem puzzling or unbelievable given your positive Church experience, President Dieter F. Uchtdorf expressed much the same idea with his customary elegance:

> But as large as the target of gospel teaching is, the bullseye—the center of the target we should never forget to focus on—it is *small.* . . . The Savior Himself gave it to us. What is it? Love God and love others. *That* is the center. Other things may be interesting to us. They may even be important. But they are not the center. . . . Our goal is to help those we teach to come closer to Christ, increase in their knowledge and love of God, and serve God by reaching out in compassion toward all His children. That is the center. And where do we find our greatest example of loving God and others? In the life and teachings of our Savior.[9]

The problem may be that we are like goldfish, unaware of the water we swim in, failing to see how cultural norms can hinder connection to divine truth and light, sometimes making the Savior and His teachings a side dish instead of the main course.

The Cultural Gospel in the Church

When the Lord taught Joseph Smith what truth is—"things as they really are" (Doctrine & Covenants 93:24)—He added, "Whatsoever is *more or less than this* is the spirit of the wicked one" (verse 25, emphasis added). Distortions of truth, even with good intentions, can be damaging. Even small distortions can damage faith, as we will see later in this chapter. Satan, the father of lies (see 2 Nephi 2:18; John 8:44), uses deception and distortion to disrupt God's life-giving light. If we build on ideas that glitter but are false, they cannot bring light, and they eventually erode trust in God and in the Church and its leaders.

Distortion happens when truth is reshaped into "more or less than this." Dial it up or down just a little, and it becomes counterfeit.

Culture sometimes acts as a Trojan horse for this. This is especially dangerous because it mixes cultural distortions with the real gospel, making it hard to separate the two. President Dallin H. Oaks taught, "It may be just as dangerous to exceed orthodoxy as it is to fall short of it. The safety and happiness we are promised lie in keeping the commandments, not in discounting or multiplying them."[10] It has been my experience that we are vulnerable to this in four common ways:

1. **Strengths:** Strengths become weaknesses when exaggerated. Zealotry and pride are born from overemphasis. Jesus rebuked the Pharisees for too much focus on laws and rituals while neglecting the weightier matters of the law—judgment, mercy, and faith (see Matthew 23).

2. **Weaknesses:** We sometimes rationalize or even elevate our weaknesses as religious virtues. Legalism, box-checking faith, and excessive focus on rules or institutions create comfort and control but shield us from the sacrifice and compassion discipleship requires.

3. **Traditions:** Beloved traditions can be mistaken for doctrine. When traditions overshadow gospel principles or harm individuals or the Church, they cause us to lose light. One powerful example is how our tradition has elevated serving a mission, something incredibly worthwhile, to the same status as a saving ordinance.

4. **The Church's Role:** Our love for and loyalty to the Church may lead us to talk as if the Church itself were the light, overshadowing and diminishing the Savior's light. For example, we often talk as if the Church or Church leaders are the gateway to salvation rather than the Savior, or that Church membership is more important than discipleship.

These distortions are inconsistent with the restored gospel and the teachings of prophets and scripture. I have seen "more or less than this" in action in well-intended but damaging ways:

> **Teaching transactional conversion:** A former member of the Church I interviewed was promised if he had enough faith he would receive an immediate and undeniable testimony at the MTC. It didn't happen, even after he fasted and prayed for many days. This promise and pattern repeated itself in the field. When the witness never came, he lost trust in the promisers. In time, he left his mission and eventually the Church. Instead of promising "on-demand" witnesses, we can teach the simplicity and power of gradual, lived conversion.

> **Exaggerating promises of protection or prosperity:** Missionaries are often told that if they serve faithfully, God will protect and bless their families. Yet many face deaths, divorces, and tragedies at home. Unfulfilled promises eroded trust in God, leaders, and family. Instead, we can teach the power of faith and patience, and the role hardship plays in life.

> **Excluding others:** Many young women refuse to date young men who did not serve missions, excluding good young men and ignoring the unique paths of some, including Presidents Nelson, Oaks, and Eyring, who never served missions. Instead, we can help people understand that character and contribution come in many forms.

> **Devaluing individuality and love:** Two untraditional but faithful missionaries wore bright socks and had unique hairstyles. A fellow missionary criticized them for not strictly fitting the missionary mold. That same day, a mother shared with me that those very missionaries had transformed her son's life and inspired him to serve a mission. They were, she said, "the perfect missionaries at the perfect time." Instead of emphasizing cultural conformity, we can focus on the goodness and fruits people offer.

I am grateful that eternal life is God's work, not ours, and that He accomplishes it through all of us—despite our different personalities, talents, weaknesses, and even the socks we wear. Recognizing and avoiding distortions preserves truth, builds trust, and keeps us centered on the gospel of Jesus Christ.

The Conflict Between Common Beliefs in the Culture versus Personal Beliefs

To more deeply understand this dynamic of "more or less than this" in the Church, we included questions in our research aimed at the prevalence and strength of certain beliefs. We asked respondents whether they agreed or disagreed with seven beliefs often expressed and emphasized in our culture. A majority agreed with only two of the seven (the first two below) and overwhelmingly disagreed with the other five.

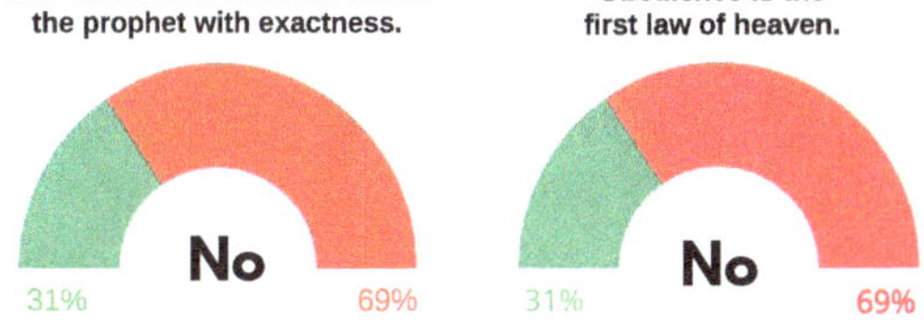

Source: Strong and Dotson, *Why People Are Leaving*, 2025.

Why? Is it a lack of faith, or has experience with life and the gospel taught many that these ideas are sometimes exaggerated or distorted in our culture? One mother I interviewed, reflecting on her son's trust crisis after his mission, said something extraordinarily instructive:

"His hurt, confusion, and even anger came from feeling he had been lied to. People he loved and trusted were not honest with him—not so much about doctrine or church history, but exaggerations of blessings, distortions of what really matters in God's eyes, and obfuscating the simple path toward the light of Christ."

These are the kinds of distortions President Dieter F. Uchtdorf warned about when he urged us to focus not only on the target but on the *center* of the target—love of God and others. Examined closely, each of these seven beliefs reflects the same temptation: the promise of an easier, more comfortable path, one that avoids the refining fire God uses to help us grow. The gospel of Christ is not meant to shield us from hardship or replace discipleship with checklists or perpetual comfort but to anchor and guide us through the challenges necessary to shape us.

Divine and Apostolic Teachings and Warnings

Not focusing on the true center is one way we "look beyond the mark" or are "deceived from the simplicity that is in Christ" (2 Corinthians 11:3). The Lord cautioned against this:

> To the Nephites: "Whoso among you shall do *more or less than* these [referring to gospel basics of repentance, baptism, and taking the sacrament] are not built upon my rock . . . and when the rain descends, and the floods come . . . they shall fall." (3 Nephi 18:13, emphasis added)

> To Joseph Smith: "Behold, this is my doctrine—whosoever repenteth and cometh unto me, the same is my church. Whosoever

declareth *more or less than* this . . . is against me; therefore he is not of my church." (Doctrine & Covenants 10:64–68, emphasis added)

› Again, to Joseph Smith in 1841: "For that which is *more or less than this* cometh of evil, and shall be attended with cursings and not blessings." (Doctrine and Covenants 124:120, emphasis added)

Modern apostles have echoed this caution. Elder Bruce R. McConkie noted how people in Jesus's time "took the plain and simple things of pure religion and added to them . . . ; and they took a happy, joyous way of worship and turned it into a restrictive . . . system of rituals and performances."[11] Elder Quentin L. Cook cautioned against pursuing perfection with such zeal that we become critical, distracted, or materialistic—forgetting our dependence on God.[12] This is the heart of the cultural gospel: inserting culture, tradition, or even the Church itself into the conduit of light between God and His children. These things may resemble the true gospel, but they do not produce lasting fruit. And this is what many who leave are rejecting.

The Church is vitally important, but it is not the light. Jesus Christ is. Elder Dale G. Renlund gave us one example: "To be clear, baptismal and temple covenants are not, in and of themselves, the source of power. The source of power is the Lord Jesus Christ and our Heavenly Father. Making and keeping covenants create a conduit for Their power in our lives."[13] Can we center the culture more authentically on Jesus Christ, allowing other good things—like the rich soil of the Church—to play their valuable supporting role?

We are torn between two worlds: one built on culture that cannot last, and one rooted in Christ. Too often, culture competes with the gospel, leaving many longing for the light they once felt and still want and need. Yet hope remains: Soil can be renewed, roots nourished, and Christ's teachings still shine to guide us. That is the work before us in part 3.

Key Chapter Takeaway

The Christ-centered gospel can quietly be replaced by cultural substitutes. Renewal and more enduring faith comes by recentering belief on our love for Jesus Christ and His teachings.

Reflection Questions

1. Where do I place my deepest trust—in Christ or in our culture, traditions, and way of life?

2. How has my understanding of discipleship changed across the seasons of my life?

3. How might others be striving to follow Christ in ways that look different from mine?

Application Suggestion

Ask yourself: When I feel threatened or unsettled, what do I instinctively cling to—Jesus Christ or the comfort of certainty, tradition, and institutional reassurance?

Then do one small, concrete act to recenter on Christ as the rock. This could be as simple as choosing a Christ-centered gospel truth you will practice this week.

Of Soil, Seeds, and the Sower

We have covered meaningful ground. The journey so far has been an investment in understanding how many are leaving and why, what culture is and why it matters, the changing factors that influence belief, and the importance of centering faith and culture in Jesus Christ and His teachings.

Whenever I feel the weight and complexity of a challenge, I am more hopeful and confident when I get focused and get to work. We are ready to do that. Part 3 begins by turning our attention beneath the surface—to the soil itself.

Healthy soil works quietly. It protects. It nourishes. It holds roots steady in wind and in seasons of heat or drought, producing slow, steady growth. When soil becomes compacted, roots cannot reach deep enough to anchor or feed. When it is depleted, growth may begin yet falter for lack of nutrients or water. Cultivation is normal and necessary. It does not require abandoning what is good. It requires keeping what is good in balance so the soil remains life-giving. Church culture is no different.

If I were to describe the Latter-day Saint community today in a single word, it would be *tension*. There are still conflicting narratives in our community about how many people are leaving the Church and why. When we gather in church settings, we speak about the gospel and the Church from different experiences, needs, priorities, and assumptions. Differences surface in tone, emphasis, and what remains unsaid. Too often, they are experienced as tension.

Many active members in our study acknowledge the conflict they feel: a sense of not belonging, discomfort in a culture that, for them, does not feel like home, and questions or concerns about the focus and priorities of the Church. Many others feel strengthened, inspired, and grateful. We sit together in the same pews and classrooms.

How can the same Church feel life-giving to some and depleted to others? We are different—in personality, experience, spiritual needs, how we experience the gospel, and what draws us to divine things. We experience the Church and its culture personally and individually.

Some of us are nourished most by institutional strength: prophetic authority, structure, order, clarity, and solidarity. Others are nourished most deeply by relational discipleship: human connection, lifting and being lifted, serving, and encountering the Spirit in personal ways. For many, it is a meaningful blend of both. But when one consistently eclipses the other, those whose needs are unmet feel the strain.

I feel this in my own life—the steadiness of the strength and structure of the Church and persistent longing for something more.

Our research reveals a disconnect between personal belief and cultural emphasis in the Church. We asked active Latter-day Saints to rank common Church priorities in importance—first, personally, and second, as they perceive the culture emphasizes. The chart that follows summarizes what they said. The pattern is clear: differences between personal beliefs on the left and cultural emphasis on the right. Where there in imbalance, there will be tension.

What Matters Most—Personal Belief vs. Cultural Emphasis
(Respondents Ranked Eight Religious Priorities)

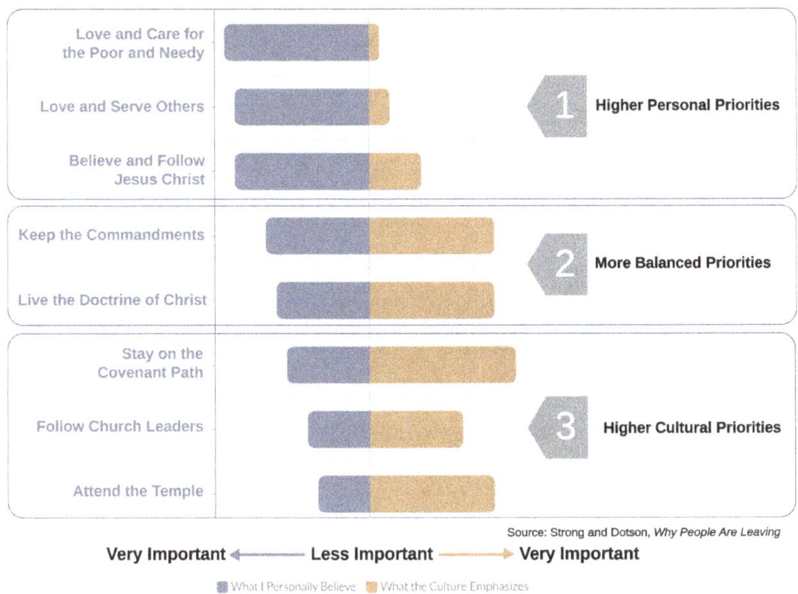

Most members believe most strongly in relational and Christlike priorities, while perceiving the culture to emphasize institutional or religious priorities more heavily. The contrast is less doctrinal than experiential. For example, respondents ranked caring for the poor and needy as their highest personal priority as disciples of Christ, yet believed the culture treats it as the lowest. I do not know Latter-day Saints who would argue that caring for the poor and needy is an unimportant doctrine. The issue is a perceived lack of emphasis. When what nourishes you spiritually feels absent in your community, you will feel alone.

Christ once told a story about soil. A sower went forth to sow (see Matthew 13). Some seeds fell upon hard ground, where roots could not penetrate. Some fell on shallow soil full of stones, where growth began but faltered. Some fell among thorns, where life was crowded and choked. And some fell onto good ground and brought forth fruit. In this parable, the soil represents the condition of the heart—our responsibility to receive the word and nourish it.

Later, the prophet Alma added something, suggesting there are *two* things we must nourish: "If ye will nourish the word, yea, nourish the tree as it beginneth to grow . . . it shall take root; and behold it shall be a tree springing up unto everlasting life" (Alma 32:41). Are we only responsible to nourish faith within ourselves, but not also in others? Is there a deeper principle from the Savior and echoed by Alma that our hearts should not only be soil that receives the gospel, but should be soil that receives and nourishes the people who are seeking it? People, who, like seeds, are planted into our Church community? Could there be a way to more deeply liken these scriptures to our time and our challenges? Perhaps a different look at the parable?

A sower went forth to sow, scattering seeds who were created by God in all their varieties. Some seeds fell by the wayside, into hard and unyielding soil, and could not find a way to take root. Some fell with shallow soil full of stones and sprang up but withered in the sun because depth was not possible. Some fell among thorns, sprang up, but wilted from lack of room and sunlight. And some fell upon soil that was good—but only for certain kinds of plants.

We are free to choose whether we embrace the gospel. None of us chooses the soil we are planted in. God places us where He sees fit. Perhaps one of the deepest acts of discipleship is when we recognize this and become cultivators of soil where every seed can grow.

A global, maturing Church will necessarily develop institutional strength—soil that stabilizes and protects. That strength is real and good. But without careful tending, imbalances form that deprive the soil of nutrients necessary for plants of all varieties to thrive. This new parable of the sower can help us see the four imbalances in our soil that require our attention:

1. **Who is the Church really for?** When culture makes love and acceptance narrow, rigid, or conditional, some quietly conclude they do not belong. This is *the tension of acceptance,* where many hunger to be embraced yet find themselves unable to take root in the community.

2. **How does the Church best prepare us for the challenges of real life?** When culture constrains the spiritual depth and strength that come from pure and simple truths of the gospel and then suffering or complexity arrive, people learn the culture they trusted did not prepare them. This is *the tension of sanctuary,* where long-held cultural traditions can prevent our spiritual roots from reaching the Savior.

3. **How do we honor God's gift of agency in a culture that expects us to comply?** When faithfully following Church leaders turns into dogmatic cultural compliance, people learn that vital spiritual growth and spiritual self-reliance cannot happen without agency and the freedom, moral reasoning, personal responsibility, and personal inspiration they require. *This is the tension of fealty,* or unconditional and unconfirmed allegiance, where obedience and agency are imbalanced.

4. **How do we become one when we are so different?** When culture reduces being one in Christ to sameness, people learn they must pretend to be something they are not to be valued. This is *the tension of conformity,* where sameness is mistaken for unity and authenticity becomes isolating.

Alma also suggested that the nourishment in the soil is *our* responsibility: "If ye neglect the tree, and take no thought for its nourishment; behold it will not get any root; and when the heat of the sun cometh and scorcheth it . . . it withers away . . . because your ground is barren" (Alma 32:38).

These are the soil imbalances we face. They influence whether roots deepen or wither, whether people's experiences in the Church bear fruit or feel barren. When fruit does not come, some eventually seek new ground where it can.

Soil can be nourished and cultivated. Compacted ground can be loosened. Stones can be lifted. Thorns can be cleared. Stability and nourishment can live together again. The question before us is not whether the gospel is true or effective. It is whether our soil allows it to flourish among us.

In the chapters ahead, we will examine these tensions and consider how to cultivate conditions where faith can take root, bear fruit, and endure for more of us.

Part 3 begins that work.

CULTIVATE THE SOIL

*Balance the Tensions
That Cause So Many to Leave*

CHAPTER 7

ACCEPTANCE

Imbalance #1:
Soil That Is Hard and Unyielding

Critical Question:
Who is the Church really for?

Much More Than a Track Meet

In March 2018, I participated in the USA Masters Track and Field National Championships in Landover, Maryland—a competition for older athletes. I took my middle son, Zach, who was excited to cheer me on. This happened while I was doing research on how people come to believe in and form relationships with their churches. I had learned a lot about what draws people toward a church and what pushes them away from it. As I reflected on how our Church's history, doctrines, standards, and culture influence why people stay or leave, I certainly did not expect new insight from a track meet.

Masters Track and Field is underrated! In this indoor arena, in front of about three thousand spectators, men and women well into their eighties and nineties defied reality—running, jumping, throwing, and vaulting. Some were still elite athletes. Others wore braces and wraps or carried visible signs of age and limitation. Yet all entered the arena together.

As the events unfolded, Zach and I began to see something more than a competition for medals. It was a gathering of people from every walk of life united by a desire to overcome whatever stood in their way—age, injury, loneliness, discouragement, or self-doubt—to become the best version of themselves. To show up. To try. To face fear. To finish. To win, yes, but far more often to lose—and to remember they were alive and that life and people were good.

Of course, a track meet isn't the Church, but a significant part of what we want and need from our Church experience mirrors what I saw there. We want to be in a community that matters, where we feel needed and that we belong. We need a place to give and receive light and love and be drawn to our highest, noblest selves—to gather, be embraced, and strive toward something greater.

One race revealed how special this competition really was: the men's eighty-and-over 1,500-meter run—a little less than a mile. Twelve competitors lined up, including one-hundred-year-old Orville Rogers. When the starter fired his pistol, the runners took off, with Orville settling immediately into last place, where he remained, alone, for the entire race, slowly shuffling along as the others lapped him multiple times. The winner, Oliver Grant, age eighty-two, finished in 7:54.07—an astonishing time for his age! When Al Ray, the last runner besides Orville, finished at 14:00.69, Orville still had about two and a half laps to go. As he continued, nearly three thousand spectators sat quietly watching him.

As he began his final lap, the crowd rose and cheered. Roughly thirty meters from the finish line, he called on his last reserves, moving from slow shuffle to something resembling a sprint. The crowd erupted as he crossed the finish line at 20:00.91 and was embraced by his fellow runners. I'll never forget watching a hundred-year-old man do something so astonishing.

Incredibly, the 1,500 was Orville's fifth race. He'd already competed in the 60-, 200-, 400-, and 800-meter races—finishing last in each. He was, after all, one hundred years old. But there was more: In each event, he broke the age-group (one hundred–plus) world record.

What struck me most was how, in a world so focused on celebrating champions (the elite, the people who do the best and are the best), the spirited crowd gave its greatest ovations to the "losers," those who did not win but finished, often against daunting odds. It takes rare courage to step into an arena knowing you will finish last.

Compacted soil often becomes hardened not because of malice but fear—fear of difference, fear of disruption, fear of losing what we cherish. There was no fear in Landover. Zach said, "I think I know what's going on here, Dad. We came expecting to watch a track meet, but instead we're watching a celebration of the human spirit." What we witnessed that day reflected what the Church can and should be—a gathering of people, imperfect yet determined, joined by love and the will to grow together.

> **"The opposite of love is not hate; it's indifference."[1]**
> **—Elie Wiesel**

Soil That Seeds Cannot Penetrate

What does this have to do with why people we love are leaving the Church? One of the reasons is they do not feel a sense of meaningful connection and belonging in our Church community. When our culture idealizes a particular profile of what it means to be a Latter-day Saint, difference becomes invisibility and even shame. When we grow hard and unyielding—so focused on ourselves that we become indifferent—faith cannot take root in the hearts of those who don't match our cultural norm.

In Landover, everyone, regardless of ability or appearance, was a vital part of what was happening. The most capable athletes showed no pride or self-absorption; they understood this competition wasn't about them but about something larger—a shared respect and love that united and lifted everyone on the track. The culture of this meet, like any healthy soil, existed for people and growth. Without the so-called "losers," it would have been sterile and lifeless.

As one of the losers that day, I felt seen, valued, unjudged, at home, and grateful. The experience was life-giving, and I wanted more. Many feel that same light in our Church, but many do not. While our cultural soil warmly invites everyone to the meet, we don't allow everyone to run or to run in a way so that they feel they matter. We implicitly (and sometimes explicitly) exclude not by enforcing God's doctrines or standards but by emphasizing lower standards or certain cultural standards above God's higher, essential standards.

We come to Church seeking to belong and to feel at home, but too many never do. In fact, 60 percent of members report they do not feel a sense of belonging in their home wards.[2] We could be discouraged by these numbers, but why? The numbers and awareness of what is

How comfortable are different people in the Church?

Source: Strong and Dotson, *Why People Are Leaving*

1 Extremely Uncomfortable — 2 Very Uncomfortable — 3 Comfortable — 4 Very Comfortable — 5 Extremely Comfortable

happening give us the power to change this. Once we see, we can choose to act—and that is what Latter-day Saints do.

I often hear people justify hard and unyielding Church soil by arguing that God's doctrines and standards can't be compromised. I agree—and therein lies the paradox God has given us to wrestle with—the tension between standards and acceptance and how to balance and prioritize both while truly loving as the Savior would.

There are certainly moments in scripture when sorting occurs—wheat separated from tares, sheep from goats, good fish from bad, the wise distinguished from the unprepared. *How* Jesus Christ taught these ideas reveals something important: not simply *that* sorting exists, but *how* it happens, *who* does it, and *when* it occurs.

He did not lower God's standards; He raised them. He deepened obedience from outward compliance to inward transformation and taught that the law finds its fulfillment in love. Standards, rightly understood, are meant to guide, protect, and elevate us—to help us grow in capacity, integrity, and Christlike character. Without them, faith loses its shape, direction, and power. The challenge is not that standards exist but how they are sometimes applied within our Church culture.

What Christ consistently resisted was the use of standards as present-day sorting tools within the community—ways of signaling who fully belongs, whose belief is most valid, or who is subtly pushed to the margins.

One of Jesus's most controversial miracles may also be one of His simplest. When He healed a man born blind, He did so by kneeling in the dirt, mixing mud with His spit, and placing it on the man's eyes— and He did it on the Sabbath.[3] In one deliberate act, Jesus crossed nearly every boundary His religious culture guarded most carefully: work on the sabbath, ritual cleanliness, and physical purity. It seems that what mattered most to Him was not the preservation of religious order or appearances but the restoration of a human life. The message was unmistakable: When love, healing, and mercy are at stake, they take precedence over even the most cherished rules—the spirit of the law above the letter of the law. When community standards harm a child of God and their belonging and growth, something essential has gone wrong.

When Jesus spoke of sorting—sheep and goats, wheat and tares, good fish and bad—He placed that work in God's hands, in God's time, and for God's redemptive purposes. His parables were not instructions for communities to measure one another but invitations for individuals to reflect inwardly. Judgment is real, but in Christ's teachings it remains patient, personal, and ultimately His.

Standards exist to elevate people, not sort them.

- God does the sorting. People don't.
- Sorting happens later, not now.
- Standards are meant to help people grow, not prove they belong.
- What matters most is what a life produces, not how it appears.
- The Church gathers; God judges.

When Church culture uses standards to sort, it moves away from what Christ taught. The result is often not deeper discipleship but soil that grows harder, less forgiving, and less able to nourish.

When our Church culture excludes or marginalizes people, it is often because that culture overemphasizes rules or cultural expectations—echoing historically problematic tendencies among believers. We repeat the mistake God's people made before: elevating visible behaviors, or what we do, while neglecting God's higher laws, which almost always center on the person, or who we are.

The Pharisees tithed with exactness yet overlooked justice, mercy, and faith (see Matthew 23:23). Israel observed sacrifices and holy days while ignoring the oppressed (see Isaiah 1:11–17). Nephi foresaw churches adorned in wealth that withheld fellowship from the poor (see 2 Nephi 28:13). And the Zoramites practiced polished and pious worship while excluding and persecuting the humble (see Alma 31:9–30). Whenever rules or cultural expectations overshadow God's higher laws, to love Him and our neighbor, belonging fades and people are sifted rather than gathered.

The solution to that tension was on full display in Landover. What we witnessed there did not require a single standard to be lowered. It required more love. Every race was measured, timed, and judged with exactness. No one cut corners or lowered bars. The rules were the same for everyone, yet everyone was allowed to run and the space overflowed with joy, respect, and belonging because everyone understood that the meet wasn't ultimately about rules or winning—it was about people. The culture was shaped by a higher law that welcomed every runner and honored every effort. That is what Christ taught: Love is the standard by which all other standards are judged and given meaning.

"But many that are first shall be last; and the last first."
(Mark 10:31)

The scriptures remind us that God gathers and lifts the forgotten, the outcast, and the least among us. He does this not only out of compassion but to redefine what it means to be acceptable to Him. Jesus praised the widow and her mite not because she was obedient but because she was full of faith and generosity (see Luke 21:1–4). The rich men, though fully compliant and confident in their giving, offered relatively little. Jesus invites us to see how easily we confuse compliance with devotion and how heaven truly measures individual worth.

In the parable of the Good Samaritan, Jesus chose an outsider—one considered unclean and unworthy—to teach who embodies the pure love of God. The priest and the Levite, the religious "all-in" of their day, passed by, indifferent and content in their correctness. He invites us to question our assumptions about who is good and who truly follows Him.

> "What man of you, having an hundred sheep, if he lose one of them, doth not leave the ninety and nine in the wilderness, and go after that which is lost, until he find it? And when he hath found it, he layeth it on his shoulders, rejoicing." (Luke 15:4–5)

When Jesus spoke of leaving the ninety-nine to find the one, He taught the very heart of His gospel. The ninety-nine represented those who saw themselves as already safe—certain of their standing, no longer needing the Shepherd. But it was the one, the "lost," who was truly secure and over whom heaven most rejoiced. Christ warned of the danger of self-assurance and showed that those who are truly found are those who know they are lost.

Healthy Soil Is Balanced

Cultivating the soil begins close to home—in the way we listen, speak, and respond when others see or believe differently. A wise gardener knows that healthy soil must be both firm and yielding—strong enough to anchor a plant yet soft enough to nourish it and allow for growth. For any church community to thrive, it must be the same. Its stability, direction, and shared identity grow from truth, divine authority, and covenants that connect us with God and provide guidance and boundaries that help us. Its nourishment, its balance of vital nutrients, comes from belonging and connection, from learning and living truth, and from the love, encouragement, and light that flow through the Savior's teachings, attributes, and example. Together, the structure the Church provides and the life the gospel gives create the conditions in which we can take root, expand, and flourish.

Of course, we all understand this and want healthy soil—a loving community and culture focused on people. Yet despite our best intentions, we often lean too heavily toward stability and protection. Faith cannot flourish until the soil receives the seed and allows it to take root. When our emphasis on the Church overshadows our emphasis on the gospel and people, our cultural soil becomes compacted and depleted, unable to nourish anyone who doesn't fit the profile of what we think a "good" Latter-day Saint looks like. When we make that profile more important than the person or the gospel, we are pruning the plant before it sprouts.

Jonathan is one example of what this imbalance can look like in real life. He was one of the most Christlike missionaries we had—bright, kind, loving, spiritually deep, and quietly capable. He loved the Book of Mormon, loved following the Savior, and was among the most effective missionaries and leaders in our mission.

Jonathan is currently married, raising three beautiful children, thriving in his career, and deeply devoted to his family. His life reflects goodness and purpose. Recently, however, I learned that he and his wife were participating less in Church, so I reached out to see how they were doing.

Jonathan shared that he loves the gospel and the Savior as much as ever. What changed was not his faith but his experience in the Church. He explained that Church no longer felt like a place that nourished his faith.

He shared an experience from when he gave a talk in sacrament meeting. In his talk, he expressed that it was okay to not have a perfect knowledge of things and that faith and hope were enough. He talked about how important it was to be honest in our faith journey and that there was no need to pretend to believe things you didn't. He bore his testimony of the Savior and the gospel. Then, with humility and honesty, he acknowledged that beyond these, he wasn't sure what he believed. He hoped the Restoration happened and that the Church was led by prophets and apostles, but he didn't *know*—and wasn't convinced that certainty itself should even matter.

After he sat down, his stake president stood and characterized what he had just said as a faith crisis and suggested he was "in need of rescuing."

Jonathan was not offended. He understood the heavy weight leaders carry and believed most act from love and sincere concern. He emphasized that this was only one leader and one moment. But he also explained that the exchange reflected something he and his wife have felt more broadly—that their way of believing does not quite fit the standard of acceptability.

I believe the problem here is not malice but something quieter and more common: a culture that too easily confuses sameness with goodness. When that happens, authenticity can feel risky, correction can eclipse compassion, and faith can slowly give way to conformity.

President Dieter F. Uchtdorf wrote beautifully, "The Savior's Church is a place of healing, not a place of despair, judgment, or sorrow. Jesus Christ, and living His restored gospel, can make of us the genuine, spiritual being of light and truth we desire to be."[4] Of course, this is true—if the soil allows us to take root.

Jonathan's story is not an anomaly—there are tens of thousands of Jonathans who look, speak, dress, learn, believe, contribute, sacrifice, obey, and love differently, and many are not finding acceptance in the Church. They believe in and love God, strive to follow the example and teachings of Jesus Christ, and want to live good, abundant, and righteous lives. They pursue truth and light as sincerely as any of us, but they don't fit the cultural profile that has come to define acceptability in the Church. Because they do not feel accepted, they often quietly step away.

Simply being aware is a beginning—if we see what is happening, we naturally want to love and include, and we can be more intentional about helping everyone feel at home.

A Conflict Between Culture and Personal Beliefs

As mentioned, what Jonathan experienced was not an isolated occurrence or the result of one leader's misjudgment. It reflects a deeper pattern within our culture—one that shapes who feels at home, whose faith feels valid, and what kinds of beliefs are considered acceptable.

To better understand this pattern, our research explored the tension between cultural expectations and personal belief across four foundational questions. Together, these questions reveal how easily a culture can drift from gathering people to sorting them—and why so many sincere, faithful individuals feel unseen or out of place even while striving to follow Christ.

The four questions we examined were simple but deeply revealing:

1. What is our most important religious role in life?

2. Who should feel most at home in the culture of the Church?

3. What is the best foundation for deep and enduring belief?

4. Why do we have a Church?

It is important to keep in mind that the questions and data that follow in this and then next three chapters provide an interpretive framework, not rigid and perfect answers. They are not intended to measure and compartmentalize us as a community, but to provide insights about our culture. What human beings think and believe is *always* more nuanced than what can be captured in a questionnaire.

Keep that in mind as you review these over the next several chapters. A good approach is to ask not "Is this right?" but "What can I learn from this?"

In response to the first question, one answer dominates in the culture: that our most important religious role is to be an active and faithful member of the Church. When a single answer becomes culturally dominant, it implicitly defines acceptability. Other ways of understanding discipleship may still be tolerated, but they are no longer visible or equally valued.

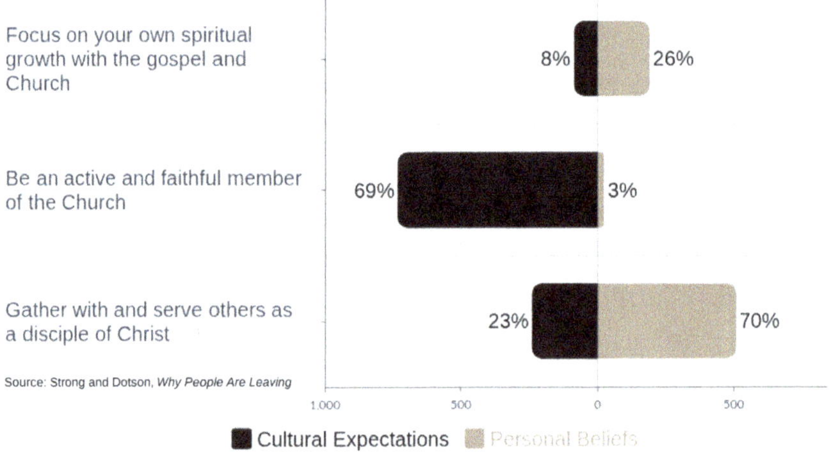

What makes this tension especially significant is the contrast between cultural expectation and personal belief. Most respondents personally believe that gathering and serving others as a disciple of Christ is their most important religious role. When the gap between what the culture signals and what individuals sincerely believe grows this wide, many begin to feel out of place, unseen, or unacceptable—especially when their belief is deeply Christ-centered. This disconnect erodes belonging and helps explain why people quietly step away.

The same pattern appears in the second question. Cultural expectations strongly suggest that the Church is primarily for those who are "all-in," while most individuals believe it should be a place for everyone—or at least anyone sincerely seeking God. This divergence directly shapes who feels welcomed and who feels marginalized.

Who should feel most at home in the culture of the Church?

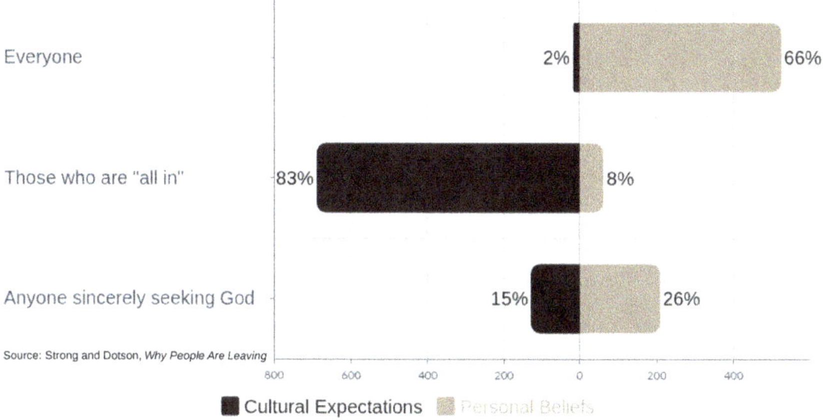

In the third question, the gap between cultural expectation and personal belief narrows somewhat. Knowledge of the Restoration remains the expected foundation for belief in the culture, but personal beliefs are more varied and balanced. Where this balance exists, individuals report feeling less isolated and more at ease.

What is the best foundation for deep and enduring belief?

The fourth question reveals a similar dynamic. While cultural expectations show somewhat greater balance here, there remains a significant disconnect between what the culture emphasizes and what individuals believe the Church exists to do. Even when the gap is smaller, its negative effects are still felt.

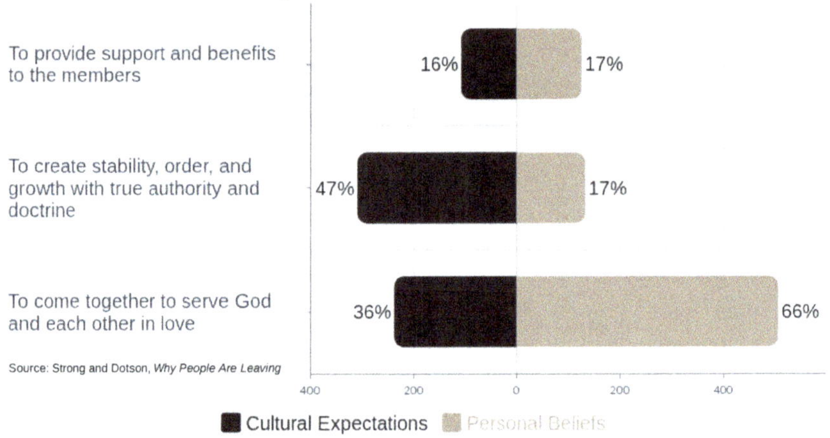

Why do we have a church?

Taken together, these four questions reveal why conformity exerts such strong pressure in our Church culture—and why so many faithful individuals experience tension between who they are and who they feel they are expected to be. When belonging depends more on alignment with cultural expectations than on sincere personal belief, even deeply committed disciples can feel unseen and unaccepted.

The good news is that cultural soil is not unchangeable. When we clearly see the pattern, we can begin to loosen what has hardened, nourish what has withered, and cultivate a Christlike balance where belief can grow without fear.

Seeds That Are Embraced

Nikki grew up in a non-Latter-day Saint home shaped by instability and hardship. His parents were loving and well-intentioned, but the circumstances of his life left him without the structure and support most young people need to flourish. Nikki did the best he could with what he had.

Several of Nikki's high school teachers and friends were members of the Church. They noticed him—not as a project but as a person. They saw his goodness, his potential, and his quiet resilience. They welcomed him, encouraged him, and helped him imagine a life that could be larger and more hopeful than the one he knew.

That love softened Nikki's heart. He began meeting with the missionaries and was baptized. As he learned the gospel, his faith grew naturally—not through pressure or expectation but through belonging and trust. Wanting to share what had changed his life, Nikki soon received a mission call to the Arkansas Bentonville Mission, where we served together.

From the beginning, Nikki was an exceptional missionary—faithful, humble, deeply devoted to the Savior, and quietly influential. Though new to the Church, his sincerity and spiritual depth made him a natural leader and a powerful witness of Christ's love. When Nikki returned home, his academic record reflected the challenges of his earlier life. He had to repeat much of his coursework before being accepted into a university. He persisted. He also married Liberty Johnson, also one of our missionaries. Over time, he was admitted to BYU, where he excelled academically and spiritually.

Today, Nikki and Liberty are thriving—raising a family, pursuing graduate studies, and living lives marked by faith, service, and quiet devotion to Christ.

Nikki's story shows what becomes possible when the cultural soil of a Church community reflects the pattern of Christ—firm in truth yet soft enough to receive. It also reminds us that Nikki was easy to embrace. There are many others whose potential is less obvious, whose paths are less linear, and whose faith looks less familiar. The question before us is whether the soil we cultivate can nourish any seed the Master Gardener places in our care.

Christ's Pattern for Softening the Soil

Christ's ministry was a master class in cultivating healthy soil. He taught truth without weaponizing it, upheld standards without turning them into walls, and lifted people pressed down by systems that valued order over openness. Repeatedly, He corrected the tendency to confuse righteousness with conformity—an organizational preference for sorting instead of strengthening. In His hands, standards were never tools of segregating and sifting but invitations to wholeness.

Christ did not resolve the tension between standards and acceptance by choosing one over the other. He resolved it by teaching us how love governs both.

1. See the One, Not Just the Ninety-Nine

The parable of the lost sheep (see Luke 15) is not a story about rescuing a rebel; it is a story about a Shepherd who refuses to let anyone disappear. While the ninety and nine remain safely within the fold, the Shepherd goes after the one who wandered—not to scold or correct but to gather and restore. Heaven rejoices not because one sheep was deficient or forced back into the flock but because one was loved enough to be seen, valued, and sought.

To see "the one" is to notice who is missing, who lingers quietly on the margins, and who does not fit the expected pattern. Christ consistently saw people, not profiles. In the Book of Mormon, He "did minister unto them one by one" (3 Nephi 11:15), establishing the pattern for His Church—not a sorting mechanism but a gathering place. President Russell M. Nelson taught that "the worth of a soul is its capacity to become like God."[5] Seeing the one doesn't weaken our standards; it deepens our love and softens the soil so *every* plant can grow.

> **"The Savior invited us to be fishers of men, not sorters of fish."[6]**
> **—Anonymous Survey Respondent**

When we see as He sees, people are known before being measured, welcomed before being refined. That is belonging. That is acceptance.

2. Make Love the Measure of Belief

When asked to name the greatest commandment, Christ chose love: "Love the Lord thy God . . . and thy neighbor as thyself" (Matthew 22:37–39). Paul and Moroni later taught that without charity, we are nothing (see 1 Corinthians 13; Moroni 7). Love is not a soft alternative to obedience—it is the lens through which obedience is rightly understood.

Christ never required full understanding before belonging. He invited people to walk with Him and learn along the way. Our culture sometimes reverses this pattern, expecting conviction before connection. But Jesus loved first, taught second, and trusted growth to follow.

President Dieter F. Uchtdorf said, "Love is the defining characteristic of a disciple of Christ."[7] President Nelson likewise taught, "Charity is the principal characteristic of a true follower of Jesus Christ."[8] When love becomes the measure of acceptance, the Church becomes less about fit and proof and more about cultivation. Faith shifts from conformity to transformation, and people grow because they are nourished by truth and light.

3. Let the Church Illuminate, Not Eclipse

The Church exists to guide us to Christ; it is not the destination. It is the vehicle. The Savior's invitation is clear: "Come unto *me* . . . and ye shall find rest unto your souls" (Matthew 11:28–29, emphasis added). Organization matters, but they are never meant to replace relationships. When the Church becomes the end rather than the means, it unintentionally eclipses the light it was built to reflect.

President D. Todd Christofferson reminded us, "We do not strive for conversion to the Church but to Christ and his gospel."[9] President Howard W. Hunter added, "The whole purpose of the Church . . . is to qualify individuals to return to the presence of God."[10]

When the Church illuminates rather than eclipses, it fulfills its sacred role. Standards remain firm, but they become signposts of hope rather than measures of worth. Leaders guide with empathy, members minister with kindness, and programs serve people rather than people serving programs. The soil softens, nourishment flows, and faith begins to flourish.

The Gardener's Call

So back to critical question #1:
Who is the Church really for?

How we answer this question determines who feels accepted in the Church.

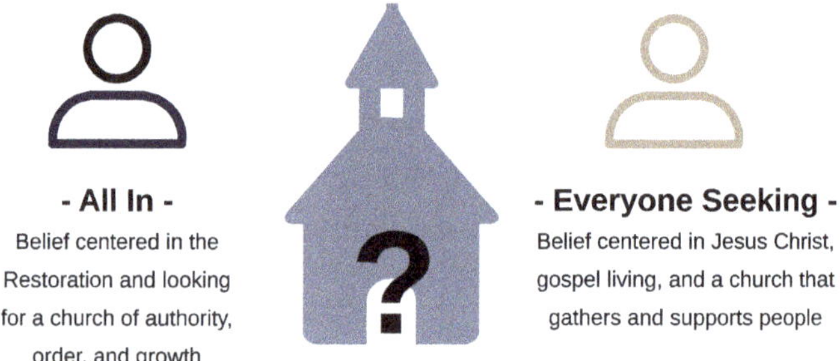

Will the prevailing belief in our culture remain that the Church exists only for those who are depicted on the left, those who are "all-in," even when most of us believe it can and should exist for everyone? And what must we do to make a hard and unyielding culture more accepting?

The Gardener's call is for us to tend the soil—to keep it living, breathing, nourishing, and able to receive. In every season, He invites us to loosen what has hardened, nourish the hungry, and make room for new roots to take hold. The measure of our discipleship is not how uniform our garden appears but how much life it sustains.

And once we see the pattern clearly, Christ's invitation becomes personal. The work is not abstract or institutional; it is ours in the way we notice, welcome, listen, and love. When the Church culture mirrors the love and light of its Master Gardener—anchored in truth yet embracing others—no one will stand unseen on the edge. All will know they are wanted, welcomed, and loved, and the garden will flourish.

Looking forward, even when the soil softens and receives the seed, it can still be shallow and full of stones, preventing the growth of deep roots. The next chapter, "Transcendence," explores this second imbalance—how Christ's gospel calls us not merely to find sanctuary in the Church but to rise, learn, and grow, transcending life's challenges as we are transformed through Him.

Key Chapter Takeaway

Because belonging is often tied to conformity, many feel marginalized. Christlike acceptance restores health by prioritizing worth before performance and making room for growth.

Reflection Questions

1. When have I felt most—and least—accepted in a Church setting?

2. How might my words or expectations signal who belongs?

3. Who in my community might feel unseen or unwelcome?

Application Suggestion

Look for moments where enforcing standards to sort instead of inspire could communicate rejection. Ask yourself: *Does this person feel valued even if they don't or can't embrace everything we teach right now?* Growth flourishes where acceptance is secure.

CHAPTER 8

TRANSCENDENCE

Imbalance #2:
Shallow Soil Full of Stones

Stopping at sanctuary on our way to transcendence

Realizing you can't grow in a sanctuary

**Critical Question:
How can the Church best prepare us
for the challenges of life?**

Roots and Stones

I have a small lavender farm. In the spring, every plant looks healthy; in the dry, hot summer, the plants with shallow roots wither, while those with deep roots flourish. People and the gospel are like those plants—deep roots in Jesus Christ and His gospel help create all-weather Saints. In seasons without heat, shallow roots can appear sufficient—sometimes for years—giving a false sense of security that is exposed when conditions change.

Missionary service turns up the heat on life's biggest questions. Over three years, I read nearly fifty thousand pages of missionary letters, conducted more than four thousand interviews, and held hundreds of meetings—each offering an intimate window into the lives of our missionaries and their wrestle with four of the most critical questions of missions and life:

1. How do I navigate the unknowns of my mission and life?

2. How can I respond to the adversity I'm facing?

3. What kind of missionary and person should I be—and how do I become that person?

4. What will make my mission and my life meaningful?

I saw extraordinary goodness in their wrestle. They were faithful, sincere, and eager to learn. But when we feel unsettled, we naturally want quick answers. Missionaries often sought clarity, relief, and a sense of safety in things they felt tradition offered them: Feeling uncertainty? Here is what you should know. Experiencing adversity? Take refuge with us. Wanting greater character? Follow our map. Need a strong sense of purpose? Our cause is the greatest of all.

Yet, as Sara and I watched closely, we noticed stones in otherwise good soil. Tradition sometimes prevented our missionaries from drawing strength from Christ and His gospel. It gave them the wrong approach to facing hard things. They wanted to resolve discomfort by avoiding it or seeking quick, superficial relief rather than patiently working through it. They felt pressured to substitute certainty for faith—projecting artificial confidence (i.e., "fake it 'till you make it") instead of the humility of learning to trust God through uncertainty and growth. They encountered cultural tendencies that turned discipleship inward rather than outward, focusing more on personal worthiness and rule-keeping than on loving and serving others. And we noticed a common inclination to confuse the map with the territory, mistaking our cultural explanations of the gospel for the lived, often complex reality of following Christ, something I discovered I was doing when Cale left the Church and it became evident that my trusted map no longer fit the terrain.

Most traditions are good. They often begin as stepping stones to truth. But over time, the same factors that formed them can also nudge us toward settling for tradition's sanctuary instead of reaching deeper with the Savior—leading us to rely too heavily on tradition itself rather than developing deep, resilient roots in Jesus Christ.

The Sun's Heat

Paul warned Timothy of religion that is "a form of godliness but denies the power thereof" (2 Timothy 3:5). The word *godliness* was translated from the original Greek word *eusebeia*,[1] which refers to *outward* devotion, including reverence, worship, and religious life. Paul was describing people whose lives were outwardly religious but inwardly untouched by the transformative power of the gospel.

When that happens, roots remain shallow. When the heat comes, faith withers. Trust in God erodes in a culture that emphasizes tradition at the expense of nourishment and growth. God's hope for us is not simply outward behavior or fitting a particular mold but inner growth and transformation. "I have refined thee . . . in the furnace of affliction" (Isaiah 48:10).

When the Savior invites us to carry His heavy, splintered cross, He does not seek to sift us out but to strengthen us. When He appeared to the Nephites who were described as "*more* righteous" amid destruction and devastation, His invitation was direct and unmistakable: He called them to repent and return unto Him, and He promised healing. "O all ye that are spared . . . will ye not now return unto me . . . that I may heal you?" (3 Nephi 9:13).

Though they were *more righteous,* He still called them to repent—to realign their hearts with Him. His invitation reframed righteousness itself: not religious devotion alone but a healed life attuned to His perspective, His priorities, and His way of being and living. As President Dieter F. Uchtdorf taught, "Faith is strong when it has deep roots in personal experience, personal commitment to Jesus Christ, independent of what our traditions are or what others may say or do."[2] Our culture and traditions—and even religious acts, like attending church or the temple, following Church standards, and even serving a mission—while very good, are not the gospel.

The Furnace of Affliction

A silversmith knows the silver is ready when he can see his reflection in it. Likewise, the Savior refines us until He can see Himself reflected in our lives as we walk by faith, choose truth even when it costs us, remain humble despite what we think we know, serve not because we need validation but because people need help, and to continue to grow.

His invitation to "return unto me . . . that I might heal you" echoes as personally today as it did then. He calls us to faith with the simple invitation to abide in Him. He calls us to growth with the summons to take up our cross and follow Him. He calls us to character with the encouragement to be not weary in well doing. And He calls us to turn outward with the life-changing charge to feed His sheep.

Yet in the swirl of cultural expectations, we must ask: Are we drawing on His power—or placing our trust in something else? Is our soil rich yet shallow, crowded with traditions that keep our roots from reaching Him? His call to return and be healed still stands—refining out of us whatever is not like Him, often through the very heat we try hardest to avoid.

Even good soil holds stones. The danger lies not in their existence but in mistaking these stones, or cultural traditions, for the gospel itself. Over time, they can make shallow faith feel dangerously safe.

The Stones of Tradition

As we watched our missionaries wrestle with uncertainty, adversity, identity, and meaning, four recurring cultural patterns emerged—four cultural "stones" that limit growth, each contrasted with a deeper root in Christ that sustains growth and prepares us for real life. The chart that follows describes the challenge and compares the stones of tradition with the roots of the gospel.

We begin with the first: How we face uncertainty—certitude versus faith.

Stone I—Certitude

Kylee's Choice

Early in her mission, Sister Kylee Denison came to an interview carrying a burden. "President Strong," she said respectfully, "there are things the Church teaches that I just don't believe or agree with. I have questions and concerns."

She spoke with clarity and grace about our history, our doctrines, and moments when we as a Church don't quite reach our own standards. Her questions came not from doubt but from a heart that loved truth, loved the Savior, and held high expectations for His Church.

That conversation began a journey for both of us. We talked about what it means to know as opposed to having faith—that discipleship is less about possessing answers and more about walking with Christ. Her questions weren't flaws in her faith; they were evidence of it.

Kylee became one of the best missionaries we ever had. She balanced her questions and faith with remarkable humility and grace. Without humility, conviction hardens into certitude—a stone that prevents deep growth of the roots, inhibiting a plant's ability to withstand life's heat. Certitude is conviction minus humility. It is the dogmatic belief that our understanding is correct and complete, that we know absolutely, and that there is no need to wrestle or consider the possibility that we are wrong, even about those things we deeply believe. It is the idea that we have to "know" with certainty to believe and act.

She flourished because she chose faith and had the courage to be honest. Without that honesty and humility, she might have been lost in a culture that sometimes pathologizes sincere and legitimate questions and rewards conformity. God taught me through Kylee and many others that questions—and even doubt—are not the enemies of faith. *Certitude* is because it closes the space where faith must live and growth happens.

Faith Is Born When Certitude Dies

In our research, when we asked respondents about these same four life challenges and how they believed we *should* respond, comparing cultural expectations with personal beliefs, their answers revealed a familiar tension, echoing what we saw in chapter 7. In the case of uncertainty, our culture tends to lean toward "knowing," while most members personally lean toward humility, trust, and learning, though there is more cultural balance here than we saw in chapter 7.

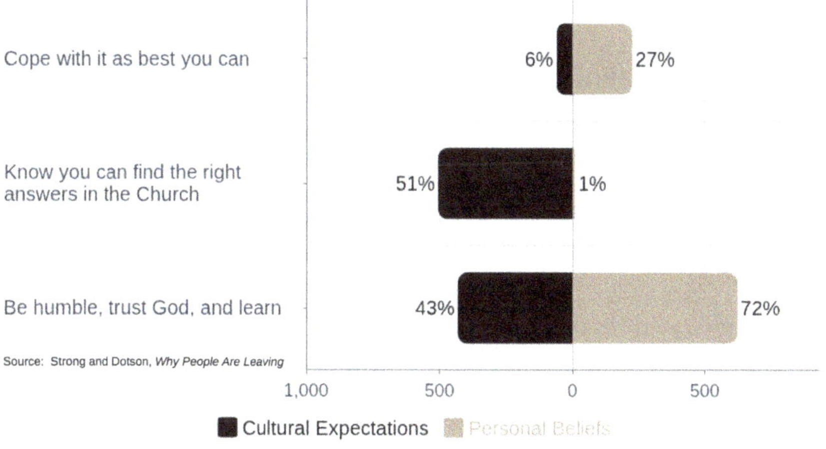

The gap between cultural expectations and personal belief, however, is significant. Over time, this contributes to conformity and feeling unseen—two factors that drive many away. Encouragingly, the data also shows some balance: There is more than one culturally acceptable way to respond to uncertainty—but the imbalance between culture and belief remains.

Fear seeks sanctuary through certitude.
Faith seeks transcendence.

Faith is forged in heat, not in shelter. Christ's invitation to Thomas— "Be not faithless, but believing" (John 20:27)—was not a rebuke but a reminder that knowing was never the goal. Peter's first steps on the water began in faith, not certainty (see Matthew 14:28–31). He did not know the outcome, but he took those steps anyway. Alma taught that faith begins as a seed, unseen and uncertain (see Alma 32).

The Book of Mormon was not written to eliminate uncertainty by making Restoration claims but to invite faith. Its real power is shown less by our authority than by the kind of people it helps us become. When Lehi and his family left Jerusalem, they had no knowledge of the promised land—only the inspiration and faith God placed in their hearts. They sailed across the great deep to an unknown place and an uncertain future, carrying seeds to plant in unfamiliar soil, hoping for a harvest they could not yet see, a small window into their faith. Terryl and Fiona Givens wrote:

> "The greatest act of self-revelation occurs *when we choose* what we will believe, in the space of freedom that exists between knowing that a thing is, and knowing that a thing is not."[3]

The gospel does not ask us to know everything. It asks us to move forward even and especially when we are uncertain. When humility and trust meet uncertainty, our roots deepen. The heat does not destroy them; it strengthens them. True faith is born when certitude dies—when we take those steps, trusting in God, without knowing the outcome.

Stone II—Refuge

Soldiers and Shoelaces

Fort Leonard Wood is a large military base in the mission. Thousands of young people—eighteen-, nineteen-, and twenty-year-olds—were there preparing for military service and the possibility of combat. We held Sunday services on the base, and those who weren't members were welcome if they came with a Latter-day Saint friend. They came in droves.

Elder Tristan Cox wrote to me: "President, I've been feeling power-less. I learned of several suicide attempts this week on the base. I went home from church the past few weeks weighed down by the darkness in the world." He continued: "Then, a young woman asked for a blessing. When she sat down, I noticed her boots had no laces—a sign she had attempted suicide. As I place my hands on her head, I didn't feel anything dramatic—just deep gratitude for her, understanding for her burden, and an easing of the chaos inside her. I felt that God was mindful of her, and I believe she felt it too."

Tristan learned a life-changing truth: God can pierce the darkness, lift us up, and strengthen us—even when the burden remains. And He most often works in small and simple ways.

Refuge versus Transformation

Our culture often encourages us to believe that if we are worthy, have enough faith, and pray, God will protect us from adversity and bless us—which may be true at times. But that idea can quietly grow into promises God never made. For example, some parents and leaders, hoping to inspire faith, assured missionaries that if they served hon-orably, the Lord would protect their families. When tragedy struck anyway, trust fractured—not because God failed but because assur-ances were offered that did not come from Him—a well-meaning but misguided attempt to allay their fears.

The significance of this cultural tendency was clear in our research. As with uncertainty, our culture embraces more than one response to adversity—a healthy sign—but the imbalance between cultural norms and personal belief remains substantial and problematic.

It is important to remember that the Savior never promised safety. He invited transformation.

"Leave your nets." (Matthew 4:19–20)

"Take up your cross." (Matthew 16:24)

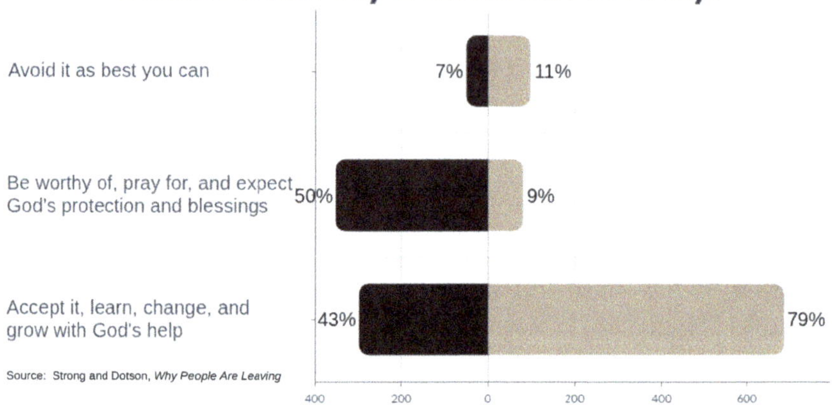

"Be born again." (John 3:3, 5)

"Become a new creature in Christ." (2 Corinthians 5:17)

Refuge has its place—a moment to breathe, to heal, to feel His peace. But growth is the destination.

The Savior taught that afflictions and weaknesses are instruments of growth. To Moroni He said, "My grace is sufficient . . . then will I make weak things become strong" (Ether 12:27). To Joseph Smith in Liberty Jail, He promised, "All these things shall give thee experience, and shall be for thy good" (Doctrine & Covenants 122:7).

Believing otherwise can lead to unnecessary disappointment and a loss of trust in God. President D. Todd Christofferson taught, "When life doesn't turn out as expected, some 'may feel betrayed by God.' However, Heavenly Father's plan is not 'a cosmic vending machine' where we select a desired blessing, insert the required sum of good works, and the order is promptly delivered.' Individuals must do their best while trusting that Heavenly Father will make good on His promises."[4]

As we choose transformation over safety and certitude, confidence grows. We learn to stand in the storm, refined by the fire rather than spared from it.

Stone III—Avoidance

Back to Jerusalem

Elder John Morgan was unmistakably good.[5] When we first arrived in the mission and met him, it was equally clear that he was lost. His lack of purpose led to mistakes that resulted in being sent home—hurt, angry, and embarrassed.

Months passed in silence. Then, through the inspired care of a wise stake president, his heart softened. He learned and grew from his choices and experiences and asked to return.

When we met him at the airport, the change was unmistakable. He carried himself with peace and purpose. He was a new creature in Christ. What once appeared to be failure became the cornerstone of his character. This was one of the most inspiring events of our mission.

Too often, we treat mistakes as failures. The Atonement is not about avoiding the furnace; it is about developing the strength to stand in it. Our research offered a clear window into this pattern. While most members perceive that our culture encourages avoiding mistakes, most people believe that growth through struggle is far more valuable.

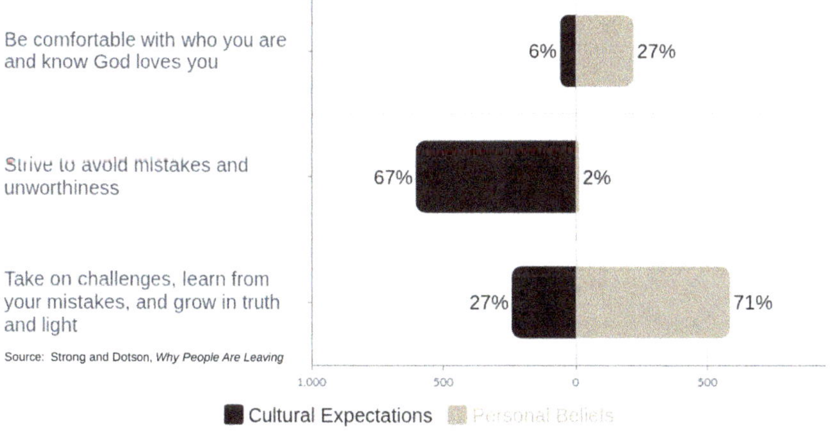

True discipleship is more than avoiding error; it is the courageous pursuit of character—the willingness to face what is hard, learn from it, and keep moving with Christ. The Greek word translated as *perfect* in the Sermon on the Mount (see Matthew 5:48), *teleios*, does not mean flawless or unblemished. It means "complete, mature, fully developed."[6] Scripture consistently follows this arc:

> - Alma the Younger turning from rebellion (see Mosiah 27:29–37)

> - Mary Magdalene rising to be the first witness of the Resurrection (see Luke 8:1–3, John 20:11–18)

> - The prodigal son returning with nothing but humility (see Luke 15:20)

> - Peter stepping back into discipleship after denying Christ (see John 21:15–19)

> - Joseph Smith finding God again in Liberty Jail (see Doctrine & Covenants 122–123)

None of them became who they were by avoiding the furnace. I've always found it instructive that Lehi's family did not leave Jerusalem in one clean, decisive departure. In truth, they left three times—first in obedience to the Lord's warning, again to retrieve the brass plates, and a third time to bring Ishmael's family.

I imagine that each departure felt like starting over—relinquishing progress, reopening uncertainty, and delaying the journey they thought had already begun. What looked like backward steps was actually preparation, forging the character their journey would require.

It was true for Lehi and his family, and it was true for Elder Morgan. Their steps backward were not failures but formation—part of how God prepares and refines us.

The Cultivation Principle: Trust

Growth requires movement—sometimes into uncertainty, sometimes against opposition, and almost always beyond what feels safe. Shallow roots avoid this kind of growth, clinging to the stones of tradition. Deep roots seek growth by reaching into the nourishing depths of the soil.

The Lord's invitation to both the righteous and the unrighteous is the same: Return to me.

Repentance is how we learn, change, heal, and transcend the tendencies of the natural man. When mistakes are treated as catastrophic, fear replaces growth. Returning, repairing, and trying again is the sacred rhythm of overcoming. It is how souls are made complete.

With this path comes real power—not the brittle confidence of outward perfection but the quiet peace Christ gives to those willing to grow. Repentance frees us from fear and from the exhausting effort to appear flawless. It frees us to act and to live as growing disciples.

The Lord is not seeking people who never falter but people who return repeatedly until His strength becomes their own. When we choose the path of returning—learning, forgiving, repairing, and moving forward with Christ—the heat does not consume us. It completes us.

Stone IV—Turning Inward

The Goat

Elder Tyler Heywood carried burdens from hardships before his mission and quietly sought healing while serving faithfully. His blessing came in an unexpected way.

"We went to help at an inactive family's farm," he told me. "While we were moving dirt, their goat was suddenly attacked by one of their dogs. The injuries were bad—deep cuts around her neck.

"I carried the goat to a trailer. Elder Peters helped when she became too heavy to carry alone. We shaved around her injuries so we could clean and close the wounds. Then we held her while Elder Peters sewed. She cried out and thrashed at times, yet I could tell she trusted us.

"As I held her, I sensed how the Savior feels when He wants to heal us. He sees us struggle and yearns for us to trust Him: *If you trust me and endure this pain, I will make you whole.* If we trust the Lord, our wounds can be healed and we become stronger."

Tyler turned outward. He lost himself in love and service and found a truth that helped heal him and will anchor his entire life: Healing often comes when we lift another.

Our research confirmed that most of us believe deeply in the transforming power of turning outward in Christlike love. Yet many also feel pressure to turn inward, focusing primarily on obedience, religious devotion, callings, worship, and ordinances. These things are vital, but they are the leaven, not the loaf.

What is the best way to find deep and enduring meaning in our lives?

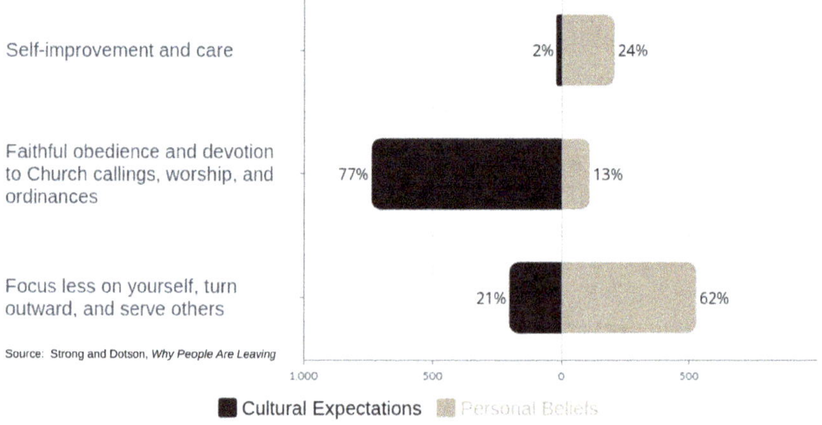

**"For whosoever will save his life shall lose it:
and whosoever will lose his life for my sake shall find it."
(Matthew 16:25)**

The Pinnacle of Discipleship: Leaven or Loaf?

There is a quiet pattern that runs throughout scripture: God uses small things that become powerful when they serve a purpose beyond themselves. Leaven remains dormant until it joins the dough and lifts the whole loaf. Salt fulfills its purpose only when it leaves the shaker to season and preserve. A mustard seed must be planted, broken open, and nourished to become a refuge for the living creatures who shelter in its branches. Nutrients in soil—precious and essential—find their highest purpose when they move into the roots and give life to the plant.

Religious devotion is one of these small and mighty things. Scripture study, sincere prayer, obedience to commandments and standards, Church attendance, magnifying callings, paying tithes and offerings, and worshiping in the temple are nutrients in the soil of the gospel. They center us in God, invite the Spirit, guide and protect us, anchor our discipleship, and connect us to heavenly things. But God provides them for something greater than ourselves.

As with salt, leaven, and seeds, their full power is realized when they give life beyond us. Scripture opens our hearts and minds to how God works with His children so we can do likewise. Prayer deepens our connection to heaven and fills us with greater compassion for others. Gathering in worship allows us to mourn with and comfort one another, especially those on the margins. The sacrament recenters us on the Savior and invites His Spirit, which works most powerfully as we lift others. Callings place in our path those God intends for us to love. Covenants and temple worship bind us to God, give our lives direction and protective boundaries, and turn our hearts outward—to those who lived before us and those who walk beside us now.

Because these things are so common and comfortable in the Church, it is easy to forget why God gives them to us. When discipleship becomes an inward accumulation of nutrients, we misunderstand their purpose and miss the heart of the gospel. Callings become résumés instead of relationships. Covenants become markers of worthiness instead of commitments to love. Devotion turns inward, salt loses its savor, leaven loses its lift, seeds fail to grow, and nutrients no longer nourish.

Reaching for Transcendence

My experience is that turning outward is the ladder of transcendence—the way God helps us become like our Heavenly Parents. We grow as we strive to love and lift others. That growth requires pushing our roots beyond the stones of tradition and deeper into a relationship with Christ. Church culture can then become the soil that fosters growth rather than something that can't sustain life—and culture begins with belief.

The Savior invites us to embrace beliefs that carry us beyond the stones of tradition and, through Him, into transcendence. We can all choose to believe and then live these simple truths:

1. Faith sees best when we realize we cannot see. When we acknowledge our limits, Christ becomes our light.

2. We are transformed and strengthened by what breaks us. The hardships we resist often become how God remakes us.

3. Character grows strongest when we are honest about being unfinished. Growth begins the moment we stop pretending we are complete.

4. Meaning is found only when we give it away. Purpose emerges not from turning inward but from offering ourselves in love.

These are beliefs we can bring to life—day by day, choice by choice.

Balancing Two Gospels

Critical Question #2 returns with urgency:

**How does the Church best prepare us
for the challenges of real life?**

Which of these two cultures will we cultivate to help us face opposition? The pull of the four stones—certitude, refuge, avoidance, and turning inward—is real and understandable. They offer refuge, or sanctuary. But sanctuary alone cannot create the deep roots required for resilient faith, strength, and maturity in Christ. Deep roots form in the soil of faith, not fear—in lives centered on Christ rather than on self-protection. His way is not to retreat but transcend—not escape from the furnace but to grow within it. This difference illustrates two versions of the gospel that quietly shape our culture:

> One offers sanctuary. The other invites transcendence.
> One protects from the heat. The other prepares us to endure it.
> One shelters. The other strengthens.

Christ does not simply lift us out of our difficulties; He prepares us to meet them with courage, integrity, and a heart turned outward.

**One reason people step away from the Church
is because a gospel of sanctuary is not enough.
God created His children to grow.**

When culture discourages growth—when only one form of faith is validated or one path of development is honored—people leave not because they reject Christ but because they seek to become who God created them to be. President Thomas S. Monson captured this truth with uncommon beauty:

> God left the world unfinished for men and women to work their skill upon. He left the electricity in the cloud, the oil in the earth. He left the rivers unbridged, the forests unfelled, and the cities unbuilt. God gives to us the challenge of raw materials, not the ease of finished things. He leaves the pictures unpainted and the music unsung and the problems unsolved that we might know the joys and glories of creation.[7]

It would be unwise to impose limits on how our Heavenly Parents help Their children grow. As our roots sink deeper—past what is shallow, familiar, or comfortable—we discover capacities we did not know we possessed. We gain resilience and hope. We learn to walk through life not fragile but fortified—not because life is easy but because we are anchored in something real.

His invitation remains: Return to Him, reach past the stones, sink your roots deep, and allow Him to transform you into what He knows you can be.

Key Chapter Takeaway

When the Church is experienced primarily as a sanctuary, faith remains shallow. The gospel prepares people to grow through challenges, not by avoiding them.

Reflection Questions

1. How has my faith prepared me for suffering or difficulty?

2. Do I experience discipleship more as a protection or something that stretches me?

3. How might others be struggling because their faith remains shallow?

Application Suggestion

Notice where fear—of loss, uncertainty, disagreement, or disruption—may be shaping your responses. Ask yourself whether your instinct is to move toward protection or toward growth and transcendence.

Identify one area where God may be inviting you to move from safety into growth through service, honest self-examination, difficult conversations, or increased responsibility. Sanctuary and rest matter, but they are not the destination. Encourage the kind of growth in yourself and others that builds resilience, capacity, and trust in Christ rather than dependence on safety alone.

AGENCY

Imbalance #3: Soil Full of Thorns

Being expected to always defer to Church tradition and leaders

The collision between authority and conscience

Critical Question:
How do we honor God's gift of agency in a culture that expects compliance?

**"When our leaders speak, the thinking has been done.
When they propose a plan—it is God's plan.
When they point the way, there is no other which is safe."
—*Improvement Era* 1945**

God's Will and Sharpies

Sister Katie Horspool served a mission for all the right reasons. She was faithful, hardworking, talented, loving, and Christlike. She went two hundred miles an hour for twelve months and then hit a wall. I'm not sure she fully understood why she hit the wall, other than maybe she served an eighteen-month mission in twelve months.

Consequently, she didn't know if she could continue serving. After thoroughly listening to and encouraging her somewhat unsuccessfully, I said, "You know, you can go home. It's an option. I'm not suggesting that to you. I'm not telling you what you should do. But you should at least contemplate whether that's the right decision for you." Though it was a difficult decision, she concluded she had done her best and decided to go home. Six months later, she sent me a letter. With her permission, I share it here.

> Hey, President, wow, it's been a second. I've learned something way cool about God and the way He works with us. I feel like my whole life, I've had this thought that God has this Sharpied-out plan for me. And if I didn't guess what was in His head, I was going to mess something up. I was always praying to find out what I was supposed to do. But then I read Helaman 10:6–11, about the time that God gave Nephi the sealing power and whatever Nephi said would be done. God said something really interesting to him . . . He said: "I will make thee mighty in word and in deed, in faith and in works; yea, even that all things shall be done unto thee according to thy word."
>
> Now here comes my point. He then said, "For thou shalt not ask that which is contrary to my will." Here's the thing, President,

I always thought of God's will as something so specific—we teach God's will in the Church in a way that is a little weird. We talk about putting His will over ours, which is good. And we talk about how we need to seek God's will, which is good. But God's will isn't just what we need to do with our lives. In this scripture, God tells Nephi that He knows Nephi isn't going to do anything contrary to His will. But it's not like Nephi had a list of the do's and don'ts of God's will. God's will is the principle that God governs Himself by.

The reason He trusted Nephi is because Nephi had chosen to govern himself by those same principles. This is a total game changer because it changes God's will from supposed-to-based to opportunity-based. I really believe that God just wants us to choose Him and to choose to live the principles He's been trying to teach us. But I didn't always believe that.

I think the realization started when you gave me the thought that I could go home. And it clicked. I had a choice. I could literally choose; and it's not like I prayed and received some magical answer that I was supposed to go home early. I didn't. And I think it would be disingenuous for me to claim that. I just chose because I was given the opportunity.

I'm realizing now that God gives us opportunities, not a Sharpie plan. He gives us options, and sometimes He prompts us to choose an opportunity over another. And sometimes He doesn't. But He is an advocate for our agency. And all this time, I felt like I had to choose what God wanted. I do, but largely, I want what He wants, and He wants me to choose like He does.

Claiming that everything we do is because God told us can be a slippery slope. It can cause us not to take responsibility for our own lives. My perspective is totally changed, and I feel I have become so much freer. Thank you for giving me the chance to choose something good.

Now, there's always the rest of the story, isn't there? What happened to Katie when she left her mission six months early? *Only good things.*

She went home. She took time to figure things out. She married a great young man. They now have two beautiful children. She and her husband are living and growing in the Church and gospel. They're doing great. She took responsibility for her choices and her life. She learned more about how to make difficult decisions. She obtained the inspiration, learning, and growth that come from wrestling with a hard decision. Exercising her agency in a way that was not traditional in our culture only brought her closer to God and caused her to grow—because she chose Him and His principles *for herself.*

Katie's experience is not about missions; it is about what happens to anyone when they believe God expects compliance rather than choice. Her story reveals a quiet tension in our culture: We speak of agency yet often operate as if our safety lies in surrendering it. Before we can understand why this hinders spiritual growth, we must understand what agency is—and what it was always meant to be.

Obedience to God is foundational in the gospel of Jesus Christ. The question is not whether we should be obedient but how we might faithfully discern God's will in a world where understanding is always partial and human voices, including our own, are imperfect. Agency does not mean acting without moral boundaries, nor does it mean choosing whatever feels right in the moment. It means taking responsibility for seeking, weighing, and responding to God's guidance with humility, effort, and integrity. When obedience is quietly reduced to unexamined deference—to tradition, culture, and even well-intended leaders—it can replace discipleship rather than strengthen it.

The Most Misunderstood Doctrine in the Church?

Good seeds flourish in good soil, but even the best seeds can be choked by thorns. In the Savior's parable, the thorns represent anything that stifles growth, and those thorns can sometimes be good but over-grown things. As I previously shared, President Oaks reminded us that excessive orthodoxy can be harmful.[1] Obedience is one of those good principles that can be exaggerated or decoupled from other gospel truths—including agency.

Agency, the divine right to choose, act, and become without coercion is the engine of eternal progression and the central reason for the War in Heaven. Real obedience always includes the exercise of agency. I believe this is one of the important reasons modern prophets and apostles frequently teach and encourage the righteous use of agency. When obedience is stripped of agency, it ceases to be obedience and becomes something altogether different, creating tremendous tension.

That something different has a name: fealty. As mentioned previously, fealty is an unquestioning, unconditional allegiance to some sovereign power where truth, goodness, choice, responsibility, reasoning, and even personal revelation are surrendered to that sovereign's authority. Christlike obedience retains these elements because they are essential for our growth as children of God. Fealty chokes the plant; obedience nourishes it. One is a thorn. The other is a nutrient in the soil.

Katie was initially suffocated by the false belief that she had no choice—a belief strongly perpetuated in our culture. When she extricated herself from that belief, she became free to grow.

The War in Heaven was fought over which plan best prepared us to become like our Heavenly Parents. Growth requires freedom. We had to be free to choose, act, and become, even with all the risks that freedom brought. Satan sought to eliminate that risk by eliminating freedom. As Moses records, Satan was cast down because he "sought to destroy the agency of man, which I, the Lord God, had given him" (Moses 4:3). Jesus sought to preserve that agency because He understood it was the only way the plan would work, with the Atonement providing a solution for the risk.

Without agency eternal progression stagnates. Spiritual, moral, and emotional growth require the freedom to choose—to love, obey, learn, decide, act, and even fail. Without unconstrained choice, no true growth can occur.

In one of the most powerful teachings in the standard works, found in 2 Nephi 2, Lehi taught that agency is not an accessory to God's plan; it *is* the plan. "There must needs be opposition in all things," he said, or else "righteousness" and even "happiness" would be impossible. Without the freedom to choose and experience real consequences and learn from them, we would "cease to be."

Christ's Atonement makes agency both safe and transformative, enabling us to "act for [ourselves] and not be acted upon." We are "free to choose liberty and eternal life," but only because God refuses to compel us. Lehi makes clear that without agency, there is no growth, joy, or becoming like our Heavenly Parents.

Just as living plants require space for roots to deepen and branches to reach toward the sunlight, we grow only when we have the space to freely choose, act, and become. Agency is the God-given space where conviction can form, where character can take root, and where spiritual strength can expand.

Fealty—The Counterfeit of True Obedience

Fealty is obedience turned into submission—the subtraction of agency that leads to surrendering judgment, responsibility, and even personal revelation to someone else. It is not loyalty or devotion. It is unquestioning allegiance rooted in the posture of "You think for me and decide for me," as if another person stands between His children and the sacred gifts of life and agency He has given us. And when that happens, growth stops. Spiritual development stalls whenever we abdicate the sacred responsibility we have to choose and become.

Fealty is a virus we all carry. Christ is the immune system that builds our faith, keeping in check the fear that activates the virus. The prevalence of this virus in our culture is very evident in our research.

We asked respondents about the most reliable way to set direction in their lives. Before you see the results, it helps to know what you are looking at. These charts reveal a cultural instinct: When life gets complex, where do we reflexively look for direction, and how does that instinct differ from what we personally believe is healthiest and most Christlike?

You'll recognize the pattern you saw in the previous chapters. In the culture, there is a strong proclivity for the answer that most emphasizes the role of the institutional Church: "Trust in the principles and guidance of the Church and the Latter-day Saint way of life and follow them." This is a clear lean toward fealty, and yet very few of us believe that fealty is the best way to set direction for our life. This extraordinary imbalance between the single acceptable way embraced in the culture and what most members believe is, again, what feeds a culture of conformity and isolation.

What is the most reliable way to set direction for your life?

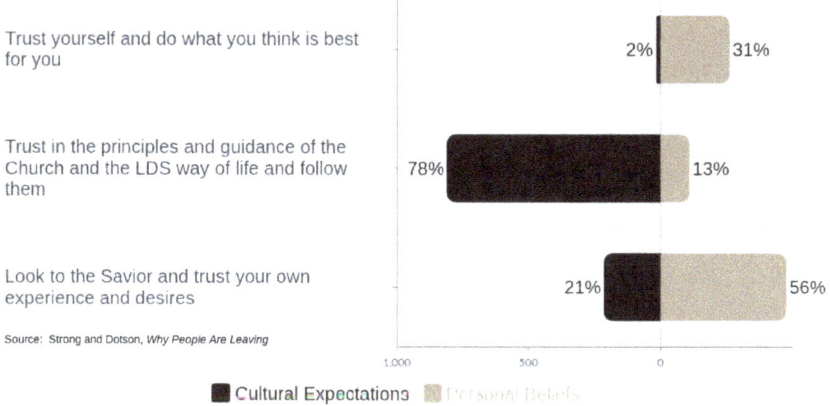

This next chart highlights the tension most of us experience in making important decisions—between what is seen as acceptable in the culture and what we personally believe—the tension of being expected to outsource vital spiritual work rather than doing it with God.

What is the best way to make important decisions in life?

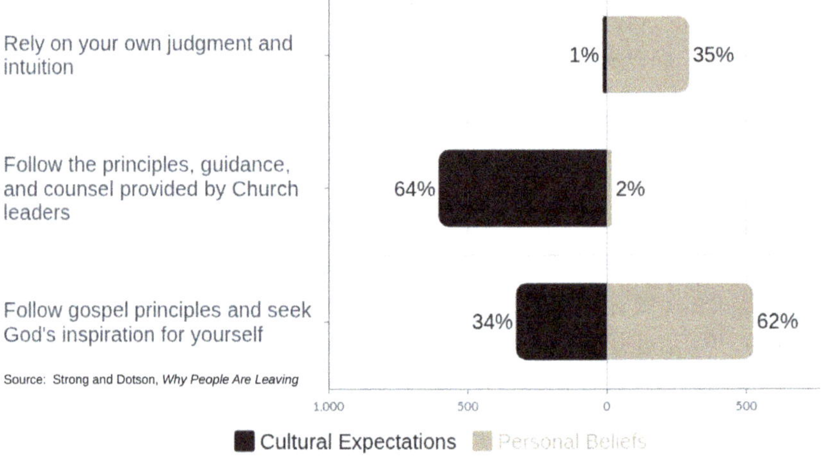

Finally, this chart helps frame why fealty is not a small quirk but both a growth and disaffiliation issue.

Perhaps the most important and sacred aspect of belief is how we come to know something is true and right. Do we get to decide for ourselves, or are we expected to follow the teachings and counsel of our Church leaders?

What is the most reliable way to know if something is true and right?

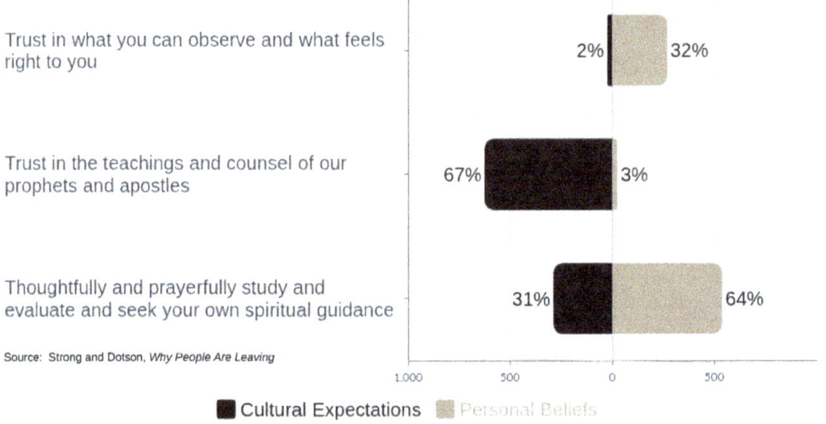

This is exactly the tension that causes many good and believing people to step away from the Church. They simply disagree with the idea that they do not get to choose for themselves what kind of life they're going to live, how they're going to make critical decisions, and how they should determine what they believe. Most of us believe that the best way to make decisions and determine the course of our lives is to look to our Heavenly Father, the Savior, the Holy Ghost, and our own ability to reason and seek spiritual guidance for ourselves. This in no way excludes the Church or its leaders. It simply places them in their appropriate and important roles as witnesses and teachers who point us to God, not gates that stand between us and God.

Why this fealty virus became part of our culture is complex. Some of it may trace to past seasons of persecution, when fealty meant survival; some to the correlation era, when it meant efficiency in a rapidly growing Church. Some of it comes from folklore, like the startling declaration I opened with: "When our leaders speak, the thinking has been done."[2] It appeared in the June 1945 *Improvement Era,* an official Church magazine, and, for reasons that are unclear, lodged itself deeply in our culture. Yet President George Albert Smith repudiated it that same year. In a December 1945 letter to J. Raymond Cope, he wrote: "I am pleased to assure you . . . that *the passage quoted does not express the true position of the Church.* Even to imply that members of the Church are not to do their own thinking is to grossly misrepresent the true ideal of the Church, which is that every individual must obtain for himself a testimony of the truth of the Gospel, must, through the redemption of Jesus Christ, work out his own salvation, and is personally responsible to His Maker for his individual acts."[3] Whatever the source, the effect is the same: a culture that sometimes leans toward surrendering judgment rather than developing it.

Of course, there are obvious and blatant situations where overt and aggressive fealty is practiced in any group or community. In my experience, this is not common in our Church. What is far more common is more subtle. We pressure people to conform to cultural scripts, imply that faithful disciples never struggle or question, treat leaders' preferences or opinions as divine mandates, and lean on fear to steer our choices. And perhaps most damaging, we sometimes make our love conditional. "I love you *if . . .*" is not Christlike love; it is the counterfeit, where what we prize is not the person but their compliance. It is love centered in what *we* need and want, not what *they* need and want. This list of patterns is not exhaustive, but it includes the most common ways agency is infringed upon in our culture, choking spiritual growth just as surely as any overt force.

The Damage

Once agency is surrendered, growth halts and the consequences are quiet, cumulative, and damaging. When obedience deteriorates into fealty—when we surrender our agency and the sacred responsibility to think, discern, and choose—something deep within us begins to die. Four quiet but damaging consequences occur.

First, our ability to judge stagnates, and we become morally dependent on others. When fealty demands we abdicate our discernment, we slip into a posture of "Just tell me what to do." We begin treating the opinions of those we perceive as holding spiritual authority as if they are God's doctrine or will, leaning on them and on tradition for every answer. Church leaders themselves have sought to correct this tendency in us. President D. Todd Christofferson taught, "At the same time it should be remembered that not every statement made by a Church leader, past or present, necessarily constitutes doctrine. It is commonly understood in the Church that a statement made by one leader on a single occasion often represents a personal, though well-considered, opinion, not meant to be official or binding for the whole Church."[4]

Instead of learning to weigh issues, evaluate principles, consider context, study scripture, pray, counsel with others, and decide based on our conclusions and the guidance of the Spirit, we become spiritually dependent—unable to stand morally upon our own feet.

Second, we lose inner strength. Fealty produces fragile people who flee from adversity and risk instead of growing from them. As a mission leader, I was surprised by how many otherwise remarkable missionaries wanted me to make decisions that were theirs to make. They believed I somehow knew better how they should live their lives than they did and that they would somehow feel better if things went wrong if I told them what to do. But discipleship cannot deepen when agency is handed to someone else. When we have someone to blame for our choices, we never learn to take responsibility. As a result, we never gain the strength that stems from freedom of choice and possibility of risk.

Third, we lose authenticity. Fealty pressures people to conform to narrow cultural scripts rather than cultivate sincere belief and honest character. It rewards appearance over substance. Thus, people often pretend so they can belong and to avoid the pain of being "othered." As Paul warned, we risk having "a form of godliness" (2 Timothy 3:5) without the inward transformation the gospel offers. Pretending replaces becoming; compliance replaces integrity.

Fourth, relationships become transactional. When compliance becomes the measure of love, relationships become conditional. We love someone only when they do what we want them to. That is not love; it is leverage. Under fealty, people feel valued for their submission rather than for who they truly are.

The human impact is profound. Many who step away from the Church do not leave because they stop believing but because the thorns of conditionality and conformity choke them out. Fealty removes from us what God most wants for us—growth, strength, authenticity, and love. Fealty is counterfeit obedience.

Authority, Truth, and the *Titanic*

Fealty often emerges when we begin to believe that authority matters more than truth. Doctrine and Covenants 121 teaches that the priesthood (authority) has no inherent power of its own. Its rights and powers are inseparably connected with the powers of heaven, and these powers can only be handled according to principles of righteousness, including persuasion, charity, virtue, and gentleness—all of which are part of the supporting framework for agency. When we disconnect authority from these principles, it has no power. And leaning on authority independent of these principles makes us vulnerable to mistakes we might otherwise avoid.

This dynamic—the elevation of authority over truth—is not theoretical. History gives us vivid examples of how misplaced confidence in authority leads to devastating mistakes. Captain Edward Smith and the *Titanic* are a spectacular, tragic, but familiar illustration.

Captain Smith had tremendous knowledge and complete authority over the ship. On that trip across the North Atlantic, he had accurate, timely information about the icebergs ahead. He received radio warnings nine times that night, yet hit an iceberg and sank the boat. Why? He misjudged the boat and the icebergs. Because he believed the boat was unsinkable, he ignored the warnings.

The boat's hull had sixteen individual chambers. It could handle a puncture of up to five chambers and still float. But it wasn't a head-on collision; the iceberg scraped along the side, tearing a three-hundred-foot gash in the hull, rupturing more than six chambers.

The captain's vast knowledge and complete authority collided with truth and the limits of his understanding and led to a terrible outcome. He was missing critical truth—truth that would have saved the vessel and his passengers in a way his authority never could. Is the lesson here that we should ignore prophetic counsel? Of course not. The lesson from this and Doctrine and Covenants 121 is that any authority, even prophetic authority, must be governed by God-given principles of righteous. It does not operate in a vacuum.

Latter-day Saint prophets understand the vital role of agency. Joseph Smith taught, "I teach them correct principles, and they govern themselves."[5] Brigham Young warned, "I am more afraid that this people have so much confidence in their leaders that they will not inquire for themselves of God . . . whether their leaders are walking in the path the Lord dictates, or not."[6]

It seems to me this same dynamic—the extraordinary respect we have for the authority of the Church and its leaders—is perhaps the primary reason that the culture encourages us to abdicate our agency to them when making important life decisions. And yet the tension persists between culture and personal belief, as most of us feel the better way is to follow gospel principles and seek inspiration for ourselves.

President Dallin H. Oaks addressed how we might wisely balance this tension when he said, "As a General Authority, it is my responsibility to preach general principles. When I do, I don't try to define all the exceptions. There are exceptions to some rules. . . . But don't ask me to give an opinion on your exception. I only teach the general rules. Whether an exception applies to you is your responsibility. You must work that out individually between you and the Lord."[7] Clearly, President Oaks believes agency and personal responsibility both play vital roles in our faith journey.

As a mission leader, I saw capable missionaries defer to my authority rather than exercise their agency and assume responsibility for their choices. This had a limiting effect on their growth. Helping missionaries embrace their agency became one of our highest priorities.

Throughout my life, I have been blessed by the guidance and example of remarkable Church leaders whose goodness, wisdom, and love have shaped and lifted me in countless ways. I'll share but three examples. As a teenager, my bishop, Stephen Nyman, guided me through my formative years, most often when we talked about life while we caught fish on Utah's Strawberry Reservoir. Bishop Nyman was a true friend and a great bishop. My mission leaders President Maurice L. and Sister Donna Watts lifted my heart and expanded my vision of what was possible for me and others, inspiring me to reach higher and serve more. They were true disciples of Christ and extraordinary leaders. And one of the important gospel teachers in my life has been Elder David A. Bednar, whom I first met in 1994 as my stake president and neighbor and whose influence has helped me over the past three decades. In each case, I sought and followed their counsel, never abdicating my agency to them; nor would they have asked me to.

I have also been richly influenced by those I have been called to serve or serve with—wonderful people who taught me much as an individual, bishop, and mission leader. The list and the lessons are endless and priceless to me.

The very best and most Christlike Church leaders I know view agency as a sacred gift and don't do things to compromise it. They know how important it is for an individual to take charge of their life and experience the freedom and responsibility that come with that.

These leaders honor agency in practice, not just doctrine. It has been my privilege over the last thirty years to occasionally talk with Elder Bednar about my personal circumstances. Of course, whenever I reach out to him, it's because I'm dealing with some difficult or complex issue and desire to benefit from his wisdom. In fact, most of the time, I would just like him to tell me what to do. I am not immune to anxiety!

Much to my disappointment, he consistently refuses to tell me what to do. He is sensitive about infringing on my agency and the responsibility I have to choose for myself. And he is skilled at giving me questions I need to wrestle with so that I can learn for myself. He has declined to give me a fish and instead concentrated on teaching me how to fish.

As a faithful people who desire to sustain our leaders, there is something else we need to remember. It is not fair to Church leaders to abdicate our agency to them. They already have plenty to worry about. They carry enough responsibility without the added burden of being responsible for others' choices. What they need from us—and what most of them value in us—is a thinking, discerning, revelation-seeking, spiritually self-reliant and courageous people who are agents and not objects. Our fealty harms our leaders as much as it harms us. And true obedience strengthens them just as much as it does us.

Elder Dale G. Renlund shared, "Our Heavenly Father's goal in parenting is not to have his children *do* what is right; it is to have his children *choose* to do what is right and ultimately become like Him. . . . God wants his children to grow up spiritually and . . . expects and directs that each of his children choose for himself or herself. He will not force us."[8]

God did not give Nephi a Sharpied list of to-dos or Lehi a map. He gave them a Liahona—a dynamic and personal guide that worked through faith, humility, obedience, and personal engagement. A map requires almost no effort or growth—only compliance. But a Liahona demands the full participation of the heart, mind, and soul to notice, discern, and act.

Christlike Obedience: How We Cultivate Agency-Rich Soil

When fealty inhibits spiritual growth in these ways, the antidote can come from Christ Himself. Clear and powerful patterns in His teachings can guide us here.

1. Christ's Pattern of Leading—Persuasion, Long-Suffering, and Love Unfeigned (see Doctrine & Covenants 121:41–42). Jesus never led through compulsion. His invitations in the Gospel of Matthew—"Come unto me" (11:28), "Follow me" (16:24), and "Learn of me" (11:29)—are rooted in trust and respect for our agency. Christlike leaders teach true principles and then trust people to govern themselves. Parents, teachers, and leaders create spiritual safety where individuals can wrestle honestly with their questions, seek revelation, and learn to walk with God. Fealty demands compliance; Christlike leadership develops capable, responsible agents.

2. Christ's Pattern of Discipleship—Ask, Seek, Knock (Matthew 7:7–8; James 1:5; Doctrine & Covenants 9:7–8). Discipleship is an active practice. Christ calls us to think, study, ponder, ask, and act. A culture of Christlike obedience expects each of us to receive revelation for ourselves and our stewardships. Instead of outsourcing our spiritual work, we seek, discern, and choose with the guidance of the Spirit. Fealty hands responsibility to someone else; disciples of Christ take responsibility for themselves.

3. Christ's Pattern of Love—I Know My Sheep (John 10; Luke 15; Mosiah 18). Christlike love is personal, patient, and without condition. Christ stayed close to people when they struggled, wandered, or questioned. Fealty turns love into leverage ("I love you if . . ."), whereas Christlike love creates belonging and honors agency in every season of a person's life.

4. Christ's Pattern of Growth—Take Up Your Cross (Matthew 16:24; Ether 12:27). Growth requires voluntary effort and voluntary becoming. Coerced righteousness cannot transform the heart. Zion is built by those who freely choose Christ, who face their struggles honestly, and who allow the Atonement to shape their experiences into something that produces growth. Fealty keeps people small and dependent; true obedience enlarges our capacities and makes us independent.

Christlike obedience allows us to move forward on the path of happiness.

The most important and sacred choice God gives us is the opportunity to decide what we believe and how we come to believe it. By following Christ's example, we can walk away from our leanings toward fealty and striking a healthy balance between learning from our leaders and taking responsibility for our choices. We simply learn to do what most of us already believe is best.

Late Latter-day Saint historian, scholar, and writer Melissa Wei-Tsing Inouye beautifully captured the risk we face in using our agency to place its beautiful, divine possibilities within our reach: "If our Heavenly Parents had intended for everyone to think alike and to follow the same path back to them, they could have endorsed Lucifer's plan. Instead, they gave us the power of agency, which is the power to make terrible mistakes and cause lasting damage. But it is also the power to be brave, to be wise, to extend the self, and to be a true healer."[9] God wants us to use our moral agency, which includes both the right to choose and the resulting consequences and possibilities.

Christ does not ask us to surrender our agency to follow Him; He asks us to use it. When we do, we become His disciples not by compulsion but by choice, and that is the soil in which we grow. This is the soil Christ invites us to cultivate—faith instead of fear, love without condition, revelation without dependency. We can become a people who choose Him freely and a community where every soul can grow with less tension and more Christlike love.

Fealty or Obedience and Agency

Critical question #3 looms over us as perhaps the most important question of all.

**How do we honor God's gift of agency
in a culture that expects compliance?**

What kind of culture will we build? How will we balance the beautiful gifts of agency and obedience? What will we do to prevent the impulses that trigger fealty? We are free to choose how to do these things. What will we do with that freedom?

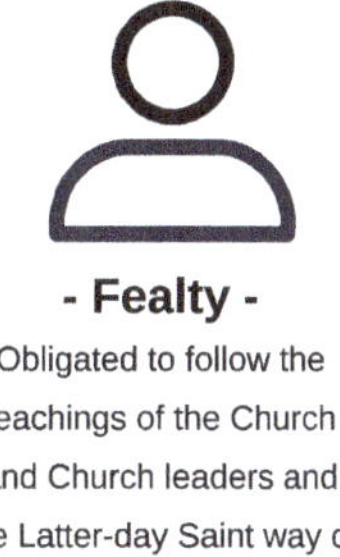

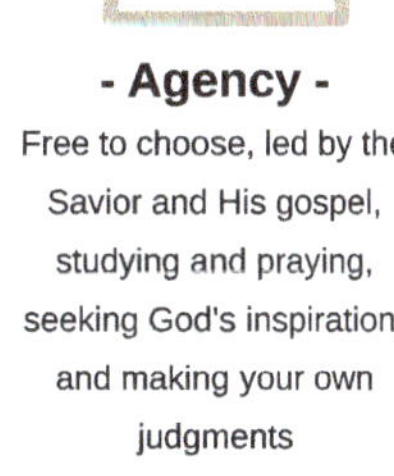

Agency is a sacred gift. Obedience must be chosen and not commanded. And that is why the gospel can never be lived by proxy. He does not want subjects. He wants sons and daughters who hear His voice and follow it—something we can all do.

Key Chapter Takeaway

If we are not careful, deference to authority can subtly replace personal spiritual responsibility. Healthy discipleship balances faithful obedience with agency and accountability.

Reflection Questions

1. How do I balance following Church leaders with personal revelation and responsibility?

2. Where might I confuse faithfulness with abdicating my agency and responsibility?

3. How can I honor others' agency even when I disagree or have concerns?

Application Suggestion

Reflect on how you relate to authority, guidance, and personal responsibility in your life. When you receive counsel, notice whether your instinct is to quickly comply or to discern thoughtfully.

Choose one decision this week where you will more fully exercise your moral agency, directly seeking God's guidance, acting with intention, and accepting responsibility for the outcome. A mature, Christ-centered faith honors inspired guidance from Church leadership while remaining accountable to God for how we choose to follow that guidance.

CHAPTER 10

HARMONY

Imbalance #4:
Soil That Grows
Only One Kind of Plant

Imbalance

Pressure to conform

Tension

Pretending to be something you are not to fit in

Critical Question:
How can we be one when we are so different?

A Kingfisher and a Flock of Magpies

My home office overlooks a pond that attracts wildlife. One morning I noticed something extraordinary—a small but striking kingfisher with slate-blue feathers, black-and-white trim, and a quiet confidence that belied her size. From a spruce branch, she watched, dove into the pond with lightning speed, and rose with her catch, sparkling water dripping from her feathers. She was being what God made her to be— uncomplicated, unthreatening, and unmistakably herself.

Before long, a few magpies showed up. They worked together to harass her, driving her off her perch and into the air. Their aggression bewildered me; kingfishers pose no threat to magpies. She dodged them with agility and grace but eventually tired and flew away, perhaps never to return. The pond feels a bit empty now—quieter, smaller, something good chased away. The kingfisher was guilty of nothing but being herself, unique and beautiful—but not a magpie.

Sameness often feels safe. We instinctively shape the soil of our communities to grow what looks familiar. But when sameness becomes the standard, we lose something vital. Differences of personality, experience, and belief begin to feel like threats instead of gifts. People hide parts of themselves to belong. Something inside them withers. But when we welcome differences, our garden comes alive with possibility. This tension is not new. It reaches all the way back to the earliest Christian communities.

The Early Saints and the Pressure to Fit the Mold

Paul's letter to the Corinthians reveals a community struggling to reconcile its differences. The members in Corinth elevated certain gifts, rituals, and leaders above others, creating hierarchies that undermined belonging and devalued anyone who didn't fit the mold. In response, Paul taught one of the most important truths about discipleship: Christ's body has many members, each indispensable, especially "those members of the body, which seem to be more feeble" (1 Corinthians 12:22). Every believer matters. The body *fails* without these differences.

Modern neuroscience helps us understand why conformity feels so natural. The amygdala scans for differences as a potential threat. Dopamine rewards group approval. In classic experiments, people agree with obviously false opinions simply to avoid standing alone.[1] These pressures can literally reshape our ability to see the truth, narrowing what we perceive long before we realize it. It is no wonder the Lord warned Joseph Smith that we could lose light and truth through the "traditions of [our] fathers" (Doctrine & Covenants 93:39).

Harmony comes when we put off the instinctive tribal reaction and look to Christ, whose way replaces fear with love and judgment with understanding. The cost of conformity can be high, especially when implemented without Christlike judgment.

Between God's Justice and Mercy Stands Christlike Judgment

Jay was a longtime professor at one of the Church's universities—faithful, devoted, and widely admired for both his character and contribution.[2] After years of service, he came to a major fork in the road.

His eighteen-year-old son shared with his parents that he was bisexual. Suddenly Jay was torn between love for his job and loyalty to the Church and his love for his son. A private, thoughtful man, he carried the tension quietly. After a great deal of soul-searching, he and his wife made a deeply personal decision of conscience: To privately show support for their son, they directed part of their tithing to organizations that assisted LGBTQ+ individuals.

This coincided with the university's new requirement for faculty ecclesiastical endorsements. When asked by his bishop if he was a full-tithe payer, Jay was honest. He described the anguish of balancing fidelity to the Church and university with his love for and desire to support his son. The bishop revoked his endorsement, and Jay was dismissed from his job.

Years of faithful service, his character, and his family's well-being carried insufficient weight; the decision hinged on a General Handbook definition of tithing. When Jay asked whether there was still a place for a man like him and a family like his in the Church or at the school, the bishop's answer made it clear there wasn't. His termination came through an unsigned form letter from an anonymous department. The dean and university president—both friends—never reached out. A few brave colleagues held a quiet off-campus dinner to thank him and wish him well. A good and faithful kingfisher flew away and began again somewhere else.

> **"He drew a circle that shut me out—**
> **Heretic, rebel, a thing to flout.**
> **But love and I had the wit to win:**
> **We drew a circle that took him in!"[3]**
> **—Edward Markham**

This example raises complex questions about authority, stewardship, and compassion. The point is not to suggest redefining doctrine, but to illustrate how cultural tone shapes pastoral interaction. In my opinion, there had to be a better way—a way truer to the complete character of Christ. The issue is not whether the Church or university should have standards; they must. The issue is how our culture influences whether those standards are administered in a way that reflects the Savior's balance of justice and mercy. No Church policy or cultural interpretation of it should eclipse Christlike goodness, which is the true measure of healthy soil.

I do not believe his bishop was bad or wrong to expect tithing to be paid to the Church—only, that he was, perhaps, discouraged by the culture from exercising the Christlike judgment he was capable of.

Joseph Smith taught in the Lectures on Faith that among the attributes of Deity are justice and mercy—distinct and paradoxical.[4]

Justice upholds law and accountability; mercy offers forgiveness and growth. How is the paradox resolved? Christlike judgment applies the wisdom needed to balance the two. Without justice, there is chaos; without mercy, hope is lost. Without judgment, there is no balance. There is no place in our doctrine where justice exists independent of mercy or where Christlike judgment is cast aside.

In Jay's case, did enforcement replaced discernment? It seems the spirit of the law was never invited into the room. Because Christlike judgment seems to have never happened, mercy appears to have played no role. That is certainly how Jay and others with first-hand knowledge of the situation see it.

President Dallin H. Oaks provided great counsel for moments like this: "In those intermediate judgments we are responsible to make, may we judge righteously and with love."[5] At moments that require balance, Christlike judgment must stand in the middle. Did that happen here? At Jay's moment of greatest need for compassion, he was cast out. The university and its students were poorer for it—all because the magpies were unable to make room for a Kingfisher.

We have the power to make a difference. Imagine what could have been if *even one* person of influence had stood with him rather than merely standing over him.

Differences, Tension, and Conformity

Culture tends to measure the outward appearance, while the Lord looks on the heart (see 1 Samuel 16:7). As with the earlier imbalances, our research shows a striking gap between what people feel the Church culture expects them to be and what they believe God invites them to become. The difference is clear in the patterns that follow. When conformity rules the culture, honesty and integrity are lost, even though most of us value them more than compliance. When that happens, people feel unable to be open about who they really are and what they believe, especially when these do not resemble the traditional profile emphasized by the culture. Social pressure begins to masquerade as discipleship. The soil hardens. And people quietly wither under the weight of being isolated in a place that no longer feels Christlike or honest.

How can we best navigate the differences among us in how we believe and how we choose to live our beliefs?

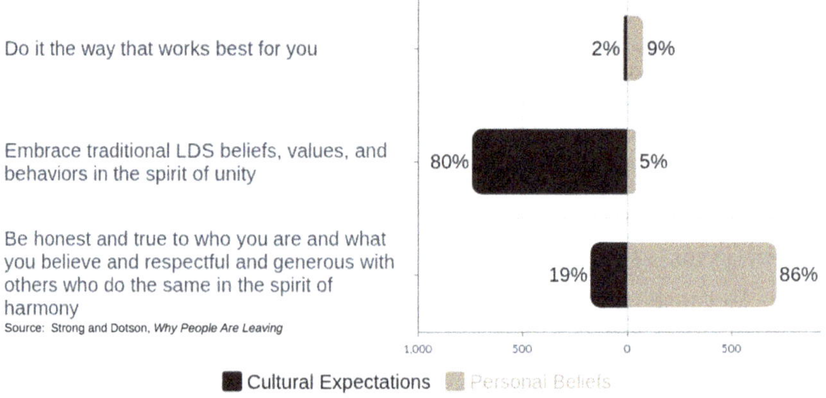

There Are Different Ways to Be a Faithful Latter-day Saint

One cause of this imbalance is a quiet but persistent myth—that discipleship has a single acceptible shape and that faithful Latter-day Saints must believe and grow in the same way. Our research on faith and religion reveals three truths: (1) People experience belief differently, (2) they grow differently, and (3) our instinct for conformity blinds us to the value of divine diversity.

The first insight—how people experience belief—reveals much about the challenges we face. Extensive research inside and outside the Church identifies several mindsets that describe the different ways Latter-day Saints experience belief. Understanding these can help us reach the unity Christ invites: "If ye are not one ye are not mine" (Doctrine & Covenants 38:27).

LDS Belief Mindsets

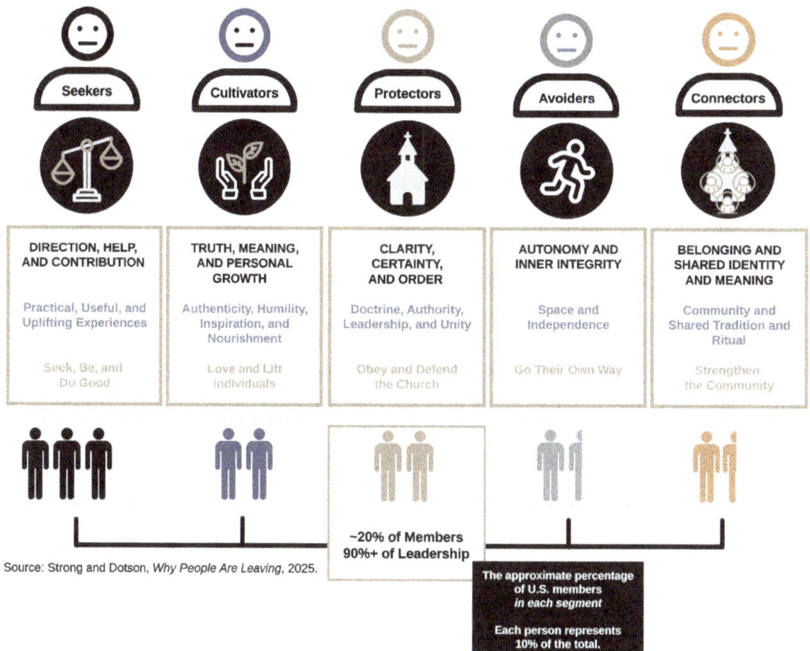

Source: Strong and Dotson, *Why People Are Leaving*, 2025.

Below is a brief overview of the five mindsets illustrated in the chart:

> **Seekers (~30 percent)—Direction, Help, and Contribution**
> These members want practical, uplifting experiences and value a Church that helps them seek, become, and do good.

> **Cultivators (~20 percent)—Truth, Meaning, and Personal Growth**
> These members thrive in an atmosphere of authenticity, nourishment, humility, and inspiration—loving and lifting each individual, specially those who may not fit.

> **Protectors (~20 percent)—Clarity, Certainty, and Order**
> These members prize doctrine, authority, leadership, and unity. They feel a sacred duty to defend and uphold the Church.

> **Avoiders (~15 percent)—Autonomy, Inner Integrity**
> These members prefer independence and space, choosing their own way without institutional pressure.

> **Connectors (~15 percent)—Belonging, Shared Identity**
> The members flourish in community, and the meaning that comes from sharing rituals and traditions with others. They seek to strengthen relationships and unity.

In our Church, our research suggests that the Protector mindset represents only about 20 percent of U.S. members—yet accounts for an estimated 90 percent of Church leadership. This imbalance—between who fills leadership roles and who fills our pews—explains much of the tension members experience.

Of course, it is natural for leaders to want to protect and preserve the institution they serve. Protector leaders value firm soil that fosters clarity, rules, order, and consistency. Cultivator members thrive in soil that breathes, with characteristics such as authenticity, individual inspiration, and pastoral care. Sometimes these needs clash within the Church. But they can be balanced.

Protector leaders rooted in Christ do this beautifully. Leaders who are uneasy with difference may unintentionally harden the soil, creating conformity pressures that push people away. This is not about character. It is about sight. Recognizing the need for balance is the first step.

The Way Our Belief Changes and Grows Can Also Differ

Belief and spirituality also develop and grow differently in different people, and recognizing these patterns can help us understand one another more generously. Brian McLaren's four stages of faith framework helps us understand spiritual differences and change. People grow differently.[6] The chart below outlines these stages.

Brian McLaren's Four Stages of Faith

Source: Brian D. McLaren, *Faith After Doubt*, 2022.

Each stage is important, legitimate, and offers something unique to the Church community. And few of us fit neatly into one stage. Perhaps you will see yourself, as I do, in more than one place. The important point is that people grow in different ways.

> **Simplicity**—Clear rules, trust in authority, confidence in right and wrong
> Strengths: Order and trust
> Risks: Rigidity and judgment

> **Complexity**—Faith becomes a system of principles that "work"
> Strengths: Competence, skill, and application
> Risk: Performance-based religion

> **Perplexity**—Pain and paradox disrupt old belief patterns
> Strengths: Honesty, depth, and humility
> Risks: Confusion and disillusionment

> **Harmony**—Faith rebuilt on love and humility
> Strengths: Compassion, wisdom, and Christlike vision
> Risk: Feeling alone

Each is valid and contributes something essential to a church community, but we tend to struggle with these different stages of belief.

Scripture repeatedly shows this dynamic growth pattern. Nephi, Joseph Smith, Peter, Paul, Alma the Younger, and the Anti-Nephi-Lehies all move through these stages in different ways. Their growth is evidence of God's hand in their lives, not of their weaknesses. One example in particular shows the beauty—and the tension—of this journey. Nephi's journey through the stages of faith shows an inspiring and instructive pattern.

1. Simplicity—"I will go and do." Nephi begins with conviction and trust in God: "I will go and do" (1 Nephi 3:7). His faith is straightforward, confident, and obedient.

2. Complexity—"And the Lord did show me from time to time." As his responsibilities expand, Nephi becomes a leader and builder—returning to Jerusalem, constructing a ship, and guiding a people. His question—"How is it that [God] cannot instruct me?" (1 Nephi: 17:51)—reveals a heart that blends skill with trust.

3. Perplexity—"O wretched man that I am." We often forget that Nephi knew anguish. He admitted his uncertainty: "I do not know the meaning of all things" (1 Nephi 11:17). Later he cried out in grief: "O wretched man that I am!" (2 Nephi 4:17). But he always returned to trust: "I know in whom I have trusted" (2 Nephi 4:19). This is sacred ground—honest, faithful, and challenging.

4. Harmony—"Unshaken faith in Him." At life's end, Nephi's faith distilled into love, humility, and hope: "With unshaken faith. . . . a perfect brightness of hope. . . . and a love of God and of all men" (2 Nephi 31:19–20).

The most constant element in Nephi's faith is not only doctrine but his dynamic beliefs and his relationship with God. Would Nephi find nourishing soil in today's Church? Or might some of today's church membership, uneasy with the nature of his growth, have struggled to recognize the faith in his unfolding journey?"

The story of Adam and Eve also mirrors this developmental arc. Eden represents simplicity. Leaving Eden brings complexity. Mortality introduces perplexity. Redemption in Christ leads to harmony. Wanting everyone to remain in Eden—to never grow, never stretch, never wrestle with truth—misses the entire purpose of mortal life.

The Limits of Simplicity

Simplicity is a beautiful beginning to faith, but for some, it can be a limiting place to stay. It is also central to many of our cultural challenges. Simplicity provides structure, protection, and direction and is rooted in faith and obedience. President Joseph F. Smith first taught and coined the phrase, "Obedience is the first law of heaven."[7]

But simplicity without growth beyond it eventually reaches its limits. It offers order without depth—like mastering grammar but lacking beautiful composition. Growth requires learning, stretching, and discovering. We often misunderstand "first law" to mean supreme rather than foundational. Paul wrote, "The letter killeth, but the Spirit giveth life" (2 Corinthians 3:6). Jesus rebuked the Pharisees for fixating on the small laws while neglecting "the weightier matters of judgment, mercy, and faith" (Matthew 23:23). Simplicity can unintentionally narrow our field of vision, leaving us unequipped to recognize faithful growth that looks unfamiliar.

When we misread others' honest questions as disloyalty, we pathologize healthy growth and risk isolating thoughtful, sincere people, and we devalue the worth of people who are different than we are. This is evident in our research, which again shows two tension-creating patterns: (1) In the culture, living an exemplary Latter-day Saint life is what defines one's worth, and (2) most of us don't believe our worth is or should be defined that way.

What primarily defines our worth in the Church community?

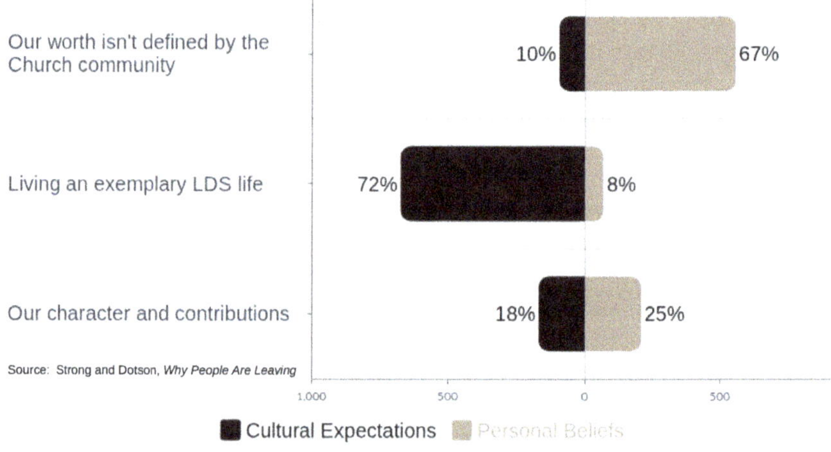

These forces create a culture where conformity is rewarded, difference is mistrusted, and belonging quietly erodes. Many feel tension between how they should be valued and what they are valued for—often conformity over character. This helps explain why 60 percent of respondents said they do not feel a strong sense of belonging in their own wards or branches.[8] Again, this tension is pushing people away.

Conformity, Love, and Fear

Why is it so hard to embrace differences in belief and spiritual growth? Often, it is fear—fear born of love. We worry about those we love. We fear that if they question what we believe or choose to grow differently, they might lose their faith. And if they lose their faith, we fear we might lose them. In a culture where conformity feels synonymous with righteousness, differences are easily interpreted as danger signs. But differences are exactly that—differences, not evidence of diminished devotion. Moroni gave us a wide, generous standard for discerning goodness: "Every thing which inviteth to do good, and to persuade to believe in Christ . . . is of God." (Moroni 7:16) The net Christ casts for goodness is far wider than the one our culture often casts.

Questions, changing beliefs, and honest doubt are not the enemies of faith—certitude is. Even Joseph Smith began his faith journey with a question. Honest seeking has always been part of God's pattern for growth. It is not inquiry that drives people away; it is our insistence, spoken or unspoken, that anything beyond simplicity is unacceptable. When we pressure people to retreat to simplicity because it makes *us* more comfortable, they feel misunderstood, unseen, and spiritually constrained. Many step away only because it is the only honest path left to them.

When Cale withdrew from the Church, I did not understand that he hadn't left faith—he left simplicity. In part, it was our insistence on simplicity as the only faithful path that made the soil too unyielding for his growth. He was still the same good, honest, truth-seeking soul he had always been—growing in his own way. One day he said to me, "Dad, the true strait and narrow path is the one from wherever you are straight to God." He was right.

Like Adam and Eve, my kingfisher son was choosing, learning, and seeking—and that is good.

Returning to the Critical Question

How can we be one when we are so different?

What path will bring us to the unity Christ encourages? Two paths exist: First, the path of conformity—unity achieved by sameness. It's predictable and orderly but ultimately small, shrinking both compassion and vision until unity becomes uniformity. Such a community becomes brittle, anxious, and easily threatened by difference. Second, the path of harmony—unity achieved through love, humility, and generous curiosity. This path makes room for different stories, different types of growth, and different ways of being faithful. It is expansive. Strong. Beautiful.

Harmony is unity without sameness, the fruit of love that grows beyond fear. Former First Counselor in the General Relief Society Presidency and director of Latter-day Saint Charities Sharon Eubank beautifully captured the spirit of this when she said, "We all have different paths, but we can walk them together."[9]

Christ never asked His disciples to become the same—only to love one another (see John 13:34–35). We come together by seeing one another as God sees us—not the same, and not at the same stage, but each growing toward Him in our own way. God created His children with differences and called them good (see Genesis 1:31).

Culture narrows us toward sameness. Christ draws us toward becoming fully alive. When we respond to difference with fear, our soil hardens. When we respond with curiosity, humility, and compassion, the soil breathes. People feel safe to be honest, to grow at their own pace, and to trust God's work in their lives—even when their path looks different from others' paths.

In communities like this, harmony—not uniformity—takes root. Christ modeled this perfectly. He honored the individual journey, lifted those on the margins, and invited growth without demanding sameness. His pattern is one of harmony rooted in love, not control. This is how we come together in a unity of faith when we are so different—by cultivating a soil where every soul can grow in the light of Christ without needing to become the same.

Part 4 turns to how we cultivate that culture—a culture rooted in Christlike faith, strengthened through relationships, knit together in community, and revealed through the fruit of the gospel.

Key Chapter Takeaway

Conformity is often mistaken for unity, suppressing authenticity and quietly fracturing community vitality. Harmony makes room for difference within a shared commitment.

Reflection Questions

1. Where have I confused unity with sameness?

2. How do I respond to those who are different but faithful?

3. What would choosing love over fear look like in disagreement?

Application Suggestion

Notice when you feel uncomfortable with difference—of belief, expression, background, or perspective—and examine whether the impulse is toward unity or conformity. Practice responding in ways that welcome diversity while remaining Christ-centered. Harmony grows when differences are treated with respect rather than suppressed for sameness.

Four Tensions in Our Cultural Soil

Hard and Unyielding Soil—Acceptance vs. Standards

Who is the Church really for?
Conditional belonging hardens the soil, and roots cannot take hold.
Emphasizing standards for sorting and sifting in judgment rather than
inspiring and lifting in love leaves many unable to take root.

Invitation:
Know, value, and embrace people first
and then inspire and lift them in love.

Shallow Stony Soil—Growth vs. Sanctuary

How can the Church best prepare us for the challenges of real life?
Focus on tradition over truth may protect stability and faith for now, but leaves
roots necessary for spiritual strength shallow and people unprepared for trials.

Invitation:
Share the beauty and value of our traditions while building deep
spiritual roots in Christ and His teachings and helping others do the same.

Thorn-Choked Soil—Agency vs. Fealty

How do we honor God's gift or agency in culture that expects compliance?
Fealty crowds out agency, slowing or stopping spiritual growth and
diminishing the influence of the Holy Ghost. People defer rather than seek
and discern and comply rather than mature and take responsibility.

Invitation:
Honor agency as a sacred gift essential for discipleship while
faithfully sustaining and embracing the counsel of Church leaders.

Single-Crop Soil—Harmony vs. Conformity

How can we be one when we are so different?
Sameness is not unity and stifles God-given differences and gifts.
It encourages pretense, causes individual isolation, and
diminishes the strength and vitality of the Church community.

Invitation:
Cultivate harmony—united in love, not conformity. Embrace who we
really are and the inherent differences we all bring to the community.

What Will We Choose?

These tensions sit with us waiting for our response. What we choose to do will be determined by what we believe and what we want. So, what do we believe about our Heavenly Parents and their love for us and all their children? What do we want for ourselves, our loved ones, and those around us—both those who stay and those who go? Will we double down on stability and protection or cultivate greater nourishment? The question is not right versus wrong, good versus evil, one side against another. It is whether we will cultivate healthy soil—where standards and acceptance, sanctuary and transcendence, obedience and agency, unity and God-given individuality can live together, and belief and faith can thrive for more of us in the Church.

One of the world's great moral storytellers, Fyodor Dostoevsky, raised a question long ago: Do we truly want the possibilities Christ offers—and the risk that comes with them—or would we rather sur-render those possibilities for security, certainty, and order? This tension is as old as the human story. From before the beginning, there have always been two ways.

Dostoevsky wrote his masterpiece, *The Brothers Karamazov*, nearly 150 years ago to explore the nature of belief in a complex, chaotic, and skeptical world—in a different time, different place, and different church but with the same tension we face now. I'd like to share some of that story.

It was a time of disruption, division, fear, and religious and political retrenchment in the city. A stranger came unannounced and walked quietly among the people. He spoke with them, listened to them, taught them, and blessed them. The city suddenly felt different—more alive, more hopeful, more whole. People gathered, drawn to Him and by the sense that something familiar yet new and important was happening, that something much better was possible.

And the old cardinal, was watching. He recognized the stranger. He understood what was happening. And he had Him arrested.

That night, the cardinal entered the prison cell. "I know who you are," he said. "I know what you are doing. You think too highly of them. What you offer them is too heavy to bear."

The man was silent. The cardinal continued. "We corrected your mistakes. We gave them something better. They are happier now." Still, silence.

"They want bread. They want certainty and miracles. They want to be taken care of." Still, the man said nothing. The cardinal's voice rose. "You offer them freedom. We keep them safe. You give them struggle. We give them security. You gave them conscience. We give them authority. You teach them faith. We give them answers." The man said nothing.

The cardinal grew angry. "You say you love them—but we are the ones who take care of them! And we cannot have you here, distracting and confusing them, teaching them they are free and giving them false hope! In the morning, you will be killed as a heretic!"

The man slowly stood, still silent, and kissed the cardinal, who staggered back, shaken and trembling. For a moment, he could not speak. Then he pushed open the prison door. "Go," he whispered. "Go—and never return." And the man walked into the night.[1]

I was baptized by my father when I was eight years old. I believe deeply in the power of ordinances. More than mere transactions, they possess the potential and power to teach, invite, remind, commit, and change us from the inside out. Perhaps this is why the Lord told Joseph Smith, "Therefore, in the ordinances thereof, the power of godliness is manifest" (Doctrine & Covenants 84:20).

Baptism by immersion is *simply* extraordinary. It is a freely chosen death of the old self that we might be reborn as something new, something better. Its power is not confined to the one moment but unfolds across a lifetime as what we are not can gradually be removed and what we were meant to be is given life in us—new creatures with new hearts, new desires, and new ways of living. Death and rebirth, again and again.

Letting go of what we are today is often difficult. I have learned that this kind of death can be painful, at least at first. God is removing from us the things we may love and lean on so that we can love and lean on Him. Looking back, I can see that what I once experienced as the painful failure of my LDS map was nothing more and nothing less than God extracting from me what needed to die so there would be room for the life He wanted to offer me.

I did not understand the power of standards leavened and lifted with love until I saw the damage my son sustained from being sorted and sifted. I did not understand the power of faith to carry us through uncertainty until God took from me the certitude I thought I needed, leaving me truly and completely free to expand my faith and choose for myself.

I did not understand the weight of spiritual responsibility before God—with the risks and growth it carries—until I saw how deferring that responsibility to the Church and its leaders quietly placed a barrier between Him and me. And I did not see the beauty of us becoming one in Christ, with honesty and vulnerability, in love, until I witnessed how superficial sameness creates pretense and diminishes and excludes anyone who is different.

Death is painful. Yet pain is our teacher. And rebirth brings healing and peace.

So, these stubborn questions loom over us, waiting for us to choose: Who is the Church really for? How can the Church best prepare us for the realities of life? How do we use the precious freedom God has given us in a culture that expects us to comply? How do we become one when we are so genuinely different?

And when the answers are unclear or seem costly—when they threaten our comfort, our certainty, our identity, even our belonging— who and what will we look to as our guiding star? Will we look to Jesus Christ and His teachings or settle for less because we think it is safer? The question is not whether Christ still calls. The question is whether we are willing to follow Him into the freedom and risk required for us to become. Because in the end, the choice is the same as it was before time began—whether we will trust Him enough to follow Him.

Part 4 turns toward that freedom, that choice—and toward Him.

PART 4

BRING FORTH GOOD FRUIT

How Christ Can Transform Our Culture

THE HARVEST

"There is nothing like a dream to create the future."
—Victor Hugo, *Les Misérables*

Gardeners cultivate the soil, and Christlike soil bears fruit in the form of resilient faith, healed relationships, and communities that move forward together in hope. J.R.R. Tolkien wrote an inspiring story designed to help a broken world remember what courage looks like and how the power of friendship and the smallest of acts can shape the future of a community. The fictional world he wrote about was nothing like ours, but the truths he raised matter for us. As *The Lord of the Rings* reaches its end, it is not armies or kings who turn the tide but ordinary people walking toward danger with nothing certain except their love for one another and their way of life. Fear calls them backward. Faith calls them forward. And that simple choice becomes the hinge point upon which everything turns.

We now face that same hinge point. Our community is full of goodness, devotion, and light—but also full of tension, pain, and questions.

We did not choose this moment, but we must choose how we will meet it. Fear narrows. Faith expands. Fear shelters. Faith transforms. And culture, the sum of our beliefs, values, and lived behaviors, bends toward whichever we feed—faith or fear.

This chapter is an invitation to dream about culture deeply nourished by faith, roots held fast despite uncertainty, and a thriving community where differences are strength and people live for each other. And like all dreams worth having, this one begins with faith.

Section 1—Soil Saturated with Faith

Faith and Fear

The battle between faith and fear is not *out there*—it lives inside our souls. Tolkien captured this tension in one character: Smeagol, the good and tender self, and Gollum, the fearful and wounded one—two beings in one body, each convinced of its own truth. One reaches toward light; the other clings to darkness. One trusts; one hides.

We are born fear-ready, wired for survival. When threatened, our breath quickens, our vision narrows, and our heart races. This isn't weakness; it's our God-given alarm system. Fear becomes harmful only when it becomes our compass—bending us and our culture toward protection rather than growth. A person can be safe inside a bunker but not free.

"Fear defeats more people than any other one thing in the world."[1]

Christ understood this, which may be why His most repeated message was simple yet powerful: "Be not afraid" (Matthew 14:27). Do we trust Him?

Faith is the alternative, but faith must be learned. It is not pretending or forcing ourselves to believe something we don't. It is the God-given power to move forward in uncertainty and opposition because we trust God. Fear comes uninvited, but faith must be chosen, coaxed, and cultivated. Faith moves us forward when we would rather retreat.

Regulation, Not Suppression

Understanding that fear is part of our biology gives us power to govern it. King Benjamin's teaching that "the natural man is an enemy to God" (Mosiah 3:19) speaks not only to appetites and impulses but also to our desires for certainty, comfort, and solidarity. These feelings may help us feel safe in the short-term. But if unregulated, they also keep us spiritually small, shallow, and anchored in safety rather than abundance. Anchors secure but also chain.

Neuroscience mirrors this spiritual truth. The limbic system initially reacts with fight, flight, freeze, or conform—the natural man. The prefrontal cortex responds with patience, empathy, courage, judgment, and restraint, regulating fear. King Benjamin did not ask us to eradicate the natural man but to put it off and yield "to the enticings of the Holy Spirit." To put off means to delay or set aside, not eliminate permanently. We can acknowledge our fears and choose to govern them. Silencing fear is simply denying it. Rather, we can place our fears under the stewardship of the Spirit and faith.

This struggle is not unique to Latter-day Saints. All people feel fear—fear of not knowing, fear of inadequacy, fear of exclusion, fear of complexity, fear of being influenced or harmed by those who differ from us. When unchecked, fear quietly hardens culture. We become careful instead of courageous, rigid instead of receptive, defensive instead of engaged, certain instead of humble. This produces a culture that is hard and unyielding, shallow and full of judgment, overrun with stifling traditions, and fit for only one kind of adherent. It's a culture that drives many of those we love away.

Perhaps this is why faith is the first principle of the gospel. In a dynamic world of growing complexity, it seems Jesus knew we would need the strength and capacity to see, learn, stretch, question, and grow. The command to "fear not" appears in some form more than a hundred times in scripture. Christ was not telling us to deny danger; He invites us to embrace transformation.

Looking Forward with an Eye of Faith

The scriptures do not exist to give us certainty but to inspire and ground us. They help us to understand and trust in God's goodness, nearness, promises, and character; to grasp the huge complexity of the human experience; and to expand our sense of what is possible.

The Book of Mormon is one of the most controversial books in the world. Critics question its origins; believers testify of its divinity. Interestingly, the disagreement usually hinges on whether the book is what it claims to be rather than on what it can teach us about life and how it can change us for the better—a revealing reflection of our culture of certitude.

I love the Book of Mormon not because it is true but because it changed me and awakened my faith. The title page declares its purpose: to testify that God remembers His children, to persuade us that Christ is real, and to remind us that there is always light in darkness. It exists to increase faith, not to prove anything.

Among its beautiful teachings is the invitation to look "forward with an eye of faith" (Alma 5:15; 32:40; Ether 12:19)—to walk when we cannot see and plant when we cannot be sure of a harvest. Faith is not blindness. Faith is trust forged by experience, refined in adversity, and nourished by God even when the outcome is unclear.

Faith is taking seeds to plant in soil you have not yet seen.

Christ never condemned fear itself. He simply asked us to choose a different friend.

How Can We Tell Whether We Are Led by Fear or Faith?

No one wants to be led by fear—yet we often are without even realizing it. Fear sometimes hides inside responsibility, stewardship, or even righteousness. We feel afraid because we care. We are concerned a child may wander, a friend may doubt, the Church may change, or truth may be lost. These fears come from devotion. But devotion does not always produce discernment; sometimes it produces blindness and defensiveness. Fear and faith bear different fruit:

Fear hardens; faith softens.
Fear controls; faith invites.
Fear reacts; faith engages.
Fear isolates; faith connects.
Fear guards; faith welcomes.

When led by fear, we clutch in desperation rather than hold in faith. We instruct more than listen. We protect more than trust. We try to fix more than strengthen. Fear makes us act from a place of anxiety rather than confidence.

When led by faith, something in us blossoms. We listen without an agenda. We speak without urgency. We extend space instead of exerting pressure. We trust Christ to meet those we love in ways we cannot—and I believe He does. When fear rises (as it will), we can pause, breathe, and invite the Spirit to lead our responses: a slower answer, a gentler tone, a question instead of a conclusion, and an open heart instead of a guarded one.

Faith does not deny fear; it simply refuses to allow fear to rule over us.

Faith as Culture

When enough individuals choose faith—not once but as a mindset—culture begins to shift. Fear becomes a warning light rather than the steering wheel. Faith becomes the air the community breathes. The soil changes. Hearts change. Our lens changes. We begin to look to Christ, not fear, to shape our beliefs, values, and behaviors.

"Look unto me in every thought; doubt not, fear not."
(Doctrine and Covenants 6:36).

What if every thought started with faith? When we sense a fearful thought, what would happen if we replaced that thought with trust in God? Faith gives us the courage to act, ask, listen, stay, and grow.

Faith does not grow in isolation. It grows in shared soil. When faith takes root, it does not end with belief; it moves outward into relationship. Faith roots us in God, but relationships root us in each other. And without those roots, even sincere faith struggles to endure. The next layer of a Christ-centered community is not agreement but belonging.

Section 2—Roots Protected and Held by Relationships

The Power of Belonging

When faith nourishes us on the inside, something changes on the outside. Relationships are one way faith becomes visible. Faith may be personal, but belonging is shared. Communities are strengthened not just by belief but by the bonds that connect us—bonds that remain strong through uncertainty, difference, and change. They are the living network that keeps us steady through drought and storm, just as roots bind and strengthen a forest.

In 2024, our Church reported just over 933,000 members in Africa.[2] The Seventh-day Adventist Church, founded thirty-five years after ours, reported more than *ten times* that many.[3] The difference is striking—and while doctrine and history certainly matter, culture is a significant factor. An individual with significant insight on our Church's presence in Africa explained it simply: "They have Ubuntu."[4] Their growth rests, in part, on a cultural strength we struggle to replicate. Ubuntu, the Zulu expression popularized by Archbishop Desmond Tutu, captures a way of seeing the world:

"My humanity is caught up, is inextricably bound up, in yours."[5]

"A person is a person through other persons."[6]

"We are diminished when others are humiliated or diminished."[7]

"We are human because we belong."[8]

Ubuntu is relationship as identity, and belonging is identity's foundation. One person's wholeness is tied to another's. That is the soil where faith helps communities flourish—particularly when a church's history, institutions, and daily practices reinforce that sense of shared life rather than unintentionally constrain it.

Wisdom from the Forest

This same truth is written into creation itself. A forest is not a collection of isolated trees; it is a living network of connection. Beneath the forest floor runs a vast web of fungal threads—an underground communication system some scientists call the "wood-wide web." Through it, trees share water, minerals, and even warning signals when danger approaches.[9]

Older, deeper-rooted trees serve as "mother trees," funneling nutrients to saplings and to trees weakened by drought, disease, or too much shade.[10] Strength flows toward vulnerability, not away from it. This allows a forest to endure. No tree thrives alone. And in healthy forests, none are abandoned.

Healthy communities work the same way. People with deep roots feed those whose roots need strengthening. Those in seasons of abundance support those in seasons of loss. When someone hurts, others quietly send what strength they can whether through presence, prayer, time, listening, warmth, humility, steadiness, or love. Belonging is not something we manufacture. It is something we grow. And it happens wherever life is shared.

Falcons Don't Have to Come Back

When Cale ended his mission at the MTC and came home, it created explosive tension in our relationship. Sara and I were confused and distraught. We saw him as immature, selfish, and making a decision that would damage the rest of his life. Many in our Latter-day Saint community saw it the same way. We all felt the need to fix him. But every conversation pushed him further away.

We could feel him withdrawing and were hurt and afraid. We wanted to control him. He was deeply hurt by the disappointment, suspicion, and rigidity he felt—so much so that he stayed home only long enough to save money for a plane ticket. Over the next six months, we had very little contact, and whatever contact we had was strained. It was a time of darkness and despair for all of us, and something had to give.

Discouraged and praying for a way forward, I boarded a flight for a business trip to the East Coast. Midair, a medical emergency forced the plane to land unexpectedly in Kansas City. As we waited, the man beside me showed me a photo album with page after page of breathtaking black-and-white photographs of falcons. He was a falconer.

I knew nothing about falconry. I asked him what he knew about falcons that most people wouldn't know. Without hesitation, he said, "They don't have to come back." Seeing my confusion, he continued. "When you release them, they're completely free. They return only if they want to. If they feel anger, disappointment, or frustration from me, they don't come back."

As he spoke, I could not take my eyes off the photographs and those astonishing, powerful, sensitive creatures. And something in me broke open. I felt God showing me my son. Cale was not broken. He was not rebellious. He was not lost. He was a falcon—intelligent, beautiful, sensitive, free, wounded—and now gone.

I suddenly understood what I could not see: I had mistaken stewardship for ownership, help for control, love for rescue. The tighter I tried to hold him, the farther he needed to fly.

I sat there undone—humbled, pierced, and *hopeful.* For the first time in a long time, I realized Cale's journey was not mine to manage. My role was not to correct him. If I wanted my son to return, I needed to be a person he would want to return to—receptive soil instead of hard and unyielding ground; a well of living water, not a stone of expectation.

That moment became a hinge point in my life. It changed how I listened. It changed how I spoke. It changed how I saw my son—and myself. Looking back on my conversations with him, I finally understood how high the stakes had been and how unprepared I was to have the most important conversations of his life. And I remain, today, a work in progress. That realization—painful as it was—became the beginning of the journey that eventually led me to this work.

What Our Faith-Transition Conversations Research Taught Us

As part of our broader study, I partnered with friend and colleague Joseph Grenny[11] to conduct extensive research to understand faith-transition conversations to learn directly from the experiences of hundreds of Latter-day Saints. We wanted to understand what strengthens belonging, what fractures it, what helps people stay connected, what pushes them away, and how that affects belief. The patterns were clear.

1. Faith transitions are more relational than informational.

Facts matter. History matters. Doctrine matters. But in our research, people did not step away primarily because of those things. They stepped away because they no longer felt like they belonged.

Emotional connection—not agreement—was the strongest predictor of a positive relational outcome. Feeling understood invigorated trust like breathing in oxygen after holding one's breath. Feeling dismissed hardened the soil and pushed people away.

Those who spoke with highly devout members or Church leaders experienced the most tension and pain and were five times more likely to have negative conversations. Unfortunately, these conversations often prioritized correction over understanding and caused the greatest harm and alienation. These people also spoke with more people on average, indicating they had greater need.

Those whose spoke with peers, close friends, or those who understood or were willing to listen to their concerns experienced the most positive conversations and relationships, and their sense of belonging was most often strengthened. They found compassion, not scrutiny; safety, not pressure, and they spoke to fewer people.

Why do people so often feel safest speaking with those who hold less authority or appear less devout? It's not because they want less faith but because they need more connection. This reveals one of our greatest opportunities: to lead not with correction but with presence.

Faith Transition Conversations Are *Critical*

- 83% reach out to others to talk.

- 40% of these conversations do not go well.

- They are 2x more likely to go badly with a parent and 5x more likely to go badly with a church leader.

- If the conversation goes poorly, relationships suffer, questions and concerns get stronger, and the individual is much more likely to withdraw.

2. What works is simple:
Listen, respect, and provide emotional safety.

Across respondents:

- Sixty-nine percent experienced healing when someone listened without challenging them.

- Thirty-six percent felt strengthened by nonjudgmental love.

- Twenty percent said the most meaningful moment was having their concerns acknowledged.

Agreement was not the point. Understanding was. People don't often leave solely because belief collapses. They leave because they don't feel like they belong.

3. Silence feels like abandonment.

For many, silence was the deepest wound of all. One gentle question—
"How are you, really?"—could have changed everything. Not to judge.
Not to debate. Simply to care.

In healthy forests, even weakened trees are not abandoned. Stronger trees increase their flow toward the vulnerable ones, and they do so naturally. Support moves toward need, not away from it. Belonging works the same way.

God does not lose those who leave. But far too often, we do. Many described leaving the Church as liberating but also disorienting and disheartening due to the loss of the community that once nourished them. They were not leaving goodness; they were losing their forest. When roots no longer hold, even the strongest trees feel it.

In our research, fortunately, we identified positive outliers—people who handled these conversations in a way that strengthened the relationship and increased the likelihood that the individual felt comfortable staying connected with the community.

It helps to remember something simple and sobering: We are human. In moments that carry deep personal and eternal meaning, we are especially prone to the very mistakes we most want to avoid. These conversations feel high-stakes because we attach to them profound significance—and paradoxically, when we most want to be at our best, we often do our worst.

The reason is not a lack of goodness or intent, but biology. Under pressure, our brain's fear response takes over, narrowing our capacity for patient, thoughtful, and loving engagement. We all understand the danger of driving under the influence, yet we often fail to recognize when we are speaking under the influence—of fear, anxiety, and urgency. And when we do, the outcomes are rarely what we hope for.

Disrupting this pattern begins within. We pause long enough to regain emotional steadiness. We examine our own feelings honestly, and the stories we are telling ourselves about the other person—asking whether they are true, fair, and generous. And we realign our purpose:

not to win, persuade, fix, or contain, but to truly understand and connect. From that place, something better becomes possible.

What follows are the patterns we've observed in those who consistently navigate these conversations well—the quiet, disciplined approaches of positive outliers who create understanding where others create distance.

What Positive Outliers Do and Don't Do When Having High-Stakes Faith Conversations

Effective	Ineffective
Take a Breather	**Talking Under the Influence**
Work on Me First	**Focus on Fixing Them**
-My feelings-	
-My story-	
-My motives-	
Seek Connection	**Expect Agreement**

Former counselor in the General Relief Society Presidency Reyna I. Aburto's words of wisdom and love capture the spirit of what these conversations can be when she said,

"Listening with love is one of the greatest gifts we can offer."[12]

Belonging is the difference between staying rooted and being uprooted. Relationships—real, enduring, Christlike relationships—are what keep us coming back. And when enough of those relationships take root, they do more than hold individuals together—they begin to reshape the community itself—and the culture starts to change.

Section 3—The Harvest: Community

A loving, life-giving community emerges when faith nourishes the soil and relationships hold the roots—and when those two forces begin to reshape culture. Tension becomes balanced and instructive rather than threatening. We begin to glimpse what the Church could become—not merely a collective but a community. A collective is where people exist for the institution. A community is where the institution exists for the people. Collectives drive differences underground or out; communities carry and explore them. Communities hold people together through love and connection rather than compliance. When faith and relationships prioritize trust and belonging, healthy culture follows.

From Fortress to Village—Belonging

A fortress protects—but only those already inside. Those who are not "in" exist cautiously, unsure how fully they can show themselves. Slowly, we learn which parts of us earn entry and which must remain hidden. Belonging becomes conditional, measured, and earned. Over time, safety is confused with sameness.

A village is different. In a village, you belong before you fit. This does not mean there are no standards or expectations or that anything goes. A village does not abandon its standards; it understands their purpose. Jesus Christ consistently honored God's commandments yet challenged culture that used them primarily to draw lines. Repeatedly, He showed that standards were meant to lift people, not hold them at arm's length. In a village shaped by His example, expectations do not function as tests of belonging but as invitations to grow—clear enough to guide, generous enough to include, and rooted in love rather than fear. This is not the absence of structure; it is structure ordered toward life.

A healthy community does not lower its moral expectations; indeed, it often raises them. But those expectations are aimed at growth, not compliance—at formation, not sorting. There are no watchtowers, gates, or checkpoints—no tests of sameness before love is given. Fortresses use standards to sift and segregate. Villages use them to call people upward and to walk with them as they rise. Paul wrote, "Ye are no more strangers and foreigners, but fellow citizens with the saints" (Ephesians 2:19). Not visitors, not suspects, but fellow citizens.

That is the paradox of our time: We speak constantly of the gathering of Israel, yet gathering is impossible in a culture that sorts, sifts, and segregates. A fortress cannot gather; it can only admit or exclude. Gathering requires openness, warmth, and space—soil where people feel safe enough to bring their whole selves and strong enough to be changed. When love is strong and expectations are used to elevate rather than divide, the courage and trust of a village make the walls of a fortress unnecessary.

Sara and I were set apart by Elder Holland and Elder Bednar in Elder Holland's office. Sara was first. Elder Holland invited all the priesthood holders to stand in the circle, and they all joined him—except for Cale, five years past his departure from the Church. Cale understood the expectations for standing in that circle and remained seated, suddenly isolated in a crowded room, completely alone in his otherness, and the heaviness of that hung in the air.

After a moment, Elder Holland looked to Cale and said, "Cale, we would love to have you join us." Elder Holland understood the standard better than anyone, but he also knew something far more important was at stake. With one simple gesture, he taught us all a powerful lesson on who belongs. Fortresses guard. Villages gather. And people stay where they feel they belong.

What does gathering look like for people going through faith transition? They need open dialogue that encourages honest conversations about faith transition, doubt, and different interpretations of history and doctrine. They need inclusivity that welcomes diversity of belief and practices within the Church community. They need active listening and support regardless of their current beliefs. They need help with Church culture that stigmatizes questioning and promotes a binary view of belief. They need an environment where people can express concerns, ask questions, and engage in discussion about complex faith issues without fear of repercussion. And, perhaps most importantly, they need Church leaders who model humility, openness to questions, and acceptance of unique and different faith journeys.

From Bunker to School—Transformation

A bunker protects what is precious, but it also shuts out light. The cost of constant shelter is stagnation. Doubt goes underground instead of being explored and conquered. A bunker preserves safety, but it inhibits faith and slowly suffocates our capacity to grow. Most people stay where they feel they are becoming better because growth creates hope and joy.

Life is a school, not a bunker. A school trusts growth enough to welcome inquiry. It does not prevent storms but prepares us to walk through them with Christ. It assumes God is present in the struggle. Questioning is part of the lesson, not a character flaw. Refinement comes through heat, not avoidance. A bunker protects; a school transforms.

From Soldier to Student—Choice and Responsibility

When a soldier blindly obeys, instruction replaces the capacity for inquiry. Obedience becomes the default posture even when discernment is what God invites us to develop. When agency gives way to compliance, we lose the very capacity discipleship is meant to cultivate.

Students live differently than soldiers. They wrestle, ask, seek, experiment, and act. They learn truth—not just rules—and then choose, taking accountability for their choices. They learn to partner with God and carry the weight of responsibility. They grow through accountability not by surrendering it to those with more authority. They trust that intelligence—not compliance—is the gospel building block of truth and light (see Doctrine & Covenants 93:36).

We often build fences to keep people in or out, but fences do not create belonging—they only create boundaries. We can choose to offer wells of living water that draw people in because they know they will find love and belonging and opportunities to grow. People don't leave living water because they know they need it.

From Subordinate to Child of God—Harmony

Sameness is tidy but fragile. Uniformity can feel safe, but it cannot produce deep growth. When unity becomes conformity, people shrink to fit the mold. Some stay silent. Others pretend or disappear. Such a community may appear stable and healthy on the surface, but one significant challenge can fracture it. Conformity may create order, but it cannot create Zion.

God's children are not carbon copies. Because they are different, they contribute in different ways, as Paul taught: "The eye cannot say unto the hand, I have no need of thee" (1 Corinthians 12:21). Difference is not a flaw in the body of Christ; it is a strength. Elder Holland expressed it simply: "There is room in this choir for all who wish to be here."[13] A children-of-God community does not ask people to fit in. It makes space for who God is inspiring them to become.

Zion is not the triumph of sameness; it is the flourishing of divinely created differences. It is harmony, not uniformity; a body, not a battalion.

The Harvest

The crops in a harvest do not appear fully grown. A harvest begins quietly—when we believe despite fear, love through uncertainty, stay soft when wounded, and show up when we'd rather turn away. It begins with faith in Christ, in one another, and in the possibility that soil can be healed. We call it Zion. Zion's soil is not safety and conformity; it is life. In a community shaped by Christ, we build connections instead of guard towers. We pass bread rather than judgment. We see people not as problems to fix but as souls to be loved. One seat always remains open. One light always stays on.

Zion will not arrive by force, spectacle, or declaration. It will grow the way a garden grows: root by root, neighbor by neighbor, act by quiet act. Not imposed—cultivated. Not uniform—beautifully varied. Not guarded—growing. Not someday—now.

Jesus Christ taught us to examine the soil to see what lies beneath the surface of our faith and community. He showed us how to prepare the soil that we might nourish, understand, and believe in ways that deepen roots and strengthen hearts. He invited us to cultivate the soil to practice acceptance, transcend fear, honor agency, and create harmony in difference. And in all of this, He calls us to bring forth good fruit—not through perfection but through His grace.

This is His harvest—a community where every soul can take root and rise. And when Zion comes, it will be because our love was greater than our fear.

Key Chapter Takeaway

Fear produces predictable outcomes that weaken trust and belonging. Renewal grows quietly through consistent acts of faith, love, and patience, producing life-giving fruit.

Reflection Questions

1. What kind of fruit does my participation in Church culture produce?

2. How do fear or trust shape my responses to others? How do I see them manifest in others?

3. What can I do to invest in rich and loving relationships?

Application Suggestion

Pay attention to your responses in moments of tension. Do you respond with faith or fear? Choose to invest in relationships even and especially when outcomes are uncertain. Focus your discipleship on good fruit: love, patience, trust, and healing. When faith leads, healthier relationships and spiritual vitality follow.

CHAPTER 12

BECOMING A GARDENER

**"For the power is in them,
wherein they are agents unto themselves."
—Doctrine & Covenants 58:28**

Stewardship

Who is responsible to care for the soil? Doctrine and Covenants 58 was given during a moment of deep frustration and disappointment for the early Saints. They had been commanded to gather to Missouri, which the Lord identified as Zion. Many expected something immediate and confirming—peace, prosperity, unity, and clear evidence that God was establishing His kingdom among them.

Instead, they encountered hardship. Poverty, internal conflict, hostility from others, disorganization, and unmet expectations marked their experience. Zion did not look the way they imagined.

Joseph sought the Lord's guidance. Why was this so hard? Why wasn't He intervening more clearly? Why did uncertainty and strain accompany their devotion? The Lord's response did not rebuke the Saints for their faithfulness, but it did correct their expectations. He taught them that Zion would not be built all at once, that blessings often followed trials, and that growth came through experience, opposition, and moral agency, not through constant instruction or immediate relief.

In that context, the Lord taught that it is not commendable to be "commanded in all things" and that faithful people are expected to learn, discern, and act without being compelled or directed. Then came the affirmation: The power is in *them*. This was not a withdrawal of divine guidance. It was an expression of divine trust. The Lord was saying, in effect, I have given you truth, principles, intelligence, and agency. Now I expect *you* to act wisely and bring to pass much righteousness of *your* own free will.

That pattern—faithfulness without the need for constant certainty, responsibility without control, trust without guarantees—has never been more relevant than it is today. I have intentionally held back throughout this book in sharing exactly what I think we should do. Instead, I have sought to build understanding. That restraint is not uncertainty. It is trust. I trust what faithful members of the Church do when they are well-informed. I trust their devotion to Jesus Christ, their moral intuition, and their capacity to act with wisdom and love.

For that reason, I don't offer prescriptions. Some of you will be grateful for that. Others will want help translating these ideas into real life. For those who want it, what follows is not instruction but a few thought starters.

1. Begin with Self

**"The greatest battle of life is fought
within the silent chambers of your own soul."[1]
—President David O. McKay**

Being a Christlike cultivator always begins with the heart. Before we engage others—before we respond to questions, disagreement, or distance—we must do our own work. That work is often quiet and unseen. It involves sitting with complexity, living with unresolved tension, and becoming grounded enough that difference does not feel threatening.

Many cultural problems are not driven by bad intentions but by insecurity and the need to protect certainty, authority, or identity at all costs. When we have not done our own integrating work, we are far more likely to react reflexively or reach for control where the Savior would invite trust. Until we are steady within ourselves, our efforts to help others will almost always be diminished by fear. Here is how that might look for someone ready to take it on.

Holding Two Truths at Once

For a long time, he tried to carry the tension. On one side was a deep loyalty to the Church—the people who had shaped him, the language of faith that still felt like home, the conviction that something sacred lived there, even if imperfectly. Walking away was never the question. He didn't want distance. He wanted less dissonance.

On the other side was an unease he couldn't dismiss. It began with Church history he hadn't known about. Over time, other things gathered around it—watching people he loved feel unseen, sitting through lessons that felt hollow, sensing a growing gap between conscience and culture. It wasn't theoretical. It was real.

What troubled him most wasn't the questions but the lack of belonging. He still believed in Christ. He still prayed. But the Church no longer felt like a place where his full conscience fit.

Eventually, he stopped trying to make the tension disappear. Instead, he learned to hold the Church with open hands—to stay but without pretending, to love but without defending, to trust God but without needing everything to feel settled.

The tension remained but found its place. And from there, he found himself on steadier ground.

2. Start Where You Have Stewardship

Once we are internally grounded, cultivation moves outward—to the places where we have stewardship: our marriages, families, friendships, and local church community. Stewardship does not require authority. It requires connection and care. Culture changes when ordinary people choose connection over correction in moments that matter. Here's an example:

Choosing Presence over Answers

They sat across from each other at the kitchen table.

"I'm not trying to tear anything down," his daughter said. "I still believe in God. I just didn't expect Church history to feel this destabilizing. And when I'm at church lately, I feel invisible."

He nodded.

"I don't want to become cynical," she added. "But I also don't want to pretend this is okay when I feel like it is not."

He felt the pull to respond—to explain, to reassure, to fix. Instead, he asked, "What part has been the hardest to deal with?"

She paused. "Not knowing what it means if I don't get clean answers. And not knowing where I belong while I'm figuring that out."

"That makes sense," he said quietly. "I am here to help," he added. "I just want you to know you don't have to sort it out alone and whatever you decide, nothing changes with me."

Nothing was resolved. But when they stood up, the distance between them was smaller.

3. When Stewardship Includes Authority

Some of the most consequential moments in Church culture happen behind closed doors, when a member speaks honestly to a Church leader. In those moments, trust is either preserved or quietly lost. Here's a positive example:

Authority without Control

"I'm not trying to be difficult," Mark said. "I just feel increasingly out of place. Some of the history troubles me, and some of the policies don't sit right with my conscience."

The bishop listened, hands folded. He felt the familiar pressure to explain the doctrine, to protect boundaries, to steady things. Instead, he collected himself before responding.

"Thank you for trusting me with this," he said. "Can you help me understand what part has been hardest for you?"

When Mark finished, the bishop nodded. "I want you to know something," he said. "I've had some of these same questions myself. They're good questions."

He didn't offer answers. He didn't redirect.

"Your honesty doesn't change your place here," he added. "We need people here with your courage and heart. Know you are among friends."

Nothing was resolved, but trust was strengthened.

4. Choosing Love without Agreement

They had known each other since childhood—Primary songs and youth conferences, late-night talks and shared prayers. They were college roommates, navigating into adulthood side by side. Their lives had taken different paths since then, but the bond remained.

"I need you to know," she said, hands wrapped around her hot chocolate mug, "this isn't about being offended—or wanting distance from you. I've tried for a long time to make it work. I just don't feel at peace here."

Her friend listened but didn't interrupt despite an unwelcome ache.

"I still believe in, but not the way I used to," she continued. "I still pray. But the way I experience the Church now—what it asks me to hold, what it asks me to set aside—it doesn't work anymore. I need to step back so I can live honestly."

There was a pause. Grief, yes, but not alarm.

"I won't pretend that doesn't hurt," her friend said quietly. "I love this Church and believe deeply in it. It's where I've found meaning. But I love you more than I love the idea that we need to believe the same way." She reached across the table. "You don't have to justify yourself to me. And you don't lose me because you're choosing a different path."

Tears came then—tears of relief mixed with sadness.

"I was afraid this would be the end of us," she said.

"It's not," her friend replied. "We still share so much—our faith, love, our values, our concern for others. We can honor what we see differently without erasing what we still hold together."

Nothing was resolved. Their paths would look different going forward. But the friendship remained—changed but intact. And both knew that whatever belief produced, their relationship was strong enough to hold it.

5. Resist the Illusion of Control

One of the most damaging distortions in Church culture is the belief that faithfulness requires control—over beliefs, outcomes, or other people's journeys. God does not cultivate faith through coercion. He invites, walks alongside, and allows people to choose—even when those choices bring Him, or us, pain. "And it came to pass that the God of heaven looked upon the residue of the people, and he wept" (Moses 7:28). Here is one example of how that might work.

When the Right Choice Still Feels Heavy

The Relief Society president lingered in the empty room after the meeting, replaying the conversation in her mind. She relived the frustration, the hurt, the temptation to explain. She had chosen restraint. Now doubt crept in. Had she done enough? Had she done too little?

That evening, she sent a single text: "I was grateful for our conversation yesterday. It helped me understand where you are coming from and even my own concerns better—and to know that I have a friend in my own questions and struggles."

The unease remained. But it was quieter—and the fact that it was shared made it easier.

A Field Guide You Can Carry with You

What these moments have in common is not resolution but orientation. When tension rises, a few reminders can help steady us:

- **Steadiness before engagement**
- **Relationship before resolution**
- **Curiosity before counsel**
- **Belonging before agreement**
- **Restraint is not weakness**
- **Measure fruit, not closure**

These principles do not remove tension. They allow faith to breathe inside it.

Sharing This Book or Its Insights without Fear

For some, the hardest part of living these principles is not practicing them but sharing them. Many may resonate deeply with the ideas in this book and still hesitate to pass them along, worried they might be misunderstood or received as pressure.

Sharing a part of yourself is an act of love, not control. If it helps, here are a few ways people have shared these ideas while preserving dignity and trust:

- "I didn't agree with everything, but it helped me be more patient and loving."

> ❯ "There are parts of this I see differently, but some insights really helped me."

> ❯ "No pressure—there were just a few ideas that helped me understand people better."

> ❯ "I'd genuinely love to hear what you think, even if you disagree."

It is okay that people think and feel differently. Conformity is not the goal. Understanding, dignity, and being one in Christ are.

Key Chapter Takeaway

Many assume cultural renewal is the responsibility of others. Change begins when we accept stewardship for the culture we shape through our everyday choices.

Reflection Questions

1. How can I shape the Church culture around me?

2. What personal responsibility have I been deferring to others?

3. What is one way I can cultivate the soil differently this week?

Application Suggestion

Identify one relationship where faith or Church experience has created tension. Consider your mindset and feelings in this relationship. Notice what you feel tempted to protect—certainty, influence, being right. Then choose one response rooted in trust rather than control.

Afterward, measure the fruit. Did it increase trust? Preserve dignity? Strengthen connection? Christ taught that truth is known by what it produces. Let that be the standard.

Conclusion

We can show each other our scars, to teach and to serve as reminders
that wounds heal. And we can walk with each other, as Christ would
do, out into the uncertain terrain, the land where Christ finds his
sheep and makes them into shepherds full of scars just like Him.
—Cale Strong, Unpublished Essay, 2025

This book began—and will end—with Cale. Thirteen years have
passed since the morning I opened his unexpected MTC email
and was torn, the moment that altered both our journeys and the
journey of our entire family, a moment experienced by so many of us.
It is true, as others observe, that life is understood only in hindsight.
Looking back, I see a young man who longed for what was real—the
fruit Lehi called "most sweet"—the kind that feeds a soul instead of
simply directing it. He believed in that promise because our Church
taught him to. He left because he could not find that fruit on a tree that,
to him, had gone barren, its soil hardened and crowded with stones
and thorns and unable to nourish a soul like his.

Disaffiliation is a crisis of trust born in a culture where the soil in
too many places has become compacted and depleted. The imbalances we have explored—standards over acceptance, sanctuary over

transcendence, fealty over agency, and conformity over harmony—do not reflect the teachings of Jesus Christ, yet they powerfully shape the day-to-day experience of our people. When the soil carries these imbalances—too hard, too shallow and stony, too crowded, or capable of nurturing only one kind of plant—even the most faithful can feel hunger.

Renewal begins in the smallest of places—in how we listen, respond, and make room for others. Culture changes when we reclaim the heart of the gospel, seeing as Christ sees, loving as He loves, and meeting people where they are rather than where we wish they were. We do not need new programs or new rhetoric. We need to loosen the soil, move the heavy stones that stop growth, and create space so Christ's light can shine on us.

Cale's experience is not unique. We're all connected to people in tension, in and out of the Church. When we begin to look at one another with a little more patience and kindness, the work of renewal becomes simpler than we think. It happens when we accept that other people's experience in the Church might be vastly different from our own. It happens when we understand that God does not lead and nourish everyone in the same way. It happens when we remove our "headlamps" and discover light outside the cone of our limited perspective.

My dream was simple: that Cale might walk the path I walked, only better. But our paths were never meant to be the same. His path is his own, and God walks with him as I watch in wonder. The deeper truth is this: It isn't about the path; it is about the fruit. We eat the fruit, not the gravel. And who are we to presume that God grows that fruit in only one orchard?

Sara and I have five children. Cale left first. Zach followed more slowly, also searching unsuccessfully for fruit on this tree. Samantha, our oldest, left next. Despite her disillusionment predating her younger brothers', she waited the longest, and by then she had a husband and three children, which meant a more complex web of concerns and impacts influencing her choice.

Like Chava in *Fiddler on the Roof,* Samantha "left our village" after we returned from our mission. When she wrote to tell us, her letter carried love, respect, conviction, and the weight and pain of leaving something her parents cherished. What she wrote afterward—her poem—became our Tevye-and-Chava moment. It is reflection, spoken in hindsight, from the heart of a parent who sees that a beloved child must go not to wound them but because staying wounds the child. The parent speaks first to their child and then turns to others who are hesitating on their own riverbanks—sharing what love and faith have to offer.

The Other Side

I see in your chart that you're fading away.
I see in your eyes that it's for me you stay.
The drip marks the seconds, and I'll be OK.
Go make light on the other side.

There's a time to take cover and a time to run bold.
Crescendo to confusion when caring runs cold.
So now is your moment—run free from the fold,
And make peace on the other side.

The river runs muddy where it used to run clear.
The river runs thicker and slower this year.
She crossed in a current of phantoms and fear,
And made fire on the other side.

The border is a whisper, a wander, a wall.
The border is not with her, not for her at all.
One hand on the Bible, she watched them all fall,
And made home on the other side.

I often wish the river between those who stay and those who leave did not exist. It is a burden we—not God—have created. Our fears, not His living water, fill it. It feels perilous to us; it is not perilous to Him. They are not lost to us, nor are they lost to God. We belong to each other. We always will. A cultural river cannot undo what God has done.

If Tevye could speak to Chava again, I believe he would want a second chance—not to change her choice or his but to quiet his fear and walk with her to the water's edge with his blessing.

Many may assume crossing the river represents leaving the Church—and that assumption makes it feel terrifying. But the river is not about leaving the Church or abandoning faith. It is about leaving fear. It is not a crossing away from God but a crossing with Him.

Crossing the river is choosing faith over fear—growth over stagnation, honesty over appearance. Where people stand afterward may differ, but what they are reaching for is the same: the life and fruit Christ promised. The real divide is not between staying and leaving but between fear and faith—and that is where we are torn.

Our history is imperfect, but we are not our history. Our doctrines are unfinished, but we are not our doctrines. Our policies sometimes fall short, but we are not defined by them. What defines us is the soil we cultivate together, the culture that shapes how the gospel is lived and experienced not by those who lived two hundred years ago but by us—right now. Culture is where that happens. It is the soil where everything either grows or withers.

Lehi saw a tree whose fruit filled the soul with joy. Alma taught that the same seed could flourish or fail as a tree depending on how it was nourished. The seed and fruit were not in question—they came from God. The soil was the question because God left its cultivation to us. Alma taught:

> **If we neglect the soil,**
> **the tree "hath no root" and withers.**
> **But if we "nourish it with great care,"**
> **it grows strong and bears fruit**
> **"sweet above all that is sweet."**
> **(Alma 32:37)**

When we insist there is fruit on a barren tree, we will never have the wisdom or courage to solve the problems in the soil. The future of the Restoration and our Church depends not on our past or our policies but on our culture. Some believe the answer is to double down—to harden the soil, revere the stones, and fortify the thorns. I am suggesting a different way.

The Church will not be defeated by the things from our past or the outside. Its greatest threat is becoming hollow, performative, less nourishing, and less alive to those who hunger for God and need it most.

> When faith is crowded out by certitude,
> when transformation is bartered for security,
> when connection hardens into conformity,
> when policies outweigh people,
> when the past overshadows the present, and
> when authority steps on grace,
> we lose the power to reach, change, and heal hearts.
> Our tree becomes barren, unable to feed the souls who come
> hungry for God.
> In such moments, we are not defeated by the world. We are
> defeated by ourselves.

The children of Israel once stood at the Jordan on the border between the wilderness and the land God promised them. They, too, faced a river that felt deeper than they could cross. It parted when the soles of their feet were wet, and then God led them out of their wilderness and into their promised land on dry ground (see Joshua 3:13–17).

We will not cross our river by a narrowed view of who is acceptable, defending stones, or fortifying thorns. We cross when, together, we step into the river with honesty and trust and when we walk with those we love, trusting that the God who moved the Jordan for Israel will move what stands in our way.

I believe that Christ is with us regardless of which side of the river we stand on. And He will be with us as we cross. He can help us make the soil good again for more of us, and the tree can bear fruit again. And we may discover—on both sides of the river—that with Him, however we have been torn, we can be whole again.

Research Methodology Summary

Purpose and Scope

Strong and Dotson, *Why People Are Leaving,* 2025 examines disaffiliation in The Church of Jesus Christ of Latter-day Saints (LDS). Disaffiliation is defined here as formerly active and faithful members who no longer participate, some of whom still consider themselves members but do not participate and have no desire to, some who no longer consider themselves members, and some who've had their names removed from Church records.

Its primary objectives are to understand how many are leaving, why they are leaving, and how respondents describe the role of LDS culture in both retention and departure. The study also explores how current and previously active members perceive the LDS culture—its strengths, weaknesses, origins, and degree of Christ-centeredness—and identifies the key cultural tensions shaping lived religious experience and disaffiliation in the Church. And finally, the study seeks to understand what the faith-transition experience is like and how respondents report that the experience influences relationships, retention, and belief.

The research focuses primarily on respondents residing in the United States, where approximately 40 percent of Church members live. A significant number of international responses were collected but were insufficient for reliable analysis and are therefore excluded. The study population includes both current members (ranging from highly active to moderately inactive) and former members at varying stages of disaffiliation, including those who are no longer members of record.

Research Design

The foundational dataset derives from a large-scale survey conducted in 2023 (n = 15,000). To aid in effective survey design, an extensive review of existing disaffiliation research, approximately a dozen focus groups, and twenty one-on-one depth interviews were conducted. The instrument included multiple-choice, Likert-scale, and open-ended questions identifying what people value in the Church, whether they have disaffiliated, and their reasons for staying or leaving. It also explored perceptions of LDS culture (belonging, judgment, openness, trust, etc.), spiritual and emotional well-being, leadership and community experiences, and collected demographic activity variables and religious-mindset typing data.

Four follow-up surveys were conducted between 2024 and 2025 to test, refine, and more thoroughly explore patterns that emerged in the initial study:

> Disaffiliation Wave and Religious Mindset Confirmation Study (2025, n = 2,306)

> Faith-Transition Experience and Culture Deep Dive Study (2024, n = 1,250)

> Cultural-Tension Confirmation Study (2025, n = 1,168)

> Faith-Transition Conversations Study (2025, n = 754)

Each study integrated quantitative measures with open-ended qualitative responses. Given the vast scale of qualitative data generated, AI-assisted tools were used to support large-scale thematic coding and pattern identification, with human review and refinement.

Expert Oversight and Review

Our research was designed, reviewed, and refined with oversight from a highly qualified, multidisciplinary advisory group. The advisory team included numerous PhD-level scholars with extensive experience in statistics, sociology, psychology, organizational culture, leadership, and the academic study of religion, including research on religious disaffiliation and extensive prior research involving Latter-day Saints. The group also included senior research professionals with decades of experience in conducting large-scale survey research, demographic analysis, and institutional research, including extensive prior research for the Church.

Advisors reviewed the survey design, analytic approach, and interpretive framing to ensure methodological rigor, balance, and alignment with best practices in contemporary social science. Their involvement provided independent critique and expert guidance. Advisory input strengthened the design and interpretation of the study but does not eliminate the methodological limitations associated with nonprobability, self-selected sampling.

Sample Characteristics and Reliability

This study does not claim statistical representativeness of the full LDS population. Because no single comprehensive public sampling framework exists for current and former members—particularly those who have disaffiliated—probability sampling was not feasible. The study therefore uses a large, diverse, nonprobability sample designed to capture a broad spectrum of the lived LDS experience. Its findings are best interpreted as substantial descriptive and analytical insights rather than precise populations estimates or establishing causal relationships.

Respondents included a balanced mix of men and women across all adult age ranges (nineteen to eighty plus). Participants represented the full continuum of Church relationship and activity, including former members, inactive members, marginally active members, conflicted active members, and fully active members reporting strong satisfaction with the Church.

The sample shows a slight overrepresentation of women and a modest bias toward more devout and satisfied participants—patterns common in voluntary survey research. This may make some findings more conservative that they would be in a less devout sample, but it does not eliminate the broader limitations associated with self-selected participation.

Observed demographic characteristics such as age, gender, and geography were broadly consistent with external benchmark studies, although such alignment does not entirely eliminate potential selection effects on unobserved variables such as belief intensity, satisfaction, or motivation to participate.

Data Analysis and Ethics

Quantitative data was analyzed using descriptive and inferential statistical techniques, including subgroup comparisons. Qualitative data—representing more than ten thousand pages of verbatim responses—was analyzed using a hybrid approach combining AI-assisted thematic coding with multireviewer human validation to improve contextual accuracy and interpretive reliability.

Findings were further explored by conducting approximately twenty one-on-one interviews with a broad cross section of disaffiliated respondents.

Participation was voluntary and anonymous, with informed consent obtained at the start of each survey. No personally identifiable information was collected. The study adheres to the principles of the Belmont Report: respect for persons, beneficence, and justice.

A fully documented methodology including survey instruments, analytic procedures, qualitative coding frameworks, AI-assisted analysis procedures, and ethical documentation is available on the project website and can be accessed via our website, tornbyjeffstrong.com, or the QR code at the beginning of this book. Taken together, the study provides a large, diverse, and analytically rich data set that offers meaningful insight into patterns of LDS experience and disaffiliation while remaining subject to the inherent limitations of nonprobability, self-selected survey research.

Other Reliable Research Showing Significant LDS Disaffiliation

Multiple independent, large-scale studies report patterns consistent with significant Latter-day Saint disaffiliation over the last twenty-five years.

For example, the 2025 Harvard Cooperative Election Study (HCES) Report shows that an increasing gap between the official number of members reported by the Church and those who claim to be members of the Church has emerged in the United States over the past seventeen years—reaching 55 percent. This gap reflects a growing divergence between institutional membership counts and personal religious identification.

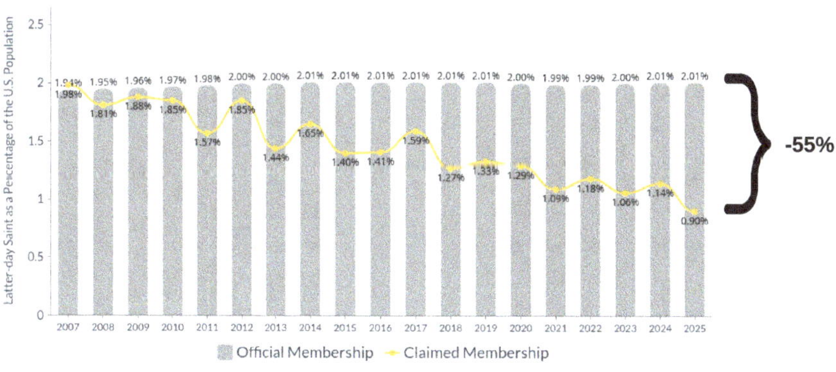

From a statistical perspective, the HCES report accurately captures the approximate magnitude of LDS disaffiliation trends. Its very large national sample size[1] minimizes random error, and comparisons with address-based benchmark studies show that HCES projections typically fall within a few percentage points of reality, making HCES trends credible evidence of real change over time, even if exact levels require confirmation from other sources, like our study.

There is a common narrative in the LDS community that, like all religions, we are losing members as more people in general disaffiliate from organized religion but that we are losing them at a much slower rate than other religions. Historically, that may have been true. But since 2009, that appears to no longer be the case. According to the HCES report, the number of people in the United States who claim membership in the Church is now declining at a *faster* rate than the other major groups, both religious and nonreligious, included in the study.

Since 2009, the Percent of U.S. Citizens Who Claim Membership in The Church of Jesus Christ of Latter-day Saints Has Declined More Than Any Other Denomination/Group

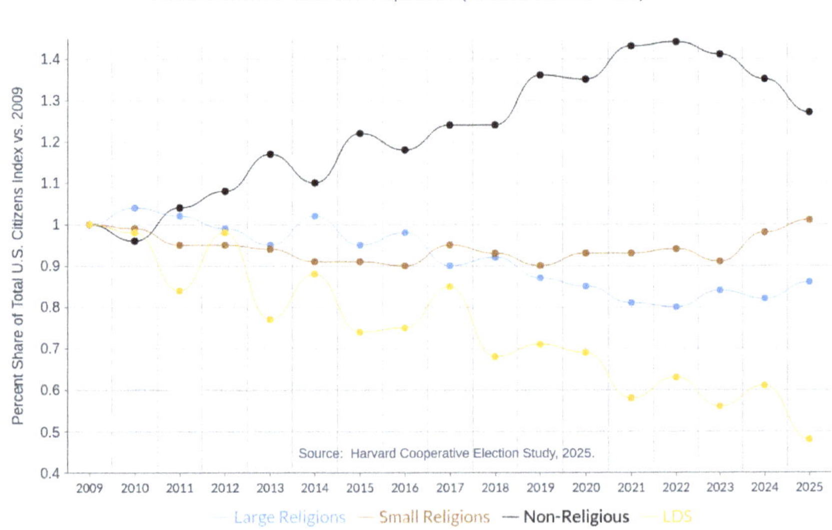

Comparing claimed membership in a single denomination to claimed membership in groups consisting of many denominations likely overstates relative disaffiliation for the single denomination. A much more accurate comparison can be made by comparing all available individual denominations included in their data set. Using this approach also indicates people claiming to be latter day Saints has declined more than every other denomination in the HCES study.

While comparing denomination-specific disaffiliation, as shown in the chart on the next page, is more precise than grouping broad religious categories, it should still be interpreted with some caution. Differences in how religious identity functions across traditions can obscure true disaffiliation rates. For example, higher birth rates and active proselytizing within the Church of Jesus Christ of Latter-day Saints introduce new members into the population, which should, in theory, sustain or increase identification—meaning the observed decline may actually understate underlying losses. At the same time, other dynamics may work in the opposite direction: some traditions retain nominal or cultural identification even after individuals disengage, and others experience significant internal switching between sects within a denomination, both of which can mask disaffiliation elsewhere and make Latter-day Saint declines appear relatively larger by comparison. Taken together, these factors suggest the data should be evaluated cautiously—but they do not negate the central finding that the Church is experiencing a meaningful and concerning loss of identification.

Since 2009, the Share of U.S. Citizens Claiming Membership in The Church of Jesus Christ of Latter-day Saints Has Declined More Than Any Other Denomination or Group

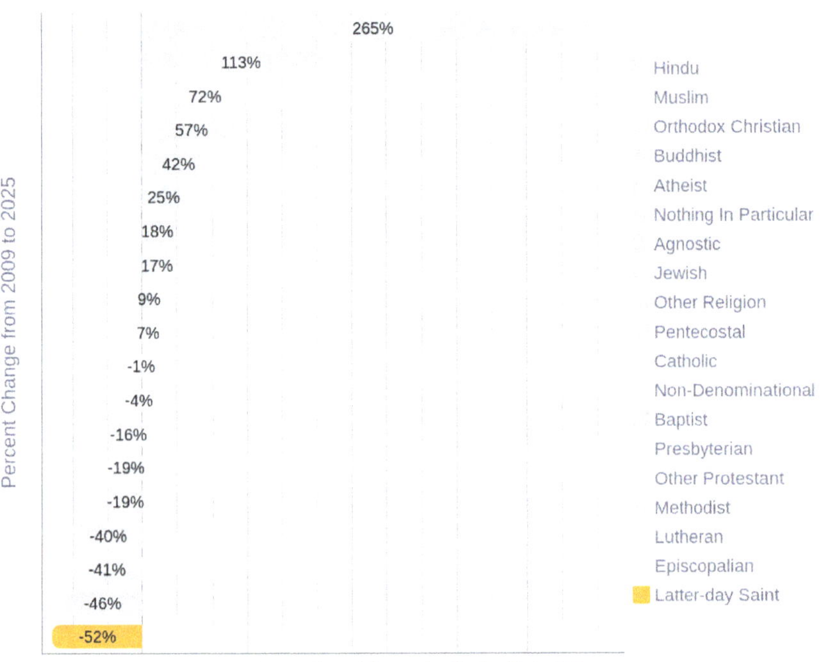

Source: Harvard Cooperative Election Study, 2025.

The HCES alone is compelling. Other credible studies support a similar conclusion. The Pew Research Center Religious Landscape (PRL) studies, also large sample size studies,[2] show a significant drop in affiliation among Latter-day Saints ages eighteen to twenty-nine who were raised in the faith declining from 75 percent in 2007 to 56 percent in 2024.

What percent of those raised as Latter-day Saints in the U.S. still affiliate at ages 18–29?

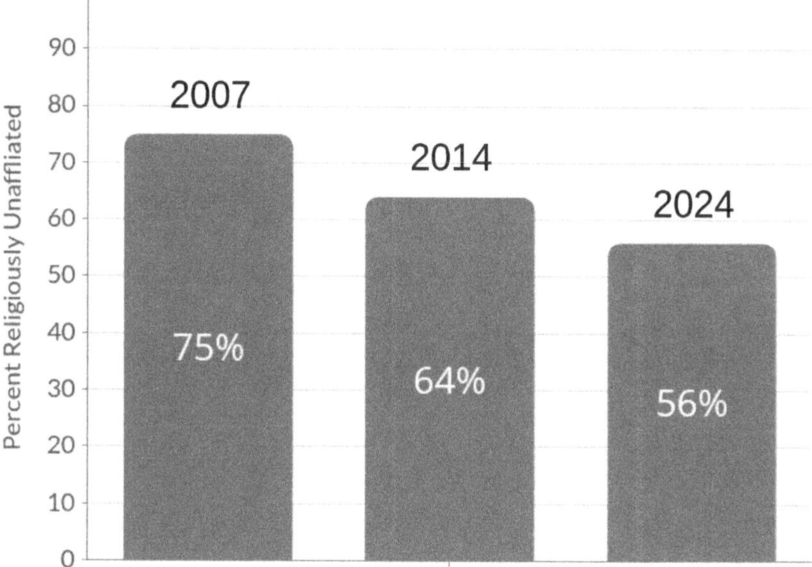

Source: Pew Research Center, U.S. Religious Landscape Studies (2007, 2014, 2024).

Though less reliable than the HCES and PRL reports due to much smaller sample size,[3] the General Social Survey (GSS) shows similar LDS disaffiliation. According to the GSS, the percent of those raised LDS who remain in the faith as adults has declined from 77 percent in the 1970s and 1980s to 38 percent in the 2020s—a nearly 50 percent reduction.

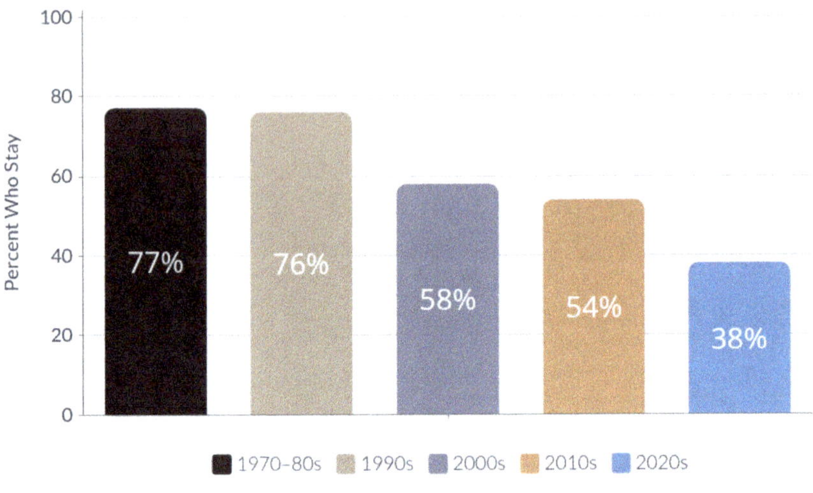

Like the Harvard study, the PRL and GSS studies suggest that LDS disaffiliation is not only significant but increasing at a faster rate than that of other major religious groups. Again, the complexities cited on page 243 require that we view these comparative numbers very cautiously.

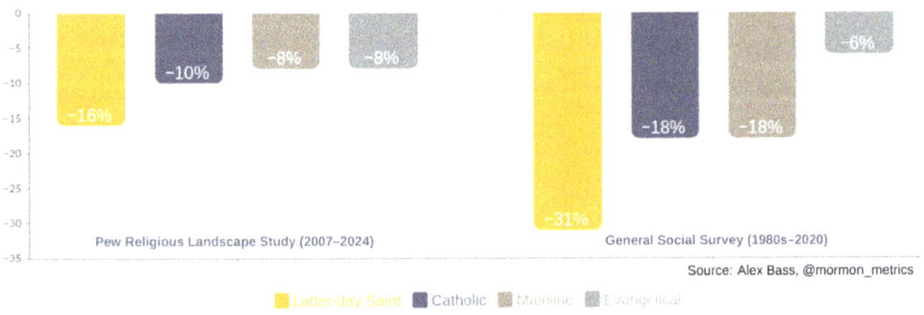

In addition to the possibility of the fastest increasing disaffiliation, Latter-day Saints are experiencing among the largest declines in positive religious practices, like church attendance, prayer, and scripture reading as well as in attitudes, like the importance of religion and certain belief in God.[4] Importantly, even with these declines Latter-day Saints compare very favorably to most other denominations.

GSS and Pew also both show a pronounced increase in disaffiliation in the LDS heartland. A GSS study showed a 432 percent increase in LDS disaffiliation in the Intermountain states since 2000.[5]

Intermountain State LDS Disaffiliation Has Increased Dramatically Since 2000

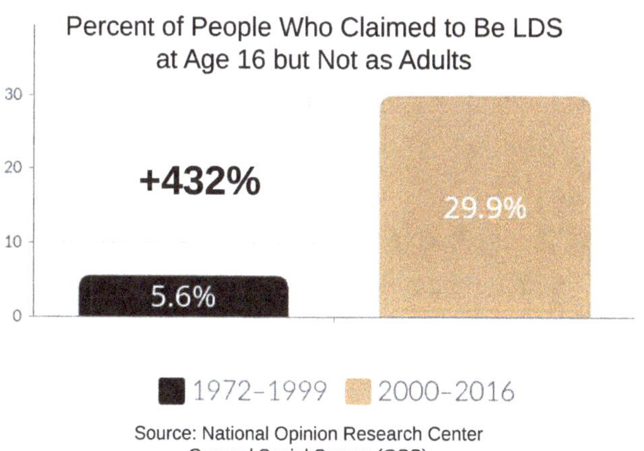

Source: National Opinion Research Center
General Social Survey (GSS)

The Pew study showed that the percent of citizens who identify as religious "nones" (i.e., when asked regarding their religious affiliation, they answer "none") increased 111 percent in Utah between 2008 and 2022, the largest increase of any state.

The Percent of People Claiming No Religion ("Nones") Grew Faster in Utah Than Any Other State in the U.S.

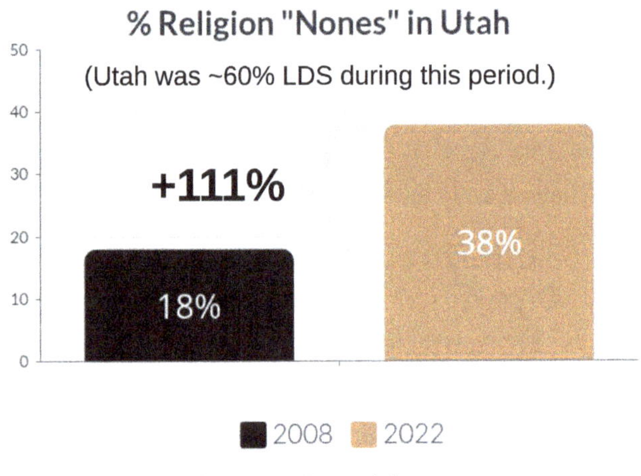

Source: Pew Research Center

Given the smaller sample size of the GSS study, it should not be relied upon for precise results but can be viewed as a reasonable directional estimate of broader trends, particularly when supported by strong studies like the Harvard and Pew reports and our study, which all indicate the same magnitude of disaffiliation.

This data alone might suggest a negative view of the health and vitality of the LDS community, but that would be incomplete and inaccurate. In "Latter-day Saint Religiousness, Well-Being, and Retention in the United States," BYU professors W. Justin Dyer, Jenet J. Erickson, Sam A. Hardy, Barbara Morgan Gardner, and David C. Dollahite analyze national and original survey data to better understand the patterns of belief, practice, and retention among Latter-day Saints. They found that Latter-day Saints consistently rank among the highest of all U.S. religious groups in core measures of religiosity and faith engagement. They report higher levels of church attendance, daily prayer, and regular scripture study, along with an exceptionally strong belief in God and the importance of religion in daily life.

Latter-day Saints also demonstrate high levels of family-centered religious practice, service, and charitable behavior.

According to the Dyer et al. study, these patterns are closely associated with elevated measures of purpose, life satisfaction, and overall well-being, reflecting a community marked by deep commitment, active participation, and strong social and spiritual cohesion.[6]

These findings are confirmed by Alex Bass's work, which shows relatively strong LDS religious devotion in many areas.

Latter-day Saints Exhibit Strong Religious Devotion Compared to Other Religions

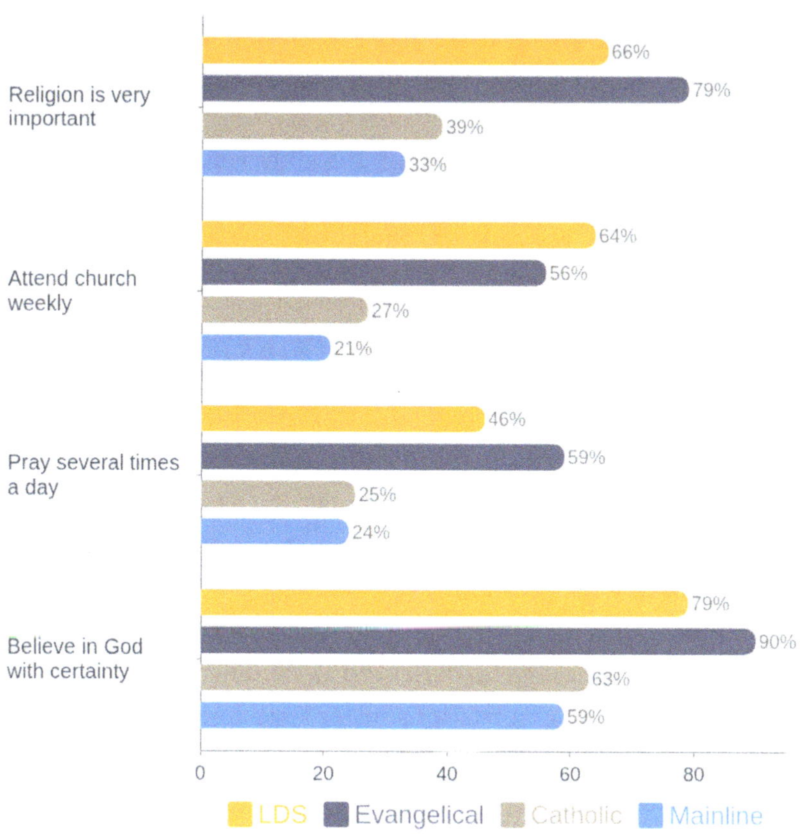

Source: @mormon_metrics data: Cooperative Election Study 2024; Pew Religious Landscape Study 2024.

What About LDS Disaffiliation by Gender?

One of the clearest findings of Dyer et al. is a distinct gender pattern: There's a sharper generational decline in retention for Latter-day Saint women than for men. While older women remain affiliated at rates near 60 percent, younger women—particularly around age eighteen—are closer to 40 percent. Men, by contrast, remain relatively stable, at 50 to 60 percent across age groups. The authors conclude that this reflects a significant generational shift, with younger Latter-day Saint women markedly less likely to remain identified with the Church than both older women and their male peers.[7]

In conclusion, though Latter-day Saints are disaffiliating in large numbers, those who stay remain highly devout and are find meaning, satisfaction, and purpose. What these contrasting views suggest is a religious community that is not working for a significant number of members who are disengaging from the faith, while it's working well for a core of committed, satisfied members. It reveals a culture struggling to meet the needs of both groups.

Across multiple data sources—including my study, the Harvard Cooperative Election Study, Pew Research Center, and the General Social Survey—the conclusion is clear: Significant disaffiliation is occurring within the Church of Jesus Christ of Latter-day Saints. The data also suggests that, since 2009, this decline may be greater than that of many other denominations, though such comparisons should be interpreted with appropriate caution and may be incorrect. Ultimately, however, the question of whether we are doing better or worse than others is not the most important one. Disaffiliation is not experienced as a statistic—it is experienced as the quiet absence of people we love. And while comparisons may preoccupy us, they can also distract from the more urgent reality: A growing number of those we care about are no longer participating in the life of the Church. *Importantly, we were unable to locate any widely cited, methodologically rigorous studies that directly contradict that significant LDS disaffiliation is highly likely.*

Testing the Validity of Our 40 Percent Disaffiliation Estimate

Appendix B summarizes several independent studies suggesting substantial Latter-day Saint disaffiliation in the United States over the past twenty-five years. The purpose of this appendix is to examine the same question from a different perspective. Rather than relying on survey data regarding religious identification, this analysis uses a simple statistical model to estimate how many formerly active members stopped participating between 2000 and 2024.

This model does not propose an exact number. It establishes a probable range based on statistical constraints. The constraints described below suggest that our 40 percent estimate is not only possible but likely conservative.

A Simple Demographic Constraint

Every religious community grows or declines through a limited set of demographic forces:

Inflows

- Convert baptisms
- Children born into member families

Outflows

- Deaths
- Disaffiliation

If we know the number of members of record, the number of congregations, and typical attendance patterns, we can estimate the approximate number of active participants at a given time. Comparing those estimates across time makes it possible to identify a range of how many formerly active members have stopped participating.

Step 1: Membership Growth Was Significant

The Church publishes official membership statistics annually. United States membership grew significantly between 2000 and 2024.

Year	U.S. Members of Record
2000	~4.24 million
2024	~6.80 million

Increase: ~2.56 million members, or 60 percent
Source: Annual Church statistical reports; Deseret Demographer analysis

Step 2: Congregation Growth Was Much More Modest

Congregation counts are also publicly reported each year.

Year	U.S. Congregations
2000	~11,500
2024	~12,760

Increase: ~1,260 congregations or 11 percent
Source: Church statistical reports; Fuller Consideration/Deseret Demographer

Step 3: Estimated Weekly Attendance Declined Significantly

An informed estimate of average ward sacrament meeting attendance is 100–150. We will use a midpoint estimate of 125 weekly attendees (as a simplifying assumption). Using an estimate of 125 attendees per congregation, weekly participation can be estimated as follows:

Year	Congregations	Average Attendance	Estimated Weekly Attendance
2000	11,500	125	~1.44 million
2024	12,760	125	~1.60 million

Despite membership growing by more than 60 percent, estimated weekly participation appears to have grown only modestly (about 11 percent).

Step 4: Participation Would Be Much Higher If Activity Rates Stayed Constant

Had activity rates remained stable since 2000, weekly attendance should have increased roughly in proportion to membership growth. Membership increased approximately 60 percent between 2000 and 2024. Applying that growth to 2000 attendance:

1.44 million × 1.60 ≈ 2.30 million expected weekly attendees

Actual estimated attendance:

≈ 1.60 million

Participation gap:

≈ 710,000 weekly attendees

Step 5: The Apparent Attendance Gap Indicates Significant Disaffiliation

Weekly attenders represent only part of the active population. Some active members attend every week, while others attend less frequently. To estimate the number of formerly active members implied by the ~710,000 weekly-attendance gap, this model converts different attendance patterns into a weekly-equivalent attendance rate. Monthly attendance is treated as twelve times per year, and low-frequency attendance as four times per year.

These estimates are derived by dividing the ~710,000 weekly-attendance gap by each scenario's weekly-equivalent attendance rate.

Scenario	Weekly	Monthly (12x/year)	4x/year	Weekly-Equivalent Rate	Estimated Disaffiliation
Low	73.8%	13.1%	13.1%	~77.8%	~912,000
Midpoint	60.0%	20.0%	20.0%	~66.2%	~1.07 million
High	49.8%	25.1%	25.1%	~57.5%	~1.23 million

Step 6: Our 40 Percent Estimate Is Reliable and, Likely, Conservative

To express disaffiliation as a share of the active population over time, the model compares total estimated disaffiliation to the average number of active members over the 2000–2024 period.

With the midpoint scenario, the weekly-equivalent attendance rate implies approximately 2.17 million active members in 2000. Had activity rates remained stable, that number would have grown to approximately 3.48 million by 2024. After accounting for an estimated disaffiliation of ~1.07 million, actual active membership in 2024 was approximately 2.40 million.

Assuming a roughly linear change over time (a simplifying assumption), average active membership during the period was therefore about 2.29 million. On that basis:

~1.07 million ÷ ~2.29 million ≈

46.9 percent

So, under the midpoint scenario, the model indicates:

Approximately 47 percent of formerly active members have disaffiliated since 2000.

Why the 40 Percent Estimate Is Valid and Conservative

Although the exact number cannot be known with certainty, several observations are clear.

First, membership growth alone cannot explain current participation levels. Had activity rates remained stable, weekly attendance would be dramatically higher.

Second, the size of the participation gap cannot be explained by deaths or record adjustments alone. The magnitude of the gap requires a substantial number of formerly active members to have stepped away.

Third, the resulting estimates align closely with the independent external research summarized in appendix B, including the Harvard CES study.

Taken together, these different lines of evidence suggest that the estimate used in this book—that approximately 40 percent of formerly active members have disaffiliated since 2000—is plausible and directionally consistent with independent data sources, like the Harvard CES and Pew Religious Landscape studies cited in appendix B.

Conclusion

While publicly available data cannot identify the exact number of Latter-day Saints who have disaffiliated during the past twenty-five years, statistical constraints provide strong boundaries on what is likely.

When official membership growth, congregation counts, and estimated participation levels are considered together, the data suggests that roughly one million—or more—formerly active members have stepped away since 2000. It could be higher or lower, but it is unlikely that it is significantly lower. So we conclude the 40 percent estimate to be reasonable.

DISAFFILIATION OUTSIDE THE UNITED STATES

The available data on Latter-day Saint participation outside the United States in our study was limited. What we provide here, from other sources, is a directional view of the best available information. We should be cautious about drawing strong conclusions at this point. Still, it is useful to consider compelling examples showing that disaffiliation is not a uniquely U.S. challenge.

Activity Levels in the Largest Countries Outside the United States

In Mexico and Brazil, the countries with the second and third largest populations of Latter-day Saints after the United States, there exists a dramatic difference between the official membership count of the Church and the number of people who claim membership on government censuses. The same holds true for Canada, though the gap is much smaller.

Additional data sources provide estimates of membership activity and disaffiliation outside the United States. One of those is Fuller Consideration's Deseret Demographer. Using a proprietary estimation methodology, they report that the percentage of members who are *fully* active (i.e., attending sacrament meeting at least forty times per year) in the countries with the largest membership centers outside the United States is about 14.5. If less active members are included, the

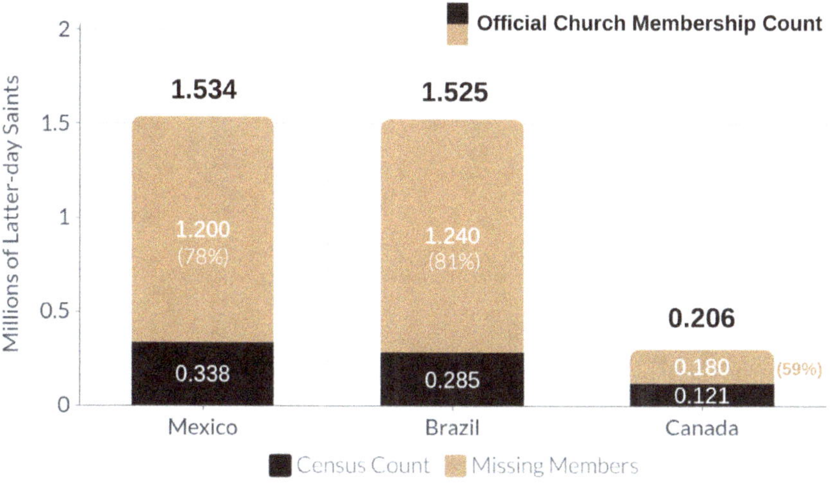

Gap between Official Church Membership Count and Government Census Counts in Mexico, Brazil, and Canada

Source: Mexico–Instituto Nacional de Estadistica y Geografia, Censo de Poblacion y Vivienda (CPV) 2020. Brazil–Instituto Brasileiro de Geografia e Estatistica, Censo Demographico, 2022. Canada–Statistics Canada (StatCan), Census of Population, 2021.

estimate of weekly sacrament meeting attendance in these countries increases to approximately 20 percent.

Six of the nine countries studied show declining participation, two show stable participation, and one shows increasing participation. These countries combined with the United States comprise approximately 75 percent of global Church membership.

While Fuller Consideration's methods are robust and may provide a reasonable estimate of actual activity levels, there is no way to verify, independent of the Church's own data, whether these estimates are accurate. They should be considered with that in mind.

There is also anecdotal data reported for the United Kingdom and Ireland that regular sacrament meeting attendance may be below 15 percent and could be as low as 11 percent of total members of record. Again, this data cannot be verified and should be considered accordingly.

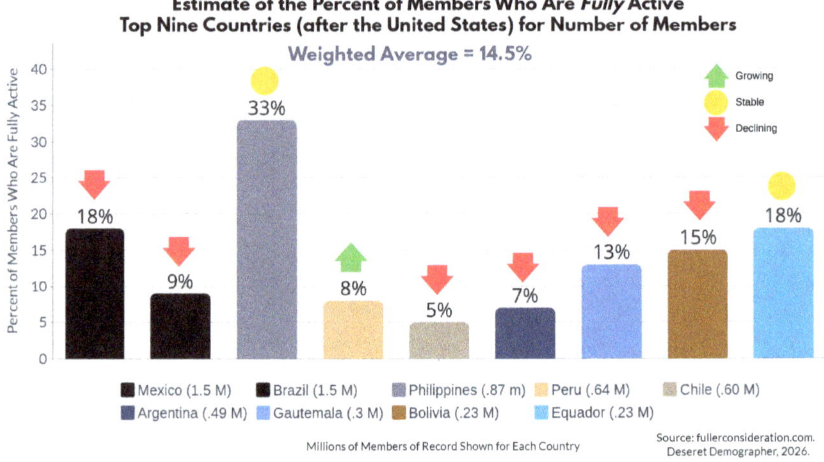

Importantly, many countries (primarily in Africa) with smaller membership numbers are experiencing strong growth, which is encouraging. But this does not appear to be the prevailing global trend.

Convert-Baptism Trends

Another narrative in the LDS community is that the Church is thriving because of recent missionary convert-baptism success. In 2025, there were approximately 385,490 convert baptisms. This figure was the largest ever with the second largest being 1997, when 317,798 people were baptized—an incredibly encouraging sign of recovery after nearly three decades of decline.[1]

It is common knowledge that the vast majority of converts do not remain active. Hopefully with the improvement in convert baptisms in 2024 and the unprecedented results in 2025, this long-term trend will change.

Whether this indicates real growth or simply having significantly more missions and more missionaries is less clear. According to the Church's statistics, converts per missionary have steadily declined from 7.6 in 1990 to 4.2 in 2024 (a decline of 45 percent). This is still the case despite noteworthy improvement from 2020 to 2023. Again, hopefully, this is the start of a positive trend. It is too early to tell.

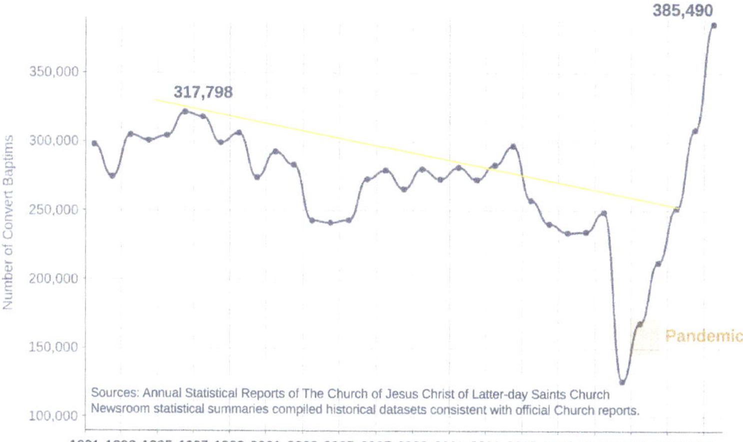

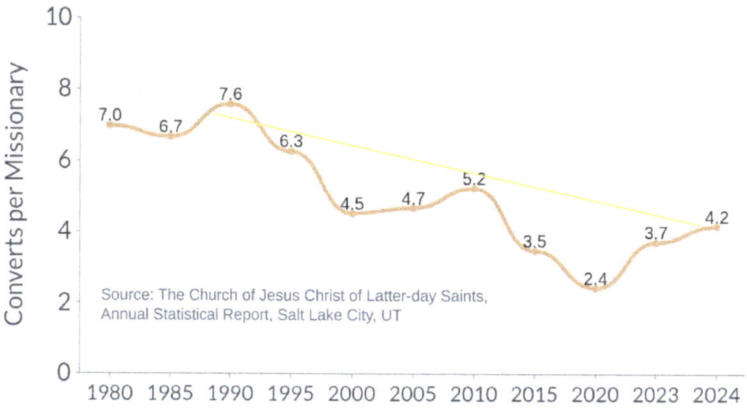

Importantly, convert baptisms and disaffiliation are, of course, not the same thing. It is entirely possible for people to simultaneously join the Church while others leave it. And as discussed earlier, the fact that member-of-record growth (+60 percent) has significantly outpaced congregation growth (+11 percent) over the past twenty-five years, another indicator that a very high number of converts do not remain active in the Church.

Reconciling Conflicting Narratives of Vitality or Disaffiliation

Because there exist contradictory narratives in our Church community about whether the Church is thriving, I often get the question: How can the Church be thriving in so many ways while also experiencing substantial disaffiliation?

Several recent academic studies, including the research I referred to by Dyer et al.,[1] emphasize the strong religious commitment of Latter-day Saints and the important indicators of vitality within the Church. These studies are valuable and deserve careful consideration, but they do not suggest that significant disaffiliation is not happening.

Clearly, both convert growth and disaffiliation are happening simultaneously in different segments of the same population.

At first glance, these two pictures may appear contradictory. They are not. Instead, they describe different perspectives on what is happening with members of the Church. Within a complex church community, many members can be growing, thriving, and experiencing the promised benefits of the gospel, while, at the same time, others are not. We have an opportunity to improve our understanding of why a significant number of members are stepping away and how we can provide a church culture that is loving and enriching for all those who are part of our community. When these views are examined together, the apparent contradiction largely disappears.

View 1: Different Groups

Three Distinct Groups

A helpful way to understand this information is to divide the Church's membership into three broad, logical groups and their levels of participation.

1. The Active Core

Globally, 20–30 percent of members of record participate actively and consistently in Church life. These members attend regularly, hold callings, may participate in temple worship, and engage in personal religious practices, such as prayer and scripture study. This group corresponds closely with the population studied in most of the research on Latter-day Saint religiosity. Surveys consistently show that this active core reports:

> High levels of religious commitment

> Frequent church attendance

> Regular prayer and scripture study

> Strong family religious practice

> High levels of personal well-being and spiritual peace

The BYU study by Dyer et al. clearly documents these patterns. Compared with members of most other American religious traditions, active Latter-day Saints demonstrate unusually high levels of religious engagement and spiritual practice. These findings are real and meaningful indicators of vitality within the Church for this group.

2. Formerly Active Members Who Have Disaffiliated

The research presented in this book focuses on a *different* population: members who were once active but who no longer participate. As stated, based on our research and the analysis summarized in appendixes B and C, roughly 40 percent of formerly active members disengaged between 2000 and 2024—approximately 900,000 to 1.2 million formerly active members in the United States and more around the world.

Importantly, this group is largely not represented in most of the studies that focus primarily on members currently identifying as LDS, yet it represents a significant part of the Church's membership who have experienced or are experiencing the Church differently. Members who are currently in the process of disaffiliation or who have disaffiliated are much less likely to respond to surveys from Church headquarters or Brigham Young University.

Many individuals in this group still value faith, spirituality, and the teachings of Jesus Christ. As the BYU study and our study confirm (see p. 31), a large share of former Latter-day Saints remains spiritually oriented even after disaffiliating.

3. Members Never Fully Affiliated

The remaining portion of members—50–60 percent of members of record—consists of individuals who were never deeply integrated into Church life. These individuals may include:

➤ People baptized as converts who quickly became inactive

➤ Individuals baptized as children who never regularly participated

Although these individuals appear on the Church's membership records, they rarely or never participated in meaningful ways, like those who are now active or who were once active and disaffiliated. Thus, members who never fully affiliated are not part of the population analyzed in this book's disaffiliation estimates.

Why the Two Narratives Appear Different

Understanding these three groups clarifies why the narrative of vitality and the disaffiliation analysis presented in this book can coexist.

Different Units of Analysis

The BYU research and much of the research done by the Correlation Research Division within the Correlation Department at Church headquarters focuses mostly on those who will respond to surveys from the Church (e.g., the active core) who still identify as LDS, while this book focuses on formerly active members who have stepped away. These are different populations within the same overall membership.

Relative Strength versus Absolute Loss

The BYU study tends to emphasize the relative strength of Latter-day Saints compared with other religious groups. In many measures of religiosity—attendance, prayer, scripture study, and family religious practice—active Latter-day Saints rank among the most religious populations in the United States. I believe this accurately describes those who identify as Latter-day Saints and includes some who may not be active.

However, strong religious commitment among those who remain does not eliminate the possibility of substantial losses among those who once participated but have since disaffiliated or the need to understand why they disaffiliate.

Polarization within Religious Communities

Sociologists of religion frequently observe a pattern known as religious polarization, where the most committed members of a religious community become even more engaged while others gradually disengage. When this occurs, surveys focused on more active participants may show increasing strength even while overall participation declines. The evidence cited here and in chapter 1 (p. 28) indicates that the Church may be experiencing a similar dynamic.

A Conceptual Model of Participation

The following simplified diagram illustrates how these three groups may coexist within the Church.

Size Ranges for Three Member Groups

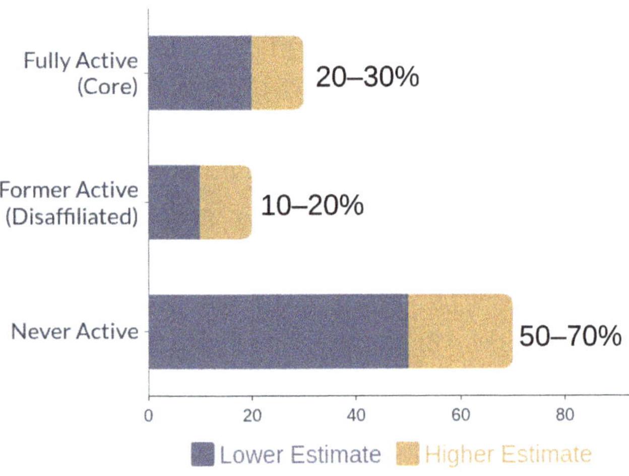

Two separate research perspectives focus on different portions of this structure:

> Studies such as the BYU religiosity research primarily describe those who still identify as Latter-day Saints, including the active core and some who are inactive.

> The analysis in this book focuses on the formerly active, disaffiliated group.

Neither perspective is incorrect or complete; each simply describes different parts of the same population.

View 2: Different Time Frames

Another important perspective that shows the two different dynamics involves looking at Latter-day Saint vitality at a point in time, or snapshot, relative to other religious communities versus looking at the trends over time, relative to other communities and to where our Church has been in the past. These perspectives also show different outcomes.

Alex Bass recently described this dynamic using data from the Harvard, Pew, and GSS studies I have cited in this book and that Dyer et al. also cite.

Bass said, "The snapshot picture actually favors the institution. Latter-day Saints in 2024 show higher levels of religious practice and commitment than Catholics, mainline Christians, and on some measures, Evangelicals. The members who show up—who pray, who attend, who say their faith is central to their lives—are doing so at rates that most Christian traditions can't match."[2] (See the chart in appendix B, p. 249, for this data)

Bass then outlines why this is an incomplete view. "When you ask not just 'how devout are members today' but 'how has that changed over time,' some important patterns emerge. Across retention, religious practice, and religious attitudes, Latter-day Saints are declining faster than comparable Christian traditions—not just losing members at the margins, but showing steeper drops in prayer, scripture study, and church attendance among those who still identify. Both things are true simultaneously."

Reconciling the Evidence

When these perspectives are combined, a more complete picture emerges. The Church retains a deeply committed core membership that demonstrates unusually high levels of religious devotion, spiritual engagement, and satisfaction. At the same time, around 40 percent of once-active members have stepped away from participation during the past several decades, suggesting there are critical issues that require attention.

Conclusion

Evidence from multiple sources indicates that the Church is experiencing both vitality *and* strain. The Church continues to sustain a remarkably devoted active core whose religious commitment compares favorably with that of almost any faith community. Simultaneously, the number of formerly active members who have stepped away from participation is large enough to merit serious attention.

Recognizing both realities does not diminish the strengths of the Church, nor does it deny the experiences of those who have stepped away. Rather, it provides a fuller and more-balanced understanding of the complex religious landscape facing the twenty-first-century Church.

Would They Return? Christlike Culture or Not?

The Dyer study also suggests that a significant proportion of disaffiliated members would return if invited to do so. That may be true for some individuals. Our research, which included many interviews with those who disaffiliated, indicates that for many, the issues are much more nuanced and contingent.

For most who step away, the process of disaffiliation is long and painful, and they have reasons for leaving that are compelling for them. In most cases, as outlined in chapters 1 and 2, there is not one single reason. The table below shows that the reasons people give for stepping away revolve around a Church culture that is perceived as rigid, prescriptive, and unloving. Until they see evidence that this has changed, it is unlikely they will return.

What would it take for you to return?

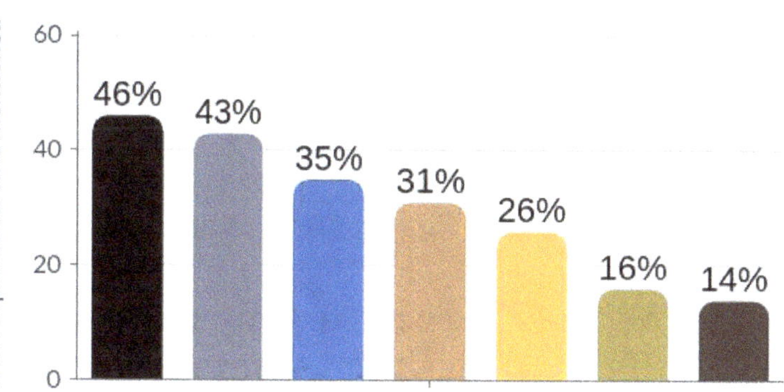

- A less rigid and legalistic culture with more love and compassion
- A more principled and less prescriptive approach to core beliefs
- Better treatment of and a greater voice for women
- Leadership honesty, humility, and accountability for mistakes
- More accepting of LGBTQ+ people
- Open and honest discussion of Church history
- Priesthood ordination for women

Source: Strong and Dotson, *Why People Are Leaving*, 2025.

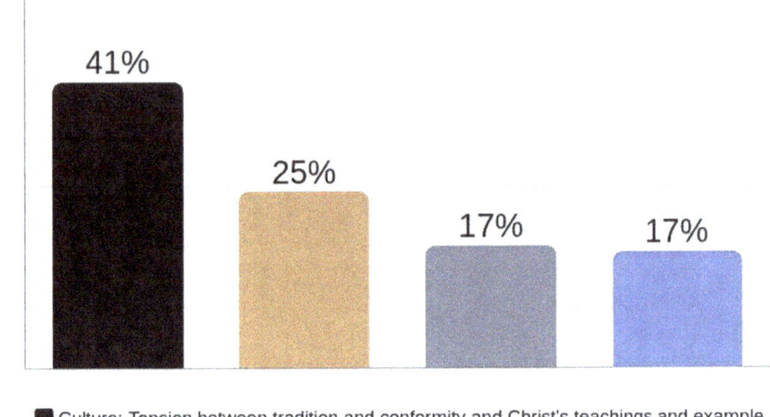

Source: Strong and Dotson, *Why People Are Leaving*, 2025.

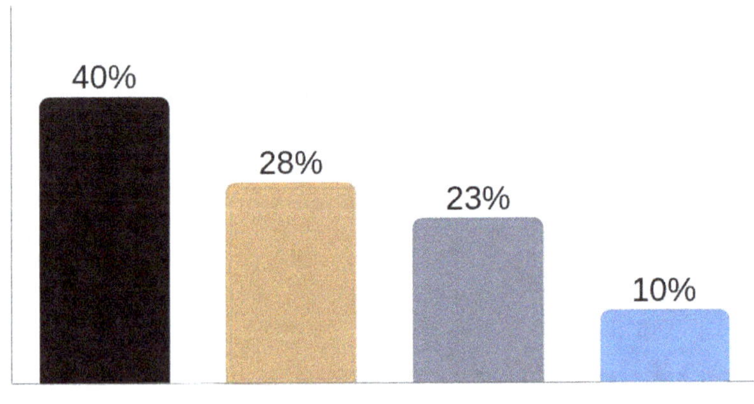

Source: Strong and Dotson, *Why People Are Leaving*, 2025.

Notes

Introduction

1. You will see the word *disaffiliation* used frequently throughout this book. Disaffiliation is different than inactivity. Disaffiliation is when an individual has been faithful and active in the Church but chooses to significantly reduce or stop that. It would include those who've had their names removed from the records of the Church, those who continue to be members of record but never participate, and those who rarely, if ever, participate. It does not include people who continue to participate infrequently or those who were never faithful and active. All people who disaffiliate are inactive. All people who are inactive are not disaffiliated.

2. Fyodor Dosteoevsky, *A Writer's Diary: Volume I, 1873–1876,* trans. Kenneth Lantz (Northwestern University Press, 1994), 68.

3. See Richard Rohr, *Falling Upward: A Spirituality for the Two Halves of Life* (Jossey-Bass, 2011).

4. Anne Frank, *The Diary of a Young Girl: The Definitive Edition,* trans. Susan Massotty (Doubleday, 1995), 208.

5. Barbara Brown Taylor, *Home by Another Way* (Cowley Publications, 1999), 42–43.

6. Stephen W. Brown, *When Being Good Isn't Good Enough* (T. Nelson, 1990), 18–19.

Chapter 1: What Is Happening

Epigraph. Attributed to W. Edwards Deming in Mary Walton, *The Deming Management Method* (Perigee, 1986), 96.

1. Appendix E provides and explanation of those narratives, showing that the Church can experience vitality and disaffiliation at the same time.

2. One compelling example is John C. Lennox, an Oxford mathematician and author known for his thoughtful engagement with science and Christian faith. His ideas for the scientific evidence of divine creation are presented in his book *God's Undertaker: Has Science Buried God?* (Lion Books, 2009).

3. Russell M. Nelson, "The Tie Between Science and Religion," *BYU Speeches,* April 9, 2015, https://speeches.byu.edu/talks/russell-m-nelson/the-tie-between-science-and-religion/.

4. For those interested, the important details regarding the summary of the research team, our methodology, and information on how to access the full report are found in appendix A.

5. Unless otherwise noted, the data and findings discussed in this chapter come from our study, Strong and Dotson, *Why People Are Leaving*, 2025. Readers may consult appendix A for the complete methodology. The full resource report, including the names and biographies of the research team and advisors, is accessible through our website (www.tornbyjeffstrong.com).

6. Strong and Dotson, *Why People Are Leaving*, 2025. Note: Our study was not designed to quantify disaffiliation outside the United States.

7. Brian Schaffner, Marissa Shih, Stephen Ansolabehere, and Jeremy Pope, "Cooperative Election Study Common Content, 2024," Harvard Dataverse, April 2, 2025, Harvard University Institute for Quantitative Social Science, https://doi .org/10.7910/DVN/X11EP6.

8. Pew Research Center, "2023–24 U.S. Religious Landscape Study Interactive Database" (2025), https://doi.org/10.58094/3zs9-jc14.

9. The information can be accessed via our website (www.tornbyjeffstrong.com).

10. For each of the four waves and in other places in chapters 1 and 2 you will see descriptive quotes regarding the sentiments of people who left the Church. These quotes are taken from the answers of anonymous responses to open-ended questions in our survey.

11. Throughout this chapter, you will see quotes that are not cited to individuals. All of these quotes were taken verbatim from anonymous respondents who took our surveys.

12. See W. Paul Reeve, *Let's Talk About Race and the Priesthood* (Deseret Book, 2018); Matthew L. Harris, *Second-Class Saints* (Oxford University Press, 2014); Neylan McBaine, *Women at Church* (Greg Kofford Books, 2014); Jennifer Reeder and Kate Holbrook, eds., *At the Pulpit* (Church Historian's Press, 2017); Tom Christofferson, *That We May Be One* (Deseret Book, 2014); and Charlie Bird, *Without the Mask* (Deseret Book, 2020).

13. The Harvard CES, Pew Religious Landscape, and General Social Survey (https://gss.norc.org/) studies all suggest similar disaffiliation acceleration. Data from each is provided in appendix B.

14. Alex Bass, *Mormon Disaffiliation: Demographic Trends and Religious Change in the United States, 2008–2024*, analysis of the Harvard Cooperative Election Study (unpublished research report, 2024).

15. Public Religion Research Institute (PRRI), *Generation Z Fact Sheet*, March 29, 2024, https://prri.org/spotlight/prri-generation-z-fact-sheet/; Gregory A. Smith and others, "The Decline of Christianity in the U.S. Has Slowed, May Have Leveled Off: Findings from the 2023–24 Religious Landscape Study," February 26, 2025, Pew

Research Center, https://www.pewresearch.org/religion/2025/02/26/decline-of-chris
tianity-in-the-us-has-slowed-may-have-leveled-off/.

16. Gregory A. Smith, "Religion Holds Steady in America," December 8, 2025, Pew Research Center, https://www.pewresearch.org/religion/2025/12/08/religion-holds-steady-in-america/; Barna Group, "Young Adults Lead a Resurgence in Church Attendance," September 2, 2025, https://www.barna.com/research/young-adults-lead-resurgence-in-church-attendance/.

17. Becka A. Alper and others, "Who Are 'Spiritual but Not Religious' Americans?" December 7, 2023, Pew Research Center, https://www.pewresearch.org/religion/2023/12/07/who-are-spiritual-but-not-religious-americans/.

18. Gregory A. Smith and others, *Religious Landscape Study* (2023–2024), "Executive Summary," Pew Research Center, accessed January 5, 2026, https://www.pewresearch.org/religion/2025/02/26/religious-landscape-study-executive-summary/.

19. Jana Riess, *The Next Mormons: How Millennials Are Changing the LDS Church* (Oxford University Press, 2019); see also Jana Riess, "Who Is Leaving the LDS Church? Eight Key Survey Findings," *Religion News Service,* March 7, 2024, https://religionnews.com/2024/03/07/who-is-leaving-the-lds-church-8-key-survey-findings/.

20. See appendix D for a detailed report on convert baptism trends.

21. Alex Bass, *Mormon Typology Report, Version 2: An Analysis of Latter-day Saint Belief and Experience Using the Pew Religious Landscape Study* (unpublished research report, 2025), based on data from Pew Research Center, *Religious Landscape Study,* latest release.

22. "Where Americans Find Meaning in Life," November 20, 2018, https://www.pewresearch.org/religion/2018/11/20/where-americans-find-meaning-in-life/; Becka A. Alper and others, "Who Are 'Spiritual but Not Religious' Americans?" Pew Research Center, December 7, 2023, https://www.pewresearch.org/religion/2023/12/07/who-are-spiritual-but-not-religious-americans/.

Chapter 2: When Belief Is Torn

Epigraph. Dieter F. Uchtdorf, "The Reflection in the Water," CES Fireside, November 1, 2009, Brigham Young University, The Church of Jesus Christ of Latter-day Saints, https://www.churchofjesuschrist.org/media/video/2009-11-0050-the-reflection-in-the-water.

1. Though often attributed to President James A. Garfield, see Jamie Buckingham, *The Truth Will Set You Free, but First It Will Make You Miserable: The Collected Wit and Wisdom of Jamie Buckingham* (Creation House, 1988), 20.

2. Paul Brand and Philip Yancey, *The Gift of Pain* (Zondervan, 1997), 188.

3. Unless otherwise noted, the data and findings discussed in this chapter come from our study, Strong and Dotson, *Why People Are Leaving,* 2025.

4. This pattern of thinking and behavior probably stems from outdated cultural patterns from the past that persist after being emphasize for decades. Old teachings and ways of thinking have been replaced by current teachings from Church leaders. And the Savior's teachings have not changed and are there to guide us. This tension will be examined in chapter 9.

5. Paul Tillich, *Dynamics of Faith* (Harper & Row, 1957), 21.

6. Anonymous survey respondent, Strong and Dotson, *Why People Are Leaving,* 2025.

7. Anonymous survey respondent, Strong and Dotson, *Why People Are Leaving,* 2025.

8. This includes the many books, podcasts, YouTube programs, or other content provided by faithful Latter-day Saints.

9. This includes the many books, podcasts YouTube programs, or other content provided by non-LDS Christian leaders.

10. This includes churchofjesuschrist.org, the Gospel Topics Essays, and other content provided by the Church.

11. Neylan McBaine, *Women at Church: Magnifying LDS Women's Local Impact* (Greg Kofford Books, 2014), quoted in "Women at Church Quotes," Goodreads, accessed January 19, 2026, https://www.goodreads.com/work/quotes/42367053-women -at-church-magnifying-lds-women-s-local-impact.

Chapter 3: Seeing

1. Daniel J. Boorstin, *The Discoverers* (Vintage Books, 1985), 86.

2. Jeff Strong and Jeff Dotson (2025), *Why People Are Leaving.*

3. Kay Halle, comp., *Irrepressible Churchill: A Treasury of Winston Churchill's Wit* (World Publishing, 1966), 133. The quote was said of Stanley Baldwin.

4. Patrick Miles Overton, *The Leaning Tree* (Bethany Press, 1975), 91.

5. David Brewster, *Memoirs of the Life, Writings, and Discoveries of Sir Isaac Newton,* vol. 2 (Edinburgh: Thomas Constable and Co., 1855), 407.

Chapter 4: Nourishing

Epigraph. Ogden translation: "Is the power of tradition to preserve the ashes or pass along the fire?" The idea of tradition being expressed as fire or ashes is attributed to Jean Jaures, a French political orator. See Romain Rolland, *Above the Battle,* trans. C. K. Ogden, 2nd ed. (Open Court Publishing, 1916), 186.

1. Norman Jewison, dir., *Fiddler on the Roof* (United Artists, 1971), film, opening monologue ("Tradition").

2. *Oxford English Dictionary,* s.v. "culture" (n.), sense I.1.a, https://doi.org/10.1093/OED/5591036717; see also *Oxford English Dictionary,* s.v. "culture" (n.), Etymology.

3. *Oxford English Dictionary,* s.v. "culture" (n.), sense III.5.a, accessed December 2024, https://doi.org/10.1093/OED/5788836946.

4. *Oxford English Dictionary,* "culture" (n.), sense III.7.a, https://doi.org/10.1093/OED/5142415889.

5. E. H. Schein, *Organizational Culture and Leadership,* 4th ed. (Jossey-Bass, 2010), 23–32.

6. Russell M. Nelson, "We Can Do Better and Be Better," *Liahona,* May 2019, 67.

7. Gordon B. Hinckley, "The Great Things Which God Has Revealed," *Ensign,* May 2005, 83.

8. Kyle Nelson (McKinsey and Company, senior strategy manager at The Church of Jesus Christ of Latter-day Saints), video conference interview with author in Dallas, Texas, April 7, 2024.

9. Kyle Nelson, interview with author, April 7, 2024.

10. Kyle Nelson, interview with author, April 7, 2024.

11. See Mark 7. The Pharisees and scribes asked Christ why He and His disciples did not observe the tradition of washing their hands before eating. He responded by pointing out their convoluted priorities and hypocrisy.

12. To share just a few of many examples: From the beginning, Eve was entrusted to courageously exercise the moral agency that made mortal life, growth, and redemption possible. Esther, facing the annihilation of her people, risked her life to act with courage and discernment, preserving the children of Israel. And Mary Magdalene, faithful when others withdrew, was entrusted by Jesus Christ to be the first witness of His Resurrection.

13. Julie B. Beck, "Mothers Who Know," *Liahona,* November 2007, 76.

Chapter 5: Understanding

Epigraph. Ralph Waldo Emerson, *Journal and Miscellaneous Notebooks of Ralph Waldo Emerson,* vol. 4: 1832–1834, ed. Alfred R. Ferguson (Harvard University Press, 1960), 86.

1. David Brooks, "Finding the Road to Character," forum speaker, Brigham Young University, October 22, 2019, 9:35, https://speeches.byu.edu/talks/david-brooks/finding-the-road-to-character/.

2. David Brooks, "The Lies Our Culture Tells Us About What Matters—and a Better Way to Live," TED Talk, April 2019, 3:01, https://www.ted.com/talks/david_brooks_the_lies_our_culture_tells_us_about_what_matters_and_a_better_way_to_live.

3. Dieter F. Uchtdorf, "It Works Wonderfully!," *Liahona,* November 2015, 21.

4. Jeffrey M. Jones, "U.S. Church Membership Falls Below Majority for First Time," March 29, 2021, Gallup, https://news.gallup.com/poll/341963/church-mem bership-falls-below-majority-first-time.aspx.

5. "Religious 'Nones' in America: Who They Are and What They Believe," January 24, 2024, Pew Research Center, https://www.pewresearch.org/religion/2024/01/ 24/religious-nones-in-america-who-they-are-and-what-they-believe/.

6. AP-NORC (National Opinion Research Center) for Public Affairs Research, "People Without a Religious Affiliation Lack Faith in Organized Religion, Not in Spirituality," AP-NORC poll, October 5, 2023, https://apnorc.org/projects/people -without-a-religious-affiliation-lack-faith-in-organized-religion-not-in-spirituality/.

7. "Americans See Catholic Clergy Sex Abuse as an Ongoing Problem," June 11, 2019, Pew Research Center, https://www.pewresearch.org/religion/2019/06/11/ameri cans-see-catholic-clergy-sex-abuse-as-an-ongoing-problem/; Harald Dreßing et al., "Sexual Abuse at the Hands of Catholic Clergy," *Duetsches Ärzteblatt Int* 116, no. 22 (May 2019): 389–96, https://doi.org/10.3238/arztebl.2019.0389.

8. Office of Public Affairs, "Wells Fargo Agrees to Pay $3 Billion to Resolve Criminal and Civil Investigations into Sales Practices Involving the Opening of Millions of Accounts without Customer Authorization," February 21, 2020, U.S. Department of Justice, https://www.justice.gov/opa/pr/wells-fargo-agrees-pay-3-billion-re solve-criminal-and-civil-investigations-sales-practices.

9. Dietrich Knauth, "Boy Scouts Victims Begin Receiving Settlement Payouts as Appeals Continue," Reuters, September 19, 2023, https://www.reuters.com/legal/ litigation/boy-scouts-victims-begin-receiving-settlement-payouts-appeals-con tinue-2023-09-19/.

10. U.S. Securities and Exchange Commission, "SEC Charges The Church of Jesus Christ of Latter-day Saints and Its Investment Management Company for Disclosure Failures and Misstated Filings," Press Release, February 21, 2023, https://www.sec .gov/newsroom/press-releases/2023-35.

11. Ronald V. Miller Jr., "Mormon Church Sex Abuse Lawsuits," Lawsuit Information Center, September 14, 2024, https://www.lawsuit-information-center.com/ sex-abuse-lawsuits-against-lds-church.html; The Church of Jesus Christ of Latter-day Saints, "Church Statement About Alleged Sexual Assault by Former Mission President," March 23, 2018, Official Church Statement, https://newsroom.churchof jesuschrist.org/article/statement-former-mission-president-alleged-abuse-joseph-l -bishop-march-2018.

12. "Order Granting Motion for Summary Judgment," *James Huntsman v. Corporation of the President of the Church of Jesus Christ of Latter-day Saints,* September 10,

2021, U.S. District Court, Central District of California, https://ia804502.us.archive.org/30/items/gov.uscourts.cacd.814559/gov.uscourts.cacd.814559.55.0.pdf.

13. "Americans Feel More Positive Than Negative About Jews, Mainline Protestants, Catholics," Report, March 15, 2023, Pew Research Center, https://www.pewresearch.org/report/americans-feel-more-positive-than-negative-about-jews-mainline-protestants-catholics/.

Chapter 6: Believing

Epigraph. David Starr Jordan, "The Strength of Being Clean," in *Inspirational Classics for Latter-day Saints,* ed. Jack M. Lyon (Eagle Gate, 2000), 179, originally published in *The Strength of Being Clean: A Study of the Quest for Unearned Happiness* (H. M. Caldwell, 1900), 7.

1. See appendix F for more information on the reasons some members feel the Church is very Christ-centered while others feel it is only somewhat so.

2. Jeffrey R. Holland, "Lessons from Liberty Jail," *Ensign,* September 2007, 31.

3. Spencer W. Kimball, *Faith Precedes the Miracle* (Deseret Book, 1972), 98.

4. Russell M. Nelson, "Drawing the Power of Jesus Christ into Our Lives," *Ensign,* May 2017, 41, emphasis added.

5. David Foster Wallace, "This Is Water," Kenyon College Commencement Address, May 21, 2005, accessed September 9, 2024, https://fs.blog/david-foster-wallace-this-is-water/.

6. Hannah Arendt, *Eichmann in Jerusalem: A Report on the Banality of Evil* (Penguin, 1963).

7. David A. Bednar, "In the Space of Not Many Years," *Liahona,* November 2024, 73.

8. "Light of Christ," Topics and Questisons, The Church of Jesus Christ of Latter-day Saints, accessed December 23, 2025, https://www.churchofjesuschrist.org/study/manual/gospel-topics.

9. Dieter F. Uchtdorf, "A Teacher's Checklist," CES Religious Educators Conference, June 12, 2022, The Church of Jesus Christ of Latter-day Saints, https://www.churchofjesuschrist.org/study/broadcasts/language-recording/2022/05/11uchtdorf.

10. Dallin H. Oaks, "Our Strengths Can Become Our Downfall," devotional address, June 7, 1992, Brigham Young University, https://speeches.byu.edu/talks/dallin-h-oaks/strengths-can-become-downfall/.

11. Bruce R. McConkie, *The Mortal Messiah: From Bethlehem to Calvary,* bk. 1 (Deseret Book, 1979), 1:238.

12. Quentin L. Cook, "Looking Beyond the Mark," *Ensign,* March 2003, 40–44.

13. Dale G. Renlund, "The Powerful, Virtuous Cycle of the Doctrine of Christ," *Liahona,* May 2024, 82.

Chapter 7: Acceptance

1. Elie Wiesel, "The Most Creative Man in the World," *U.S. News and World Report,* October 27, 1986.

2. Strong and Dotson, *Why People Are Leaving,* 2025.

3. The Holy Bible, King James Version (Salt Lake City: The Church of Jesus Christ of Latter-day Saints, 2013), John 9:1–41.

4. Dieter F. Uchtdorf, Facebook post, November 25, 2024.

5. Russell M. Nelson, "An Invitation to Exaltation," *Ensign,* June 1989.

6. Strong and Dotson, *Why People Are Leaving,* 2025.

7. Dieter F. Uchtdorf, "The Love of God," *Ensign* or *Liahona,* November 2009.

8. Russell M. Nelson, "Peacemakers Needed," *Liahona,* May 2023.

9. D. Todd Christofferson, "Why the Church," *Ensign or Liahona,* November 2015.

10. Howard W. Hunter, "Chapter 12: 'Come Back and Feast at the Table of the Lord,'" in *Teachings of the Presidents of the Church: Howard W. Hunter* (The Church of Jesus Christ of Latter-day Saints, 2015).

Chapter 8: Transcendence

1. Johannes P. Louw and Eugene A. Nida, *Greek-English Lexicon of the New Testament* (United Bible Societies, 1988), §53.5, hereafter cited as Louw-Nida.

2. Dieter F. Uchtdorf, "Nourish the Roots, and the Branches Will Grow," *Liahona,* October 2024.

3. Terryl and Fiona Givens, *The God Who Weeps: How Mormonism Makes Sense of Life* (Deseret Book, 2012), 5–6, emphasis in original.

4. D. Todd Christofferson, "Our Relationship with God," *Church News,* April 3, 2022, https://www.thechurchnews.com/2022/4/3/23217417/elder-christofferson-april-2022-general-conference-relationship-with-god/.

5. The individual's name has been changed to protect privacy.

6. Louw-Nida, §88.100.

7. Thomas S. Monson, "In Quest of the Abundant Life," *Ensign,* March 1988, 5.

Chapter 9: Agency

Epigraph. Lee A. Palmer, ed., "Ward Teachers' Message for June, 1945: Sustaining the General Authorities of the Church," *Improvement Era,* June 1945, 354.

1. Dallin H. Oaks, "Our Strengths Can Become Our Downfall," devotional, Brigham Young University, June 7, 1992, BYU Speeches, https://speeches.byu.edu/talks/dallin-h-oaks/strengths-can-become-downfall/.

2. Palmer, "Ward Teachers' Message for June, 1945."

3. This is in a letter from President George Albert Smith to Dr. J. Raymond Cope dated December 7, 1945. See "A 1945 Perspective," *Dialogue: A Journal of Mormon Thought* 19, no. 1 (1986): 38–39, emphasis in original.

4. D. Todd Christofferson, "The Doctrine of Christ," general conference address, April 2012, accessed February 25, 2026, https://www.churchofjesuschrist.org/study/general-conference/2012/04/the-doctrine-of-christ.

5. John Taylor, "The Organization of the Church," *Millennial Star,* November 15, 1851, 339.

6. Brigham Young, in *Journal of Discourses,* 26 vols. (Liverpool, 1855–86), 9:150 (January 12, 1862).

7. Dallin H. Oaks, "Elder Dallin H. Oaks: The Dedication of a Lifetime," *Church News,* May 1, 2005, accessed February 25, 2026, https://www.thechurchnews.com/2005/5/1/23236626/elder-dallin-h-oaks-the-dedication-of-a-lifetime/.

8. Dale G. Renlund, "Choose You This Day," *Liahona,* November 2018, 104, emphasis in original.

9. Melissa Wei-Tsing Inouye, "A Church That Is Real: Walking the Path of Most Resistance," *Wayfare,* January 7, 2025, https://www.wayfaremagazine.org/p/a-church-that-is-real.

Chapter 10: Harmony

1. Gregory S. Berns et al., "Neurobiological Correlates of Social Conformity and Independence During Mental Rotation," *Neuron* 58, no. 3 (2005): 245–53.

2. Jay is not the professor's real name. I chose a different name to protect his privacy.

3. Edwin Markham, *The Shoes of Happiness and Other Poems* (Doubleday, Page, 1913), 127.

4. See Lecture 4 in "Doctrine and Covenants, 1835," in *Revelations and Translations,* vol. 2: *Published Revelations,* ed. Richard E. Turley Jr., Robin Scott Jensen, and Riley M. Lorimer, Joseph Smith Papers (Church Historian's Press, 2011), 44–52.

5. Dallin H. Oaks, "Judge Not and Judging," Brigham Young University devotional, March 1, 1998, *BYU Speeches,* https://speeches.byu.edu/talks/dallin-h-oaks/judge-judging/.

6. Brian McLaren, *Faith After Doubt: Why Your Beliefs Stopped Working and What to Do About It* (St. Martin's Essentials, 2021).

7. Joseph F. Smith, "Discourse," in *Deseret News,* October 29, 1873, 644.

8. Strong and Dotson, *Why People Are Leaving,* 2025.

9. Sharon Eubank, "The Promise of Belonging," broadcast address transcript, April 1, 2021, ChurchofJesusChrist.org, https://www.churchofjesuschrist.org/study/broadcasts/miscellaneous-events/2021/04-01/11eubank

Interlude: What Will We Choose?

1. Fyodor Dostoevsky, *The Brothers Karamazov*, trans. Constance Garnett (Lowell Press, 2009), part 5, chapter 5, EPUB.

Chapter 11: The Harvest

Epigraph. Victor Hugo, *Les Misérables*, trans. Lee Fahnestock and Norman MacAfee (Signet Classic, 1987), 646.

1. Walter Lowen, *How and When to Change Your Job Successfully* (Simon and Schuster, 1954), 31.

2. "Statistics and Church Facts," Newsroom, The Church of Jesus Christ of Latter-day Saints, accessed November 29, 2025, https://news-africa.churchofjesus christ.org/facts-and-statistics.

3. Andrew McChesney, "Explosive Growth Drives Adventist Church in Africa," March 1, 2023, Adventist Review, https://adventistreview.org/news/explosive-growth -drives-adventist-church-in-africa/, referencing the 2025 Annual Statistical Report.

4. Name withheld by request.

5. Desmond Tutu, *No Future Without Forgiveness* (Doubleday, 1999), 31.

6. Desmond Tutu, quoted in Michael Battle, *Reconciliation: The Ubuntu Theology of Desmond Tutu* (Pilgrim Press, 1997), 65.

7. Desmond Tutu, quoted in Battle, *Reconciliation*, 35.

8. Desmond Tutu, *No Future Without Forgiveness*, 31, 196.

9. Peter Wohlleben, *The Hidden Life of Trees: What They Feel, How They Communicate: Discoveries from a Secret World*, trans. Jane Billinghurst (Greystone Books, 2016), 10–11.

10. Wohlleben, *Hidden Life of Trees*, 33.

11. Joseph Grenny is a New York Times best-selling author, social scientist, and cofounder of VitalSmarts. He is the author or coauthor of *Crucial Conversations*, *Crucial Accountability*, *Influencer*, and *Change Anything*, with more than ten million copies sold worldwide. His work focuses on leadership, influence, organizational culture, and the social dynamics that shape individual and institutional behavior.

12. Reyna I. Aburto, "Thru Cloud and Sunshine, Lord, Abide with Me!," *Liahona*, November 2019, 58.

13. Jeffrey R. Holland, "Songs Sung and Unsung," *Ensign*, May 2017, 51.

Chapter 12: Becoming a Gardner

1. Quoted by David O. McKay, "Choose You This Day," *Official Report of the One Hundred Thirty-Seventh Annual General Conference*, April 1967, The Church of Jesus Christ of Latter-day Saints, 84.

Appendix B: Other Reliable Research Showing Significant LDS Disaffiliation

1. The Harvard CES study sample size varies year-to-year. In a typical year, it would have approximately 50,000-60,000 participants, including 1,000–1,500 Latter-day Saints.

2. The Pew Research Center Religious Landscape studies typically include 35,000–40,000 participants, including 700–800 Latter-day Saints.

3. The General Social Survey typically includes 3,000–3,500 participants, including 50–75 Latter-day Saints and should be interpreted cautiously.

4. Alex Bass, "Are Latter-day Saints Beating Secular Headwinds? Analysis of the Cooperative Election Study, Pew Religious Landscape Study, and the General Social Survey," March 13, 2026.

5. The Intermountain states include Arizona, Nevada, Utah, Wyoming, and Idaho.

6. W. Justin Dyer, Jenet J. Erickson, Sam A. Hardy, Barbara Morgan Gardner, and David C. Dollahite, "Latter-day Saint Righteousness, Well-Being, and Retention in the United States," Working Paper, Family Foundations of Faith, https://foundations.byu.edu/0000019b-1343-d613-a59b-17df82980000/latterdaysaintreligiosity-pdf, find that Latter-day Saints consistently rank among the highest of all U.S. religious groups in core measures of religiosity and faith engagement. They report higher levels of church attendance, daily prayer, and regular scripture study, along with exceptionally strong belief in God and the importance of religion in daily life. Latter-day Saints also demonstrate high levels of family-centered religious practice, service, and charitable behavior. These patterns are closely associated with elevated measures of purpose, life satisfaction, and overall well-being, reflecting a community marked by deep commitment, active participation, and strong social and spiritual cohesion.

7. W. Justin Dyer, Jenet J. Erickson, Sam A. Hardy, Barbara Morgan Gardner, and David C. Dollahite, *Latter-day Saint Religiousness, Well-Being, and Retention in the United States* (Provo, UT: Brigham Young University, 2025), https://foundations.byu.edu/0000019b-1343-d613-a59b-17df82980000/latterdaysaintreligiosity-pdf.

Appendix D: Disaffiliation Outside the United States

1. The Church of Jesus Christ of Latter-day Saints, "Statistical Report, 1991–2025," https://www.churchofjesuschrist.org/study/general-conference.

Appendix E: Reconciling Conflicting Narratives of Vitality or Disaffiliation

1. Dyer, Erickson, Hardy, Gardner, and Dollahite, "Latter-day Saint Righteousness, Well-Being, and Retention in the United States"; see also Justin Dyer, "Latter-day Saints Are Retaining Faith at Uniquely High Levels in a Secularizing Society," *Deseret News,* December 15, 2025.

2. Alex Bass, "Are Latter-day Saints Beating Secular Headwinds? Analysis of the Cooperative Election Study, Pew Religious Landscape Study, and the General Social survey, March 13, 2026.

Acknowledgments

This book exists because thousands of people were willing to be vulnerable. I am profoundly grateful to the nearly twenty-thousand individuals who participated in surveys or interviews and the dozens who generously shared their stories with me in more personal conversations. Their willingness to open up and share deeply personal experiences and perspectives about their journeys in the Church gave this book its substance and soul. I have tried to listen carefully, to represent their experiences accurately, and to honor their trust.

I am deeply grateful to my editors—Lisa Roper, Katie Lewis, Lori Forsyth, and Michele Preisendorf—for their discernment, precision, and commitment to clarity. Their gift for extracting water from a stone was extraordinary. Their guidance made this book possible. They made it so much better and strengthened and sustained me through its many revisions.

I owe particular thanks to Dr. Jeff Dotson, my research partner, whose intellectual rigor and methodological care were foundational to this project. I am also grateful to the other researchers and advisors who contributed to the research and work that informs this book.

I am thankful for the friends, colleagues, and trusted counselors, including many Church leaders and some former Church members, who offered encouragement and feedback along the way, and for my family's patience over the years this project took shape. I am also grateful for the mentors and teachers who shaped my faith and the over seven hundred missionaries with whom I had the privilege of serving. Finally, I am grateful for the many dear friends—both those who remain in the Church and those who have stepped away—whose lives, relationships, and stories helped me see why the questions explored in this book matter. I remain a committed member of the Church that, warts and all, formed my faith that remains deep to this day.

About the Author

Jeff Strong spent nearly three decades in the global consumer products industry, serving in senior executive roles at Procter & Gamble and Johnson & Johnson, including as global president and chief customer officer. His professional experience in general management, research, strategy, and organizational leadership shaped both the rigorous national study behind this book and his insights into how culture forms, flourishes, and sometimes falters.

In addition to his corporate leadership, Jeff has served as a bishop and mission president in The Church of Jesus Christ of Latter-day Saints and as a faculty member at Brigham Young University. He also worked for a time as an advisor to the Church. Drawing from both executive and pastoral experience, he brings a rare combination of deep research experience, analytical depth, and lived faith to one of the most consequential and personal questions facing the Church today.

Jeff and his wife, Sara, live in Midway, Utah. They are the parents of five children and grandparents to six.